VOCATIONAL TEACHERS AND THE LAW

Vocational Teachers and the Law

Michael Farry

B.C.L., D.Ed A., M.Litt., Ph.D.
of Kings Inns, Barrister-at-Law,
Lecturer in Law,
Carlow Regional Technical College

WITH A FOREWORD BY
The Honourable Mr Justice Peter Kelly
The High Court

BLACKHALL
Publishing

This book was typeset by
Gough Typesetting Services Dublin for
BLACKHALL PUBLISHING,
26 Eustace Street, Dublin 2.
(e-mail: blackhall@tinet.ie)

A catalogue record for this title
is available from the British Library

ISBN 1 901657 03 5 hb
ISBN 1 901657 02 7 pb

The material contained in this book is not published or presented as legal
advice and the author and publishers do not accept responsibility for any
errors or omissions or for loss or damage howsoever caused to any person
acting or refraining from acting as a result of the material in this
publication.

Printed in Ireland by
Betaprint Ltd

Foreword

I was delighted to be offered the chance of reading this book in draft because it is a truly scholarly production. The scholarship, however, is transmitted lightly and in a most readable and digestible form.

This is Dr. Farry's second book in the field of education law. It follows within a year of the publication of his seminal work, *Education and the Constitution*. Education law is now a developing area of Irish jurisprudence. It should form an essential input into teacher training and legal education courses.

I found the historical introduction to be particularly interesting. Until I read this book I was unaware of the fact that references to vocational education were to be found in the Brehon law tracts.

The book contains interesting insights into the relationship between Church and State in the vocational sector. The author has also addressed the difficult issue of the confidentiality of interview procedures for public appointments. Interviewers would do well to read that part of the book dealing with discovery and the author's comments contained in section 5(19) on the burden of proving discrimination.

Vocational education has enjoyed a statutory basis for close on a hundred years. Nonetheless, it is bedevilled with departmental memoranda, circulars and regulations, none of which are readily accessible and all of which are free from parliamentary control. One can only hope that new education legislation which is at present in preparation will improve this unhappy situation.

This book is essential for every lawyer who has any involvement in matters pertaining to the field of education. It will also be a welcome addition to the shelves of any vocational teacher who has any interest in his/her profession.

Peter Kelly,
The High Court,
St. Andrew's Day, 1997.

Table of Contents

Part 1: Origin and Structure of Vocational Education

CHAPTER 1: EARLY IRISH VOCATIONAL EDUCATION

CHAPTER 2: MODERN VOCATIONAL EDUCATION

CHAPTER 3: VOCATIONAL EDUCATION COMMITTEES

CHAPTER 4: BOARDS OF MANAGEMENT

Part 2: Appointment of Vocational Teachers

CHAPTER 5: RECRUITMENT

CHAPTER 6: QUALIFICATIONS

CHAPTER 7: APPOINTMENTS

CHAPTER 8: DISQUALIFICATION FROM HOLDING OFFICE

Part 3: Discipline of Vocational Teachers

CHAPTER 9: SUSPENSION

CHAPTER 10: REMOVAL ON STATUTORY GROUNDS AFTER A LOCAL INQUIRY

CHAPTER 11: REMOVAL BY MINISTER WITHOUT A STATUTORY LOCAL INQUIRY

CHAPTER 12: REMOVAL BY A VOCATIONAL EDUCATION COMMITTEE

Part 4: Procedure

CHAPTER 13: LOCAL INQUIRY

CHAPTER 14: THE RULES OF NATURAL JUSTICE

CHAPTER 15: CONDITIONS OF APPOINTMENT AND MEMO V.7

Introduction

Since the origin of the system few books have been published dealing with vocational education or indeed by those who work within it. In my opinion the system has been the poorer on that account.

The scope of this book is confined to exploring some of the effects of legislation and judicial decisions on vocational teachers' employment.

Recourse to law and reliance on legal rights is not a characteristic of good industrial relations and this book is not presented to suggest that it is, but rather in the hope that an appreciation of the legal implications may prevent unpleasantness and help the resolution of disputes among those working within the vocational system.

It gives me great pleasure to acknowledge the help and assistance which I obtained from many people while writing this book. My thanks to my staunch friend and colleague Martin Nevin for his help and encouragement, Dr. Damien Ó Muirí B.L, NUI Maynooth, former colleagues Padraig Naughton (*The Examiner*), and Paul Muldowney of the High Court Press Office, George Maybury AGSI, Peter McMenamin, Deputy General Secretary, TUI, the late Joe Rooney IVEA and other persons with knowledge of the subject matter who desire to remain anonymous.

In particular I wish to thank Chairperson, Dr. Mary Upton, Acting Director Seamus Puirséil, the Council and staff of the NCEA and Austin Waldron, former CEO of Co. Carlow, who read the typescript and made many helpful suggestions.

My special thanks to the Hon. Mr. Justice Peter Kelly of the High Court for writing such an interesting foreword.

My thanks are also due to the Director and Governing Body of Carlow RTC, Richard Lennon, Librarian and the staff of Carlow RTC Library; Margaret Byrne, Librarian and Mary Gaynor, Assistant Librarian of the Law Society, Jonathan Armstrong, Librarian, Kings Inns.

Readers should note that as of 1 October 1997, the title of Minister for Education has been changed to Minister for Education and Science and the title of Department of Education to Department of Education and Science.

Michael J. Farry
8 December, 1997

To Veronica

Abbreviations

A.C.	Appeal Cases
All E.R.	All England Reports
Beav.	Beavan
C.L.Y.	Current Law Yearbook
CH.D.	Chancery Division
DEE	Determination under Employment Equality Act
D.L.R.	Dominion Law Reports
EAT	Employment Appeals Tribunal
E.H.H.R.	European Human Rights Reports
E.C.R.	European Court Reports
I.C.R.	Industrial Court Reports
I.L.T.R	Irish Law Times Reports
I.L.T.SJ	Irish Law Times and Solicitors Journal
Ir. Jur. Rep.	Irish Jurist Reports
I.R.	Irish Reports
I.R.L.R.	Industrial Relations Law Reports
JCC	Justiciary Cases
J.I.S.L.L.	Journal of the Irish Society of Labour Lawyers
J.P.	Justice of the Peace Reports
K.B.	Kings Bench
L.R.	Law Reports
L.G.R.	Local Government Reports
L.T.	Law Times Reports
N.Z.L.R.	New Zealand Law Reports
N.I.	Northern Ireland Law Reports
Q.B.	Queens Bench
SJ	Solicitors Journal
T.L.R.	Times Law Reports
UD	Unfair Dismissal
W.L.R.	Weekly Law Reports

Table of Cases

Table of Statutes

CONSTITUTION OF IRELAND

CHAPTER I

Early Irish Vocational Education

Better build schoolrooms for the boy
Than cells and gibbets for the man.

Eliza Cook, A song for the ragged schools

Vocational education is not a modern phenomenon. The concept of educating
or training a person for their station in life has existed since the earliest times.
Modern Irish vocational education is merely continuing a process that has
existed for thousands of years

Early Irish history shows that there was a recognised approach for dealing with vocational education. Even before St. Patrick there were specific
legal provisions relating to syllabi, and relating to teachers. There were also
legal provisions regarding social recognition in terms of status which determined the particular vocational training a person was to receive.

1.1 The Brehon Laws

The earliest written provision for Irish vocational education is contained in
the Senchus Mór, the most important law tract of ancient Ireland, more com-
monly referred to as the Brehon Laws.

They contained sections governing the colour and type of clothing to be
worn by persons of different social rank as well as the subjects considered
appropriate for different classes of students.

The Milesians (3,500) are credited with introducing the distinction of
rank by the wearing of colours. A slave was permitted to wear only one colour, a peasant two, a soldier three, an Ollamh six. Cusack[1] suggests that this
was probably the origin of the Scotch plaid.

1.2 The Subjects Taught

The subjects to be learned also depended on the vocation or station in life of
the student. The children of "Og-Aire" chiefs were to be taught "The herding
of lambs and calves and kids and young pigs and kiln drying, and combing
and woodcutting" to boys; the use of the quern and kneading trough and the

---

[1] M.F. Cusack, *The Patriots History of Ireland* (Dublin, 1871), p. 28.

use of the sieve to daughters.[2] The sons of a noble were to be taught horse-manship, swimming, chess playing and brann-playing; the daughters were to be taught sewing, cutting-out and embroidery. Sons of the Feini grades were not to be taught horsemanship.[3]

A teacher who failed to teach the required subjects was obliged to repay most of the fee paid to him by the parent. The Senchus provides "If these things be not taught them, there is a fine of two-thirds of the price of fosterage to be paid to the father, on account of the negligence of the foster-father." The herding of sheep, one of the occupations referred to in the Senchus, was a common feature of both Irish and ancient Greek civilisation. Homer in his great epic the Illiad (77 B.C.) refers on a number of occasions to the skills of the shepherd.

The Brehon Laws were collected into one volume about the time of St. Patrick in the late 430's. Linguistic evidence shows that parts of the text are in the Bearla Feini dialect of the fifth century and the glossary of Cormac Mac Airt (227-266 A.D.) written in the ninth or tenth century quotes the Senchus Mór a number of times. These Laws "persisted after the Norman conquest side by side with English law until the destruction of the old Gaelic order which followed the battle of Kinsale (1601)."[4]

1.3 Trial Pieces

Much of the evidence of early Irish vocational education relates to attempts at designs called trial pieces. These are on bone or slate and were produced by individual trainees or apprentices rather than by groups in a formalised school structure. They date from the early sixth century onwards and some such arti-facts have been found during the excavations of medieval Dublin at Wood Quay and are now in the National Museum.

Many of the great examples of Irish technical skills are religious objects or associated with religious, *e.g.* The Book of Kells, The Chalice of Ardagh, The Cross of Cong, but by no means all. Silver shields were made (1383 B.C.) at Airget-Ros, by Eanna Airgtheach while Eochaidh Eadghadach, king of the Milesians had a goldsmith and specimens preserved in the Royal Irish Academy may have been made during his reign.

Perhaps the best illustration of technical innovation is the artificial silver hand created by an artificer and a physician for King Nuad of the Tuatha Dé Danann (AM. 3303). The Brehon Laws required that a king should be free from personal defects. When King Nuad lost a hand in battle, a substitute hand had to be made if Nuad was to retain the crown. One was successfully

---

2 Senchus Mór, p. 153.
3 Senchus Mór, p. 157.
4 Fergal McGrath S.J. *Education in Ancient and Medieval Ireland* (Dublin, 1979), p. 36.

designed and made and ever afterwards the king was known as Nuad of the Silver Hand.[5]

1.4 Schools

One of the earlier examples of a formalised school structure is probably the famous military college called the "House of the Red Branch" (Craebh Ruadh) at the fort of Eo-Main or Emania built by Queen Macha, near Armagh, about 400 years before Christ. This institute flourished for more than 600 years but according to Dr. Healy[6] when St. Patrick came to Ard-Macha, this school no longer existed having been destroyed by the Three Collas about the year 322 A.D.

Most of the early Irish schools developed in the monasteries which further organised and developed the systematic and formal transmission of skills.

Students in these monasteries copied scriptures and manuscripts, some of which were illuminated with intricate designs. They also engaged in architecture and building. The first building in stone is said to have been erected by Malachy O'Morgair who died in 1148 A.D.

1.5 Medieval Developments

There seems to have been little educational progress on a national level until the early fourteenth century when both civil and church authorities thought it desirable that a university be established not for the native Irish but "for the Engleis lieges of the Norman Kings".[7] Both powers pursued this objective in a sporadic but determined fashion over the centuries.

In 1311, the Archbishop of Dublin was granted a papal bull by Pope Clement V to found the first university of Dublin. This attempt did not, however, prosper and in 1320 Alexander de Bicknor, Archbishop Lech's successor to the see of Dublin, applied for and procured a Bull from Pope John XXII confirming the former Bull and the statutes drawn up for the earlier foundation.[8]

Edward III supported this university, lectures were given in St. Patrick's Cathedral and degrees conferred, but this initiative also failed as did another attempt in 1475. Contemporary accounts, however, indicate that the absence of university status did not affect the high academic standards which existed in Irish schools.

---

[5] For a fuller account see Cusack, *The Illustrated History of Ireland* (Kenmare, 1868), p.61

[6] Dr. J. Healy, *Ireland's Ancient School's and Scholars* (Dublin, 1890).

[7] T. Corcoran S.J., *Education Systems in Ireland* (Louvain, 1928).

[8] W. MacNeile Dixon, Trinity College Dublin (London, 1902), p. 3.

1.6 The Gaelic Schools

Edmund Campion (Oxford Fellow, later martyred) in his Histoire of Ireland 1570-1571 comments on a visit to a gaelic school in 1570:

> Without either precept or observation of congruite, they spoke Latin like a vulgar language, learned in their common schools of leechcraft and laws, whereat they begin children and hold on sixtene or twentie yeares, conning by rote the Aphorisms of Hippocrates, and the Civil Institutes. . . .[9]

Corcoran[10] confirms that, like the universities of Europe, these schools taught medicine on the lines of Galen and Hippocrates and that a considerable body of traditional (chiefly herbal) medicine was taught in Irish. The Institutes of Justinian (the new code) was taught in Latin, the Brehon Law in Irish.

One such school was the law seminary of the MacEgan family in Tipperary in the reign of Charles 1 (1600-1649).[11] Corcoran states that twelve generations at least of the family of brehons and historians lectured in at least eleven different regions:

> Their chief school was at Ballymac Egan in the North of Ormond. Another great law school, enjoying large revenues from land was that of O'Daveren at Caher mac Naughten in Burren, it was still powerful in 1603.[12]

The Corpus Juris Civilis of Justinian, an elementary synopsis of the new code and digest of Roman Law commissioned by the Emperor Justinian, became law in 533 A.D. In the twelfth century a school of commentators (glossatores) in Bologna began the modern research and revival of the Institutes. Their work the glossatores was found in Pisa, and brought to Florence where it remained to the end of the last century.[13]

1.7 Teachers

In Roman Law tutors seem to have been custodians of students entrusted to their care in a way which bears a striking similarity to fosterage under the Brehon Laws. The students were boarded with the teacher who was paid an

---

[9] Edmund Campion, *Histoire of Ireland, 1570-711* and McGrath *op. cit.* p. 56.
[10] Corcoran, *op.cit.,* p. vi.
[11] Edward Ledwith, *The Antiquities of Ireland* (Dublin, 1814.)
[12] Corcoran., pp. v-vi.
[13] Bryan McMahon, Ph.D., *Some Fundamental Concepts in the Civil Law System*, JISEL, 1977, p. 8.

appropriate fee depending on the social status of the pupil and the life style in which he had to be maintained.

The Institutes state:

> *Tutores autem sunt, qui cam vie ac potestatem habent, exque ree ipsa nomen ceperunt.*

> Tutors are those who have this authority and power, and they take their names from the nature of their office.

> *Est autem tutela, ut Servius definivit jus ac potestas in capite libero ad tuendum eum, qui propter aetatem se defendera nequit, jure civili data ac permissa.*

> That tutelage, as Servius has defined it, is a right and power over a free person, given and permitted by the civil law in order to protect one whose tender years prevent him defending himself.[14]

1.8 Fosterage under the Brehon Laws

It appears that children were boarded with their tutors and regarded under the Brehon Law as being foster-children. Fosterage derived from the Latin alo, to nourish.

There were two kinds of fosterage under Brehon Law, fosterage for affection, and fosterage for payment. The price of fosterage depended on the social rank of the child's parent. The fosterage of a son of a king cost thirty "séds", of a son of an Og aire three "séds".

1.9 Teacher's Powers of Discipline

There were three ages of foster children. The first age was one to seven years, the middle age, seven to twelve years, the last age twelve to seventeen, and the power of the foster parent to chastise the student depended on the age of the child. "He is to be castigated in the first age; and he shall be without food, with castigation, in the second age; and restitution shall be made during the last age, from twelve years out. And no difference is observed between their assault and their larceny until they reach twelve years.[15]

> *Is i lanamanacht athfethair itir in dalta ocus in taite forcetail, for-cetal cen dicell (ocus a fuirmid an grad), ocus cosc can acgairbe on oite for in dalta, ocus a biathad ocus eitiud in airet bes ac denam dana dligthig, muna fagba'o neoc aile;*

---

[14] The Institutes of Justinian, See Imperatores Justininiani institutionum, J. B. Moyle D.C.L., (Oxford, 1912).

[15] Hiberniae Leges et Institutiones Antiquae, Senchus Mór (Dublin, 1865) Vol. 11, p. 1187.

The social connection that is considered between the student and the literary foster-father is; that the latter is to instruct him to the best of his ability, and to prepare him for his degree, and to chastise him without severity, and to feed and clothe him while he is learning poetry or law, unless he gets such from someone else.

ocus o scoil Feniusa Forrsaid anall gabair in foscud sain; ocus faigdi fri dommataid, ocus gaire fri sennataid on dalta don aite, ocus log enech in graid a fuireama he, ocus a etail dana uile in airet bes aca foglaim, ocus cet tuilleam a dana iar ndul a tig a aite.

and from the school of Fenius Forsaidh onwards this custom prevails; and the student is to assist his tutor in poverty, and to support him in his old age, and the honour price of the degree for which he prepares him, and all the gains of his art while he is leaving it, and the first earning of his art after leaving the house of his tutor, are to be given to the tutor.[16]

1.10 Demands for a University

The persistent demand for a university was conceded in response to a petition presented by the Mayor and Corporation of Dublin to the Privy Council in 1590. A Royal warrant was granted "to erect a college on the site of the Abbey of All Hallows for learning in the said place . . . in such manner and with such good orders and statutes as some other of our colleges here in England." The college was to be *mater universitas*, for the better education training and instruction of scholars and students. The College, *Sacrosanctae et Individuae Trinitatis* opened in 1593 and celebrated its quatrecentenary in 1993.

This development did not satisfy Catholic needs and in 1600 Hugh O'Neill the Earl of Tyrone demanded: "That there be erected a university upon the crown rents of Ireland, wherein all sciences shall be taught according to the manner of the Catholic Church"[17] and again in the peace negotiations of 1644 the same demand was put forward with the addition of "Innes of Court and free and common schools."[18]

1.11 The Act of Uniformity

These requests were followed by the Act of Uniformity 1665 which exacerbated the Catholic situation by providing that every school master and every teacher should make a declaration that he would conform to the Church of

---

[16] *Ibid.,* pp. 348-349.

[17] Corcoran, *op. cit.,* Hugh O'Neill's *Educational Demands, 1600* and Calander S.P. *1599-1600 Ewstopia.*

[18] Corcoran, *op. cit., Education in the Peace Negotiations 1644,* Corwen, p. 24, Carte Papers, x, 46.

Ireland, take an Oath of Allegiance and Supremacy and not undertake any teaching before obtaining a licence from the Church of Ireland Ordinary of the diocese.

The famous Kilkenny born Bishop and Philosopher George Berkeley (1685-1753) questioned;

> . . . *whether, in imitation of the Jesuits at Paris, who admit Protestants to study in their colleges, it may not be right for us also to admit Roman Catholics into our college, without obliging them to attend chapel duties, or catechisms, or divinity lectures and ... keep money in the Kingdom, and prevent the prejudices of a foreign education.*[19]

There was no response to Berkeley's query. Some twenty years previously he had been unable to obtain an appointment in Ireland because he was suspected of being a Jacobite after the publication of a sermon on passive obedience which he gave in Trinity College Chapel.

Establishment opinion against the education of Catholics above their station in life was allied to the need to control the educational system and to use it as an *instrumentum regnum.*

1.12 Charter and Private Schools

The response to the demand for schools was, therefore, met by the foundation of the Charter Schools in 1733 to teach English, Scripture, Principles of the Protestant Religion, Writing and Arithmetic. The Charter schools were also to cause Popish children and other poor natives *"to be instructed in Husbandry and Housewifery, or in Trades or Manufactures, or in* **suchlike manual occupations, as the society shall think proper."**

Private schools did provide instruction in the classics, mathematics and commercial subjects and Edmund Burke (1729-97) and Cardinal Cullen (1803-1878) are among those to receive such an education at the famous Quaker boarding school founded at Ballitore by Abraham Shackleton. There is some evidence that shorthand was among the commercial subjects taught in the school, even at this early date.[20]

Although the Act for the establishment of Maynooth seminary was passed in 1795 the official attitude toward the native Catholics was reinforced by the belief that schoolmasters had assisted the insurgents in the Rebellion of 1798, and Castlereagh refused to introduce legislation to provide a popular system of education, ostensibly on this account.

---

[19] George Berkeley, *The Querist*, 1750, also Corcoran *op. cit.,* p. 38.
[20] See Thomas Pim's *Stenography Book*, 1786, Ballitore School Collection, Y. M. Historical Collection, Box 1078, Religious Society of Friends (Quakers) 4-5, Eustace Street, Dublin 2.

1.13 The Royal Dublin Society

In 1731 members of the new protestant landlord class established the Dublin Society for improving Husbandry Manufactures, and other useful Arts[21] at a meeting in the Philosophical Society Rooms in Trinity College Dublin.

The society which encouraged new methods of land cultivation and technical education provided education in Botany, Veterinary Science, Art and Architecture. The Metropolitan School of Art was established by the Dublin Society in 1746.

1.14 Early Legislation

The Public Libraries Act (Ireland) 1855 contains the first statutory provisions for Schools of Science and Art in Ireland. It was introduced to give greater facilities for the establishment of free public libraries and museums or schools of Science and Art and was amended in 1877 to include the science and art of music. Borough councils or Boards and Town Commissioners were given liberty to apply part of the rate toward the payment of salaries of music teachers

1.15 The Department of Agriculture and Technical Instruction

The second Report of the Royal Commissioners on Technical Instruction (1884) collated evidence relating to technical Instruction in Ireland and led to unsuccessful attempts to introduce legislation in 1886 and 1887. Eventually the Technical Instruction Act 1889 (amended in 1891) was enacted and applied to Ireland but there was no real progress until the establishment of the Department of Agriculture and Technical Instruction under the Agriculture and Technical Instruction (Ireland) Act 1899. During the parliamentary recess of 1895 a committee was convened by Sir Horace Plunkett to report on the establishment of a department of Agriculture and Industries for Ireland. This committee became known as the Recess Committee and their report in 1896 stated that practical education in Ireland barely existed because there was no system of local administration to enable the 1889 Act to have any effect. It was only when the Grand Jury system was replaced by the Local Government (Ireland) Act of 1898 that it became possible for local bodies to contribute funds for technical instruction.

In some respects the 1899 Act was a turning point in the development of technical education in Ireland. It established an administrative educational structure and a statutory system of financing from central and local funds.

Another commission established to determine "how far, and in what form, Manual and Practical Instruction should be included in Primary Schools un-

---

[21] Henry F. Berry, *A History of the Royal Dublin Society* (London, 1915), p. 22.

der the Board of National Education" made three reports in 1897[22] and a final report in 1898.[23]

1.16 Archbishop Walsh

One of the great pioneers of industrial education in Ireland was the famous Archbishop of Dublin, Most Rev. Dr. Walsh who called for the establishment of a system of industrial training in 1886, some ten years before Plunkett or the Recess Committee. In a speech delivered at St. Joseph's Blind Asylum, Drumcondra in October, 1886 he stated;

> It is a sad commentary on the working of the system . . . that in our department of primary education-no place, or practically no place has yet been found for a system of industrial training for our industrial classes.[24]

He pointed out that the great bulk of the population had to live by the labour of their hands and he continued "an education that is purely literary, and in no sense industrial, is not only useless but positively unfits them for the work of their lives."[25]

Although the Agriculture and Technical Instruction (Ireland) Act arose out of Horace Plunkett's Recess Committee Report and Archbishop Walsh's concern was predominantly with the primary system,[26] there is little doubt that the Archbishop's speeches played a seminal role. It may be, however, that his preoccupation with the primary system left the Catholic church with no formal role in the new structure.

In a speech at Goldenbridge, Dublin, a month later, he stated that he did not mean that the schools should undertake the teaching of trades. Significantly section 30 of the Agriculture and Technical Instruction (Ireland) Act 1899, in defining technical instruction, specified: "It shall not include instruction given in elementary schools or teaching the practice of any trade or industry or employment. . . ."

1.17 Department of Education

The Department of Agriculture and Technical Instruction continued to con-

---

[22] First Report; 1897 (c.88383) XL111.1, Second Report; 1897 (c.8383) XL111.109, Third Report; 1897 (c.8618) XL111. 401.

[23] Final Report; 1898 (c.8923) XLIV.1.

[24] Patrick F. Walsh, *William F. Walsh* (Dublin, 1977), pp. 504-507.

[25] *Ibid.*

[26] See Letter to Plunkett, 25 August 1896, T.P. Gill Letters, National Library, Kildare Street, Dublin, 13 509.

trol technical instruction until the Department of Education was established under the Ministers and Secretaries Act 1924 and its powers and duties were assigned to be administered by the Minister for Education. The business and functions relating to agriculture were separated from technical instruction and were assigned to the new Department of Lands and Agriculture, while technical instruction under the 1899 Act continued to be administered by the Department of Education until the enactment of new legislation in the form of the Vocational Education Act 1930.

CHAPTER 2

Modern Vocational Education

Technical Education is
the exaltation of manual labour.

W. E. Gladstone, *Speech*, Chester, 12 September 1890

Modern Vocational Education is principally regulated by the Vocational Education Act 1930, and the Vocational Education (Amendment) Act 1944. There have been a number of other Amendments in the main relating to VECs *e.g.* the Vocational Education (Amendment) Act 1970 which enabled a VEC with the Ministers consent to engage in jointly maintaining a school. This facilitated the development of Community schools.

2.1 The Vocational Education Act 1930

Prior to the 1930 Act, vocational education was governed by the Agriculture and Technical Instruction (Ireland) Act 1899. The change of nomenclature has never been justified or explained despite the previous designation but the Commission established to review and advise on the new Act was entitled the Commission on Technical Education.

The Minister in a letter to the inaugural meeting of the Commission referred to the need to have the fullest information in the matter of Technical Instruction and to his conclusion that the Commission should examine how far trade and industry were being kept back through "lack of technical training." He thus used the terms technical education, technical instruction and technical training. Perhaps the terms were being used loosely with no particular significance attaching to any of them or alternatively the use of the new title may have been intended to place more emphasis on the work related aspects of the education to be provided.

However, as pointed out later the Minister's assurance to the Catholic Hierarchy that the Act introduced nothing new in relation to control of the system, would have been better facilitated had the title of the new Act not been changed.

The Act does not define the term vocational education but presumably it encompasses technical education and continuation education both of which are the only types of education referred to and defined in the Act.

In 1943 the Commission on Vocational Organisation referring to the word vocation stated that it had the advantage of being a comprehensive term which covered all forms of occupation whether profession, industry, trade or craft and that it avoided difficulties as to whether certain occupations were to be called profession, industry, trade or business.

This explanation is not applicable to the 1930 Act because professional education had never been provided within the technical instruction system of the nineteenth century or indeed within the manual instruction system which preceded it. The Commission on Technical Education[1] referred to the fact that secondary schools were not concerned with the special preparation of youth for employment at the normal age of 16. "They have maintained a tradition of preparing young people for university and professional life and for appointments in the civil service."

2.2 Technical and Continuation Education

The 1930 Act obliges a VEC to provide both "technical" and "continuation" education and defines both of these terms. Clearly it was envisaged that the main emphasis would be on continuation education and the Act imposes more onerous obligations on a VEC with regard to it than it does with regard to technical education. The Commission on Technical Education recommended[2] continuation schools as well as classes.

The term vocational education is not referred to in either the definition of continuation education or technical education, but trades, manufacture, commerce and other technical pursuits are common to both definitions. Section 3 of the Vocational Education Act 1930 states:

> For the purposes of this Act the expression "continuation education" means education to continue and supplement education provided in **elementary schools** and includes general and practical training in preparation for employment in trades, manufacture, agriculture, commerce and other industrial pursuits, and also general and practical training for improvement of young persons in the early stages of such employment.

In a letter to the Bishop of Limerick,[3] the Minister referred to the instruction to be given as **continuation instruction** and stated:

> "It is not, however, and was never intended to be, continuation education in the sense that it continues the type of education given in primary schools or continue the atmosphere that prevails in them.

---

[1] Report of the Commission on Technical Education, Stationery Office, Dublin, 1927, p. 49.
[2] *loc. cit.* recommendation 16, p. 30.
[3] See Dr. S. O'Buachalla, *Education Policy in Twentieth Century Ireland*, Appendix B.

The use of the words **continuation instruction** instead of continuation education in the letter might seem a little ingenious but the use of the phrase elementary schools in the Act is strange, given the fact that the term "elementary schools" has never been explained.

The late Sean O'Connor, a former secretary of the Department of Education, said[4] it would seem farfetched to suggest that it was used deliberately to assure the Catholic bishops that continuation instruction did not mean a continuation of the type of education in primary schools but he offered no other explanation.

2.3 Development

For over thirty years the vocational sector was severely restricted in its operation and did not develop its core activity, partly because of the compliant acceptance by successive Ministers of limitations on competing with the Church controlled second level schools.

In 1963 Dr. Hillery proposed to introduce Comprehensive schools and a Technical Schools Leaving Certificate to achieve "a technical educational standard comparable in esteem, but differing in kind, from that available in the secondary school."

The author believes that when this new development in technical education was proposed by Dr. Hillery, at least one Catholic Bishop felt that they (the Catholic Bishops) had been deceived by O'Sullivan and that the contents of his letter and the assurance they thought it contained was cited against the Minister. The late Sean O'Connor substantiates the view that the Bishops felt that they had been deceived, in his reflections entitled *A Troubled Sky* in 1986.

2.4 Main Provisions

"Technical education" is defined by section 4(1) as meaning:

> education pertaining to trades, manufactures, commerce and other industrial pursuits (including the occupations of girls and women connected with the household) and in subjects bearing thereon or relating thereto and includes education in science and art (including, in the county boroughs of Dublin and Cork, music) and also includes physical training.

While the only training mentioned is physical training, the words "pertaining" and "pursuits" in the definition and the general drafting of the section cover a multitude. Music is not defined as technical education except in the County boroughs of Dublin or Cork.

---

4   Sean O'Connor, *A Troubled Sky* (Dublin, 1986), p. 11.

Vocational education areas are established by Part II which also provides for the establishment of vocational education committees, hereinafter referred to as VECs in and for, each such area. Continuation education and technical education are dealt with Part III and a duty is imposed on every VEC to establish and maintain a "suitable" system of continuation education and to supply or aid the supply of technical education in its area.

There are 10 parts of the Act which contain a total of 126 sections. There are also 5 schedules to the Act. Part II the major part of the Act contains 23 sections dealing with VECs. The Act has been amended seven times[5] and mainly in relation to VECs.

The accent on manual instruction and the concept of learning by doing[6] was an old one, but the statutory description as education of what was previously called instruction may have been an effort to influence public opinion. The Commission on Vocational Organisation pointed out some years later[7] that the status of the educated person was almost in direct ratio to his inability to work with his hands.

2.5 Not General Education

The secular nature of the Act was the subject of comment by those who noted that the new co-educational multi-denominational schools could create dangers to the religion and morals of pupils. Monsignor Cummins, Chairman of the Roscommon Technical Committee denounced the Bill in such terms while an anonymous veteran Christian Brother pointed out[8] that "the Bill was received with 'paens of praise' by those . . . not familiar with educational problems...followed by silence broken by a startling and scathing denunciation" by Monsignor Cummins. The editor of the Irish Rosary in the same edition stated that "the priests and people of Ireland would need to sit up and take notice. The new 'Vocational Education Bill' is a further step in purely secular education under local authorities." To him it seemed to be a most dangerous measure, by reason of its secular tendency and its exclusion of religion. The editor also claimed that the new Bill was "a menace to religious education" and that it would provide, a host of new jobs for a horde of new job-seekers at the public expense.

The Minister for Education told the Catholic Hierarchy in a letter of 31 October 1930 that both continuation and technical education provided for by the Act remained essentially vocational and that vocational schools were distinctly not schools for general education. General education would continue

---

5 In 1936, 1944, 1947, 1950, 1953, 1962, 1970.
6 Rousseau (1712-1778), Pestalozzi (1746-1827), Frobel (1782-1852) and many others.
7 Report of the Commission on Vocational Organisation 1943, Chapter 1, p. 7, paragraph 9.
8 *Irish Rosary*, June 1930 p. 433.

to be given in primary and in secondary schools. Some commentators claim that the Catholic Bishops were assured that the vocational system would not compete with schools controlled by Catholic authorities and that it would not be allowed to infringe on the type of education they provided. Others claimed that it was "the same old train on the same old tracks".[9] The Bishops reservations about the provision of co-education and about night schools under the Act were also addressed by the Minister in his letter.[10]

2.6 Effect of the Act

While the objectives of the Act were clear, its shortcomings were: (1) that it did not deal with Apprenticeship because the Department of Industry and Commerce were preparing the Apprenticeship Act 1931; and (2) although many vocational schools were to be located in country areas, the Act did not deal with agricultural training or education (it did deal with horticulture). The Departments of Agriculture and of Industry and Commerce had each protected their own areas and imposed limitations on the new system. The Hierarchy apparently, had done likewise.

2.7 Marcus O'Sullivan

When it was introduced into the Dáil by Professor O'Sullivan, the then Minister for Education, he stated that the Vocational Education Bill was only envisaged as a stop gap measure "to deal with the problems that will face us at least in the course of the next five or ten years." This public statement of the Minister contrasts strangely with the private view. When the draft Bill was discussed with the Department of Finance[11] the records show that "[t]he Department of Education contemplates that the developments provided for in the Bill may not be fully secured inside a period of 20 years." In addition, at a conference with the Minister for Finance on 14 August 1929, the Minister for Education intimated that he was most anxious that Vocational Education schemes should proceed only by gradual steps, and he wished to receive suggestions as to means of providing a brake against over-rapid development with consequent reaction upon public funds. The Department of Finance noted that continuation education must contain a practical manual training for both sexes. This would put a brake on the speed of development. The difficulties of providing a sufficient number of trained instructors would also slow down development. A further brake could be achieved by limiting the rate that committees could levy to finance the system.

The Minister for Education was not totally compliant because a Department of Finance minute of May 1930 states:

---

[9] Rt. Rev. Mgr. Cummins, D.D., P.P. *Irish Independent*, 7 May 1930.
[10] See O'Buachalla, *loc. cit.*
[11] Department of Finance File S84/13/29, para. 9.

So far as our control of finance is concerned the reins seem to be on the horse's back at the moment. A long list of amendments have not been examined from our point of view.[12]

A further note later that same month protests:

The Dept. of Ed have "sold a dummy" and not sent us revised draft for printing as arranged. We are now confronted with the final text of the Bill which has been printed and circulated to Deputies without our prior concurrence.[13]

According to the late Dominic O'Laoghaire[14] the instincts of John Marcus O'Sullivan for discerning how much he could "get away with" were wonderfully accurate and he was wise enough, in making concessions to entrenched interests, to preserve the minimum flexibility to achieve viability for the new departure." O'Laoghaire says that it has sometimes been fashionable in academic circles to decry the quality of O'Sullivan's real achievement in "securing acceptance of his Vocational Education Act 1930 and in getting the new school system off the ground in its early years." This may be to overstate the case. It was an achievement but in O'Sullivans own words it was not a new system and lay technical instruction committees were already an accepted feature of Irish education. In the present author's view the introduction of the technical instruction system which preceded the Vocational Education Act was a significantly greater achievement. Attributed to Horace Plunkett, it would not have been possible without the consent of Archbishop Walsh.

Despite the foregoing, it is doubtful that the Act was ever intended to last a generation. The fact that there have been relatively few legal challenges to its provisions has meant that no substantive body of case law has emerged. While the number of amendments testify to Government readiness to enact amendments to the Act when such are considered desirable. O'Laoghaire states "In fact the flexibility preserved in the 1930 Act has been unbelievably extensive." and he comments[15] on its wonderful adaptability in situations of increasing complexity. A view which the present writer would endorse.

The present Minister for Education, Micheál Martin T.D. has announced[16] that he intends to introduce new vocational education legislation (the first for 67 years) to govern the vocational sector and underpin its future.

In addition to Acts of the Oireachtas, vocational education in this country is regulated by Statutory Instruments, Memos, Circular Letters, and Agreed Reports.

---

[12] Department of Finance, 3 May 1930.
[13] Department of Finance, 28 May 1930.
[14] Dominic O'Laoghaire, *The Missionary Impulse*, NCEA, 1991, p. 35.
[15] *Ibid.*, p. 35.
[16] See *Irish Independent*, 3 September 1997.

CHAPTER 3

Vocational Education Committees

Education makes a people easy to lead,
but difficult to drive;
easy to govern,
but impossible to enslave.

Lord Brougham, *Speech*, House of Commons, 29 January 1828

The legislative origin of all of the present Vocational Education Committees is section 7(1) of the Vocational Education Act 1930 which provides:

> There shall be a committee (in this Act referred to as a vocational education committee) in and for every vocational education area to fulfil in respect of such area the duties assigned to vocational education committees by this Act.

The creation of such committees was not a new initiative because they were, in fact, the successors of the technical instruction committees established under section 14 of the Agriculture and Technical Instruction Act 1899.

3.1 Composition of a VEC

The Agriculture and Technical Instruction (Ireland) Act 1899 merely stated that a Technical Instruction Committee might consist partly of county council or urban district members and of other persons. Section 8(1) of the Vocational Education Act 1930 specifies that a VEC shall consist of fourteen members of whom not less than five nor more than eight should be persons who were members of such councils unless it was a county VEC containing urban districts.

On 11 October 1996 the Steering Group on School Accommodation recommended the following membership of VECs:

seven public representatives from the council/s within the Vocational education area,
three parents/guardians of current school students,
four teaching staff of the VEC, and
one clerical/administrative staff of the VEC

These 14 members to form a Bun Choiste which would organise the completion of the Mór Choiste with the adition of:

> three nominees of the local economy and trade unions,
> three nominees of the voluntary and community groups

This Committee of 20 members will have the option of co-opting up to 2 further members.

Under the 1930 Act the local authority did not have a free hand in selecting the non members. Section 8(4) states that in electing members of a VEC under this section a local authority "**shall** have regard"[1] to the interest and experience in education of the person proposed to be elected and to any recommendations,[2] made by bodies interested in manufacturing or trades[3] in the committee's area and **shall**[4] where it "**appears desirable**" and "**circumstances permit**" make the election so as to provide for the representation of such bodies on their VEC.

3.2 Parents and Teachers

On 23 April 1991 Deputy Jim Higgins (Fine Gael) introduced a private members Bill entitled the Vocational Education (Amendment) Bill, 1991 in Dáil Éireann. The Teachers Union of Ireland supported the Bill, the object of which was to grant membership of VECs to two parents and to two teachers. The Deputy outlined the observer status of vocational teachers at VEC meetings, some having no right of comment, while others had a right of comment only. Some VECs had a welcome practice of nominating a vocational teacher. He sought to amend section 8 of the Vocational Education Act 1930. At the second stage of the Bill, on 28 May, the Minister for Education stated that she was in sympathy with the thinking behind the proposals in the Bill, but pointed out that, on legal advice, the Bill was flawed and inoperable.

To achieve what the draftsman wanted, the Bill would have to provide that, in addition to the membership already specified in the Act, there should also be additional members, not less than two of which would be parents, and not less than two of which would be teachers.

As recently as July 1997, parents were calling for proper representation on all VECs. The Parents Association for Vocational Schools and Community Colleges (PAVSCC) called on Environment Minister Noel Dempsey to

---

[1] The phrase "shall have regard to" is not defined and means "must consider" but "considering" is the total obligation.
[2] These bodies are not given a power of nomination, they can recommend.
[3] By section 8(4) Vocational Education Act 1930 bodies of employers or employees are included in this phrase.
[4] If it "appears desirable" and "circumstances permit" the local authority can give a power of nomination to these bodies.

amend the Local Government Act to legislate for the nomination of two parents — by parents — to all VECs.[5] The present Minister for Education, Micheál Martin, intends to amend the legislation to provide for extended representation of parents, teachers and industry.

3.3 Number of VECs

At the time of writing there are thirty eight VEC's, twenty seven county committees including one each for Tipperary North Riding, and Tipperary South Riding), four city committees. (*i.e.* Dublin, Cork, Limerick and Waterford), and seven (scheduled urban districts) town committees. (*i.e.* Bray, Drogheda, Boro' of Dun Laoighaire, Galway, Sligo, Tralee and Wexford) The White Paper on Education[6] proposed the rationalisation of the number of VECs and comments that the area of jurisdiction of many of the existing ones appears to be too small to be cost effective and that this applied in particular to the urban district VECs but extends also to some county VECs. It also stated[7] that there will be legislative reform and rationalisation of the system.

The Technical Working Group appointed by Education Minister Bhreathnach, T.D., in its report of 27 June 1996 on Rationalisation of VECs for the Commission on School Accommodation Needs, recommended that the number of VECs be rationalised from thirty eight to eighteen, in stages and that the Minister use her power under section 100 of the Vocational Education Act 1930 to amalgamate the urban district VECs of Bray, Drogheda, Sligo, Tralee and Wexford with their county vocational areas. It was also recommended that the Department of Education establish a mechanism for further reviewing the number of VECs in the light of demographic trends and developments in educational provision.

On the 11 October 1996 it was announced[8] that Minister Bhreathnach accepted in principle the steering group recommendations on rationalisation of VECs. The first step would be the amalgamation of the five town VECs — Bray, Sligo, Tralee, Drogheda and Wexford — with their county committees.[9] On 21 February 1997 the Minister signed amalgamation orders to come into effect in January 1998. All of the indicators are that the amalgamations will

---

5 See *Irish Independent*, 1 July 1997 and *TUI News*, September 1997.
6 at p. 175.
7 at p. 162.
8 See *Irish Independent* 16 October 1996).
9 Vocational Education Urban District of Bray/Co. Wicklow Vocational Education Area Order 1997 S.I. 91/1997; Vocational Education Borough of Sligo/Co. Sligo Vocational Education Area Order 1997 S.I. 92/1997; Vocational Education Urban District of Tralee/Co. Kerry Vocational Education Area Order 1997 S.I. 89/1997; Vocational Education Borough of Drogheda/Co. Louth Vocational Education Area Order 1997 S.I. 90/1997; Vocational Education Borough of Wexford/Co. Wexford Vocational Education area Order 1997 S.I. 88/1997.

proceed. The Minister for Education told an IVEA delegation in September 1997 that he could not rescind the amalgamation orders. Legislation would be need to do so.[10] The second phase would probably be the amalgamation of Dun Laoghaire, Waterford, Limerick, and Galway city VECs with their county committees and the third phase would see the amalgamation of the Longford/ Westmeath, Clare/Tipperary N.R., Mayo/Roscommon, Waterford/Tipperary S.R., Carlow/Kilkenny, Laois/Offaly, Sligo/Leitrim and Cavan/Monaghan. The VECs for counties Cork, Donegal, Kildare and Meath and for the cities of Dublin and Cork were to remain unchanged.

Following the General Election of June 1997 the new Minister for Eudcation, Micheál Martin T.D., took the view that a 10-year programme of amalgamating VECs was underminig confidence in the VEC sector and that while his plans still involved some rationalisation it would not be to the extent envisaged by the Commission.[11]

3.4 Duties of a VEC

Section 30, Vocational Education Act 1930 specifies the duties generally of a VEC as being:

    (a) to establish and maintain in accordance with this Act a suitable system of continuation education in its area and to provide for the progressive development of such system; and

    (b) to supply or aid the supply in accordance with this Act of technical education in its area.

3.5 Meetings

Meetings may be held by a VEC whenever or wherever it deems necessary (see section 13 Vocational Education Act 1930) but an annual meeting and at least one monthly meeting must be held during the months of October to June.

3.6 Confidential Matters and Defamation

The law accords qualified privilege to both written and oral reports made in carrying out a private or public duty provided that they are made without malice. This means that remarks made which otherwise would be defamatory and actionable at law may be privileged because of the occasion involved where they are uttered. Confidential matters relating to the performance of duties by a VEC officer or servant should be discussed in confidence. In order

---

[10] See *Irish Independent*, 30 September 1997.
[11] See *Irish Times*, 3 September 1997.

to do so a proposal must formally be made to exclude the public and the press and a resolution passed to that effect.[12]

Matters discussed in committee are privileged but if repeated outside could be defamatory and lead to an action on that account.

3.7 Surcharge

In October 1985 VECs and CEOs were warned by the Department of Education to stop "illegal payments". A circular letter stated that the Minister was concerned that a number of chief executives had failed in their duties under section 26 of the Vocational Education Act 1930 and that large amounts of public funds had been paid illegally. This included payments made to teaching staff in excess of allocation and payments made from revenue funds for capital projects. From 1986 the Department would no longer consider retrospective sanction for such transactions. The circular warned that CEOs could be dismissed and VECs liable for prompt disciplinary action. Some VECs despite the fact that they were given formal warning about illegal payments nonetheless decided to go ahead and make such payments.[13]

That same year eighty one rebel Labour councillors in Britain were faced with financial ruin when auditors issued surcharge certificates for "wilful misconduct" in delaying setting rates. In Lambeth, South London, 32 councillors were named on a certificate issued for £126,947, while in Liverpool 49 councillors faced a bill for £106,000. In May 1996 the District Auditor of Westminister City Council imposed a surcharge of £31.6m on six councillors for wilful misconduct and in the alleged use of tax payers' money to finance the sale of council houses at cheap prices to people likely to vote Conservative.[14]

Section 5 of the Agriculture and Technical Instruction Act 1889 provided that Managers were to be personally liable for money not shown to be properly applied for the purposes for which it was granted and that the accounts were to be audited.

Section 58 of the 1930 Act provides for the audit of VEC accounts by the Local Government auditor and that sections 20 and 21 of the Local Government (Ireland) Act 1902 as amended or adapted shall apply to the audit.

Section 125 of the Vocational Education Act 1930 gives the Minister for Education the power to make regulations in respect of the accounts of a VEC and their audit. In exercise of this power the Minister for Education made the

---

[12] See *Nevin v. Roddy and Carthy* [1935] I.R. 397 and *McCarthy v. Morrissey* [1939] Ir. Jur. Rep. 82.

[13] *Irish Press*, 10 October 1985.

[14] *Irish Times*, 10 September 1985 and 10 May 1996. On 19 December 1997 the High Court in London reduced the amount to £27m and upheld the surcharge on the leader and deputy of the Council.

Vocational Education (Accounts, Audit and Procedure) Regulations 1931. Section 58(1) of the Vocational Education Act 1930 applies section 20 of the Local Government (Ireland) Act 1902 and allows the Auditor to charge a deficiency or loss caused by negligence, misconduct, or failure to bring money into account against a member or officer.

3.8 Misconduct of Members

Where members of a VEC pass unlawful resolutions or incur expenditure or deficiency, in the face of advice against such action by the CEO they may be guilty of misconduct. The CEO is obliged to record precisely what happened and to record the names of the members who voted in favour of the action despite the advice.[15] If the members honestly but wrongly believe that their action is authorised by law, it would not amount to misconduct.[16]

3.9 Notice of Surcharge

Paragraph 39 of these regulations states:

> If the auditor finds that any deficiency or loss has been incurred by the negligence or misconduct of any member or officer of a committee, or that a sum which ought have been brought into account by such officer was not so brought into account, and in pursuance of section 20 of the Local Government (Ireland) Act 1902 as applied by sub-section (1) of section 58 of the Act charges against such member or officer the amount of such deficiency, loss or sum, the chief executive officer shall, if so required by the auditor in writing, send as soon as he conveniently can, by post or otherwise, a statement of such deficiency loss, or sum to such member or officer and to each other member of the committee.

3.10 Service of Notice of Surcharge

Paragraph 40 states:

> "The CEO shall deliver, or send by post or otherwise, to each person against whom the auditor makes any surcharge or charge a copy of the certificate of dis-allowance and surcharge or charge within twenty-four hours after the making of the surcharge or charge.

---

[15] *Davies v. Cowperthwaite* [1938] 2 All E.R. 685.
[16] *Annison v. District Auditor for St. Pancras Borough Council* [1962] 1 Q. B. 489.

3.11 Surcharge against Committee Members

Surcharge against committee members was considered in *The King (Kennedy) v. Auditor of the Local Government Board*[17] where it was held that the committee members of Ennis Rural District Council who were merely parties to a resolution authorising the employment of solicitors for the performance of a purely clerical function, did not make or authorise the making of payment within the meaning of section 12 of the Local Government (Ireland) Act 1871.

There was nothing in the action of the council in employing the solicitors for the work in question to render the payment illegal or unfounded within the meaning of section 12 and the employment of the solicitors was not negligence or misconduct within the meaning of section 20 of the 1902 Act. It was also held that the members who passed the resolution were "persons accounting" within section 20.

3.12 Surcharge against an Officer

Surcharge against an officer arose in the case of *Rex (O'Carroll) v. King*[18] when an officer of Dublin Corporation, who was an "accounting person" within section 20 of the Local Government (Ireland) Act 1902 was held to be rightly surcharged. The case arose from an audit of the accounts of the Technical Education Committee of Dublin Corporation for the year ending 31 March, 1910. Mr. O'Carroll was Manager and Secretary of the City of Dublin Technical Schools and secretary to the committee. His duties included *inter alia* "checking of all accounts" In the opinion of the Auditor, he was responsible for all sums of money received in his department. A subordinate, Mr. D., had charge of all accountancy matters and this was approved of by the committee. A sum of over £200 was not brought into account. A warrant was obtained for the arrest of Mr. D. who pleaded guilty to embezzlement and falsification of accounts and was imprisoned.

The Auditor made a charge against Mr. O'Carroll and his subordinate Mr. D. for not bringing the money into account and certified that the money was due from them jointly and severally. The court held that the prosecutor was rightly surcharged with the loss caused by his negligence in failing to check the accountant's receipts with the dockets. He was accountable for receipts (fees etc.) although their actual receipt by him was through the hands of a subordinate officer.

It would have been competent for Mr. O'Carroll to rebut the *prima facie* case by showing that the sum in question had been lost without negligence or default on his part but in relation to charging, it was sufficient, without affirmatively avowing any negligence to state that there were sums which ought to have been brought into account.

---

[17] [1907] 2 K. B. 505.
[18] [1916] Vol. L I.L.T.R. 193.

The auditor may permit errors in accounts, which in his opinion, have been caused by inadvertence to be corrected. In England negligence is now dealt with by the local authority and negligence which amounts to "wilful misconduct" can be dealt with by the district auditor.

3.13 The Data Protection Act 1988

Paragraph 6 of the Third Schedule, of the Data Protection Act 1988 as applied by section 16(1)(a) requires bodies established by or under any enactment, and financed wholly or partly by moneys provided by a Minister of the Government to register as a Data Controller, if they hold personal data capable of being processed automatically. A VEC is such a body and, therefore, is obliged to register. Circular Letter DPA Ed 3/89 points out that registration of a VEC covers all the vocational schools under its control. Registration must be renewed every year, the current fee being £100.

Data capable of being processed automatically includes personal data held on word processors, telephone logging equipment, computers, flexi-time systems etc. and schools which hold such personal data must observe the provisions of the Act in relation to it.

These are that the personal data must be:

- obtained and processed fairly;
- held for specified lawful purposes;
- not used or disclosed in any way incompatible with the specified purposes;
- adequate, relevant, and not excessive for the specified purposes;
- accurate and up-to-date;
- not kept longer than necessary;
- available to the data subject; and
- kept secure.

3.14 Common Law Duties of VEC as an Employer

Every employer has a duty to take reasonable care for the safety of his workers during the course of their employment.[19] This involves not exposing them to unreasonable or unnecessary risk.[20] The duty is personal to the employer and it is no defence for an employer to claim that he delegated this function to a school principal, manager or another person.

---

[19] *Wilsons and Clyde Coal Co. v. English* [1938] A.C. 57.
[20] *Street v. B.E.A.* [1952] 2 Q.B. 399.

3.15 Negligence of VEC (Staff)

This duty to take reasonable care, includes the duty; to provide a safe place of work, to provide safe plant and machinery, to provide a safe system of work, to provide competent fellow workers, and to provide proper and adequate supervision. In order to succeed in an action an injured worker must prove that the employer was negligent, that the employer committed a breach of his duty to take reasonable care for his safety and that the injury he has suffered resulted from this breach. In *Bolton v. Stone*[21] Lord Reid said it is negligence to allow even a small risk to arise if it can easily be avoided.

In *Butt v. Inner London Education Authority*[22] the Court of Appeal upheld a county court decision that, although the Factories Act 1961 applied so as to impose a statutory duty and despite the fact that the plaintiff pupil at a technical school was adequately supervised, the school authority was negligent in not fencing a machine.

3.16 Negligence of VEC (Students)

The duty of care owed by a school authority to children on the schools premises was reviewed by Mr. Justice Barr in *Mapp (an infant) v. Gilhooley*[23] when he held that the duty owed to pupils on school premises in the course of normal school activities is **to take reasonable care to protect them from foreseeable risks of personal injury or harm**. In measuring that duty; the Court must take into account all relevant factors, including:

• the ages of the children in question;

• the activities in which they may be engaged;

• the degree of supervision; and

• the opportunity which those in charge had to prevent or minimise the mischief complained of.

3.17 The Safety, Health and Welfare at Work Act 1989

A VEC is deemed to be an employer for the purposes of this Act. The result is that it has a number of statutory duties with which it must comply.

The first and most important duty is to ensure as far as is **reasonably practicable**, the safety, health and welfare at work of all of their employees (section 6). Vocational teachers although officers, are covered by this injunction.

---

[21] [1951] A.C. 850 .
[22] [1968] 66 L.G.R. 379.
[23] *Mapp (an infant) v. Gilhooley* [1990] I.T.L.R., 5 March.

In relation to places of work used in connection with work activities by persons who are not their employees, there is a duty to ensure that the place, the entrances and exits and articles or substances in them, do not endanger the persons using them at work (section 8).

The VEC is obliged to identify and assess hazards at work, to specify the manner in which the safety, health and welfare of persons at that place of work will be secured and to prepare a Safety Statement (section 12). A consultative mechanism on safety and health at the place of work must be established and safety representatives appointed. Each school within a VEC's area is a separate place of work and a separate safety statement is required in respect of each school.

"Reasonably Practicable"   The word "practicable" on its own has been held in *Adsell v. K&L Founders and Engineers Ltd.*[24] to imply possibility in the light of current knowledge and invention, but the addition of the qualification "reasonably" mitigates this so that the duty imposed on an employer is thus not an absolute one.

The meaning of "reasonably practicable" has been subject to judicial scrutiny on a number of occasions, most notably in *Edwards v. NCB*[25] where it was stated that "it seems to imply that a computation must be made by the owner in which the *quantum* of risk is placed on one scale and the sacrifice involved in the measure for averting the risk (whether in money, time or trouble) is placed on the other, and if it is shown that there is a gross disproportion between them — the risk being insignificant in relation to the sacrifice — the defendants discharge the onus on them."

While some commentators consider that the "reasonably practicable" test bears a remarkable resemblance to the employer's common law duty of care, based in negligence, it must be noted that in *Trott v. Smith*[26] it was pointed out that this expression when used in relation to a charge of breach of statutory duty "places a stricter obligation on an employer than that imposed at common law."

A failure to take "reasonable precautions" occurred in *Wrenn v. Bus Éireann*[27] when a conductor left a **potentially violent group** of passengers and returned downstairs. He had quietened a fracas on the top deck of the Artane bus but did not ask the assailant to leave or notify the Gardaí. When the conductor went downstairs it started again and the plaintiff was slashed with a razor blade. Regulation 44 of the Road Traffic (Public Service Vehicle) Regulations 1963 imposes a duty "to take all reasonable precautions to ensure the safety of passengers" on vehicles.

---

[24] [1953] 1 All E.R. 97.
[25] [1949] 1 K.B. 702.
[26] [1957] 1 W.L.R 1154
[27] Unreported, Supreme Court, 31 March 1995.

In *Larner v. British Steel plc*,[28] the Court of Appeal held that section 29 of the Factories Act 1961 must be read without implying any test of reasonable foreseeability.

"safety, health and welfare" are not defined in the Act. Some indication of the meaning of safety may be derived from the Fourth Schedule to the Act.

"at work" This phrase would apply to a teacher injured while taking refreshment at a permitted hour or relieving necessities of nature is in the course of his employment.

Section 7 imposes a duty on an employer to persons other than his employees not to expose them to risk to their health or safety in the way he conducts his undertaking. This is an obligation to the general public but would apply to students, visitors, self-employed and employees of another. Students attending a school or college as well as those on industrial trips to factories or business premises would obviously be included.

Persons engaged in maintenance, upkeep or repair of schools and colleges would be covered by section 6.

Duties of Employees Section 9. The duties of an employee while at work are specified in general terms to take care for his own safety health and welfare and that of others, to co-operate with the employer, to use protective clothing and equipment, to report defects in plant, equipment, place or system of work and not to intentionally or recklessly interfere with or misuse any appliance, protective clothing convenience or equipment provided for securing health, safety or welfare.

In addition to taking care for themselves workers now have a statutory duty to report defects in equipment, *e.g.* lathes, extractor fans but also defects in the premises, *e.g.* worn floor covering, slippery floor surfaces, damaged steps, broken glass, damaged desks, damaged electrical sockets etc.

Identification of Hazards Section 12(3) requires employers to examine the place of work and to identify potential causes of harm. The nature of the work, previous accidents and ill health of employees can help in this respect. Physical hazards, chemical hazards, biological agents and human factors must be considered. Noise, dust, vibration, over-exposure to ultra-violetlight, radiation, hot surfaces or substances, faulty equipment, machinery, electricity, handling of goods or equipment are among the physical hazards.

Chemical hazards include carcinogens, explosive substances, skin irritants, acids, dyes, solvents and items likely to cause chest problems. Biological agents include viruses and bacteria.

The human factors to be taken into account include age, mental and physi-

---

[28] T.L.R., 15 February 1993.

cal capability, pregnancy, new workers, and the avoidance of sustained stress.

3.18 The Occupiers' Liability Act 1995

Subject to section 8, the common law rules relating to occupiers liability have been replaced by duties, liabilities and rights under this Act.

Section 8 provides that nothing in the Act shall be construed as affecting any enactment or any rule of law relating to:

(a) self defence, the defence of others or the defence of property,

(b) any liability imposed as a member of a particular class of persons including the following classes:
  (1) Persons by virtue of a contract for the hire of, or for the carriage for reward of persons or property in, any vessel, vehicle, train, aircraft or other means of transport;
  (2) persons by virtue of a contract of bailment; and
  (3) employers in respect of their duties towards their employees or

(c) any liability imposed on an occupier for a tort committed by another person in circumstances where the duty imposed on the occupier is of such a nature that its performance may not be delegated to another person.

Categories of entrant　　The Act specifies three types of entrant on to property: (1) visitors, (2) recreational users, and (3) trespassers.

A "**visitor**" is:

(a) an entrant, other than a recreational user, who is present on premises at the **invitation or with the permission**, of the occupier (while present for the purpose for which invited or permitted) or any other entrant specified in paragraph (a) (b) or (c) of the definition of recreational user;

(b) an entrant, other than a recreational user, who is present on premises by virtue of an **express or implied term in a contract** (while present for the purpose of performing the contract);

(c) an entrant **as of right** (while present for the purpose of exercising the right);

(d) it also includes an entrant whose presence has become unlawful after entry and who is **taking reasonable steps to leave**.

A "**recreational user**" is an entrant with or without the occupiers permission or implied invitation present **on premises without charge for** the purpose of engaging in a **recreational activity** including an entrant without charge to a national monument. It does not include:

(a) a member of the occupier's family who is ordinarily resident on the premises;

(b) an entrant who is present at the express invitation of the occupier or such member; or

(c) an entrant who is present with the permission of the occupier or such a member for social reasons connected with the occupier or such member.

A "**trespasser**" means an entrant other than a recreational user or a visitor.

Duty of occupier

(1) An occupier of premises owes a duty to take **such care as is reasonable in all the circumstances** to ensure that a visitor does not suffer injury or damage by reason of any danger existing on the premises;

(2) An occupier owes a duty to a recreational user or trespasser:

 (a) **not to injure** the *person* or damage their *property* **intentionally,**

 (b) **not to act with reckless disregard** for the *person* or *property* of the person.

Extension, Restriction, Modification or Exclusion of Duty   An occupier may by *express agreement* or *notice* **extend** his duty towards all categories of entrant and restrict, modify or **exclude** his/her duty towards visitors.

A restriction, modification or exclusion shall not bind a visitor unless: (a) it is **reasonable** in all the circumstances; and (b) if done by notice, that the occupier has taken reasonable steps to **bring the notice to the attention** of the visitor. Unless the contrary is shown an occupier is deemed to have taken reasonable steps to do so if the notice is displayed prominently at the normal means of access to the premises.

Criminals   Where a person enters unto premises for the purpose of committing an **offence**, or commits an offence on premises, the occupier shall not be liable for breach of the duty under sub-section (1)(b) not to injure or damage his property and not to act with reckless disregard etc., unless a court determines otherwise in the interests of justice.

3.19 Education Boards

For a number of years it has been suggested that Local Education Authorities similar to those in Britain, should be established to manage and co-ordinate the provision of educational services in an area. They would deal with primary, secondary, third level and adult education as well as youth and recreation activities and school transport. Proposals were mooted in an IVEA document in 1974 and the National Planning Board Report of 1984 also commented on this matter.

On 2 December 1990 the IVEA accepted a new policy document on education structures and agreed to seek meetings with Catholic Bishops and other interested groups to reform local education structures.[29]

In March 1994 Minister Niamh Bhreathnach, T.D. issued a position paper on Regional Education Councils to advance the debate on intermediate education structures before putting proposals to Government. This position paper was followed in 1995 by the White Paper which devoted a whole chapter[30] to Education Boards. Part II of the Education Bill 1997 dealt with the establishment and function of such boards.

Fianna Fáil in opposition, opposed the Boards on the grounds of cost and remoteness from local education interests and pledged to abolish any which had been set up. In office, Micheál Martin T.D. confirmed that the establishment of the ten Regional Education boards would not be included in the redrafted Education Bill which he intended to introduce.[31]

---

[29] See *Irish Times*, 3 December 1990.
[30] Chapter 14, White Paper on Education, *Charting our Education Future*, Department of Education, 12 April 1995.
[31] See *Irish Times*, 5 August 1998 and *TUI News*, September 1997.

Chapter 4

Boards of Management

Education is an admirable thing,
but it is well to remember from time to time
that nothing that is worth knowing
can be taught.

Oscar Wilde, *The Critic as Artist*

A Boards of Management of a vocational school or a community college is a sub-committees of a VEC. There is no specific provision authorising the appointment of Boards of Management but each VEC is entitled to appoint sub-committees by virtue of Section 21 of the Vocational Education Act 1930 which provides:

> A vocational Education Committee may from time to time appoint such and so many sub-committees as it thinks proper for the exercise or performance of any of its powers, duties, and functions which in its opinion can be better or more conveniently exercised or performed by a Sub-Committee.

Further the Minister for Education may[1] require a VEC to appoint a sub-committee to exercise and perform such specified powers, duties and functions of such committee as in the opinion of the Minister can be better or more conveniently exercised or performed by a sub-committee and whenever any such order is made and in force it shall be the duty of such committee to comply with the requirements thereof.

4.1 Section 21, Vocational Education Act 1930

Section 21 also provides that a sub-committee appointed by a VEC shall consist of not more than twelve members, and may, at the discretion of such committee, consist exclusively of persons who are members of such committee or partly of persons who are and partly of persons who are not members of such committee.

---

[1] The Minister can by order require a VEC to appoint a sub-committee and s/he can specify the powers, duties and functions but I cannot find any authority for the proposition that he can prescribe its composition. Section 59 of the Education Bill 1997 proposes the transfer of the functions of the Minister under the Vocational Acts 1930-1970 to the relevant education board in the region.

The acts of every sub-committee of a VEC are subject to confirmation by the VEC except where such VEC with the sanction of the Minister dispenses with the necessity for such confirmation. The acts of a Board of Management are, therefore, subject to confirmation by a VEC except where the need for confirmation has been dispensed with and the dispensation sanctioned by the Minister.

In 1974 the Minister for Education suggested[2] that VECs should avail themselves of the powers conferred upon them by section 21 of the Act to set up sub-committees in respect of each vocational school in their schemes which would act as a Board of Management of these schools. The composition,[3] procedure and functions which the Minister considered appropriate to these suggested[4] Boards of Management were set out in an attached memorandum. Each board must consist of four members of the VEC and two parents[5] of children attending the school, elected by the parents of the children attending the school.[6] Circular Letter No. 73/74 suggested a membership of six although section 21 of the 1930 Act provides for a maximum of twelve.

4.2 VEC Representatives

VEC representatives sit at the pleasure of the VEC during their term of office, if they wish to do so.[7] Parental representatives hold office as long as a child of theirs is a pupil attending the school or for the term of office of the VEC.[8] Vacancies are filled by VEC nomination and by election of parents.

The nomination and election of an incoming board should normally be made and done not later than 31 October following the first meeting of the incoming VEC and the first meeting of the incoming board should be held not later than two weeks after its constitution.

Former members of Boards, who are still qualified are eligible for re-election or nomination. There is an important provision[9] that, in general, no board members should have any interest in property used by the school or be

---

[2] Circular Letter, June 1974.

[3] The Minister has no statutory function in deciding the composition. The maximum number of people is twelve and the VEC has absolute discretion as to how the twelve are arrived at. However the composition, procedure and functions which the Minister "considers appropriate" to the suggested Boards was set out in Circular Letter No. 73/74.

[4] Note that the word "suggest" was used. The Minister could by order require a VEC to appoint a board of Management by using his powers under section 21(2) Vocational Education Act 1930, but that was not done.

[5] One of the parents must be a mother.

[6] Rule 1 CL 73/74.

[7] Rule 2(a) CL 73/74.

[8] Rule 2(b) CL 73/74. NOTE: Boards of Management constituted in accordance with the terms of circular letter No 73/74 were to come into operation by the 31 October 1974.

[9] Section 21(4).

interested in supplying goods or work to or for the purpose of the school. Rule 2(f) of Circular Latter 73/74 provided that with the Minister's written approval a person can be excepted from this rule. It seems unfortunate that such a worthwhile protection anticipated by the section should be qualified, particularly when the "special circumstances" are not spelt out or defined.

4.3 Procedure

The first procedure of the Board is to elect a Chairperson who presides at meetings. The school principal acts as Secretary and has no voting rights.[10] The Board should meet at least monthly[11] and **a quorum is three members**. Four members may convene a meeting of the Board. The Teachers Union of Ireland considered[12] that the Boards should consist of: members of the VEC, parent representatives, representatives from interests in the community served by the schools, and teacher representatives. They pointed out that this would require a larger Board than indicated in the Minister's proposal. No concession is made to the imbalance of VEC members as opposed to parent members in CL No 73/74 but some Boards of Management are more democratically composed with educational interests holding only 50% of the seats. The VEC is the sole arbiter of the composition of its own sub-committees.

4.4 Notice of Meetings

Notice to attend the meetings, specifying the business proposed to be transacted shall be sent by the Secretary under his signature, to the usual place of residence of each member of the Board, at least seven days beforehand. In the case of a meeting requested by four members the notice must be signed by the four members concerned and the Secretary notified. The names of the members present at the meetings must be recorded in the minutes of the meeting by the Secretary and the minutes sent to the VEC where receipt of such minutes should be recorded and forwarded to the Department of Education.

4.5 Functions and Duties

Every VEC which is an enforcing authority and which has appointed a sub-committee to exercise and perform any the powers, duties and functions of such committee under Part V of the Act "shall be required to keep a minute book and to enter in such minute book minutes of the proceedings at every meeting of such sub committee'.[13]

---

[10] Rule 5(f). Circular No. 73/74.
[11] Section 18(5) of the Vocational Education Act 1930.
[12] Section 21(4) of the Vocational Education Act 1930.
[13] *per* Rule 6 Vocational Education Act 1930 [Part V] [Registers and Records] Regulations 1938 No. 29.

The Board of Management has responsibility for the general management of the school, subject to the Department's regulations. It should ensure: (a) that the school is adequately equipped and maintained and must report any deficiencies to the Committee for remedy; (b) and that classes are held on time and in accordance with the time-table.[14]

The Board of Management determines the uses for community purpose of the school building or grounds at the times which will not affect school work.

The Board submits an estimate of the income and expenditure required for the school during the following financial year to the VEC before a date appointed by them. This is to facilitate the VEC in submitting its annual scheme to the Minister.[15]

If delegated by the VEC to do so, it arranges for payments out of petty cash for minor expenditure and it can delegate responsibility for this to the Principal,[16] who is answerable to the VEC through the CEO.

Through the Principal, the Board exercises general control over the conduct of the school.[17]

The Board is charged to ensure that there is religious worship and instruction for the pupils in accordance with the rites, practise and teaching of the religious denomination to which the pupil belongs.

It must also ensure that there are sufficient teachers in the school appointed with the approval of the competent religious authority to give religious instruction.

The CEO may attend any meeting of the Board.[18] A Department of Education inspector is entitled to be present at any meeting of a sub-committee and to address such meeting, including Boards of Management but he is not entitled to vote on any matter to be decided at the meeting.[19]

The Vocational Education Act 1930 provides[20] that a sub-committee of a VEC may contain members who are not members of the VEC, and the discretion of the VEC in this matter is absolute.

---

[14] Section 21(2) of the Vocational Education Act 1930.

[15] One wonders how the figure of 4 VEA members and 2 parents was arrived at (section 2). Local Elections (Petitions and Disqualifications) Act 1974.

[16] Unless clerical assistance was provided and the necessary office equipment, the additional burden of servicing Management Boards would be the last straw and the TUI would instruct the Principals to refuse to serve these Boards. *TUI News & Views,* Vol. 3, No. 1, 1974.

[17] More often if necessary but not during the months of July and August.

[18] *TUI Views & News,* Vol. 3, No. 1, 1974.

[19] Rule 6, Circular No. 73/74. The acts of the Board must be confirmed by the VEC except where the need for confirmation has been disposed with by the VEC with the sanction of the Minister 20 Every VEC has to submit an estimate referred to as an annual scheme to the Minister for Education for the following financial year, on or before the 1 December. Section 14(1) of the Vocational Education Act 1930.

It would seem that while the Minister may encourage, or indeed, order[21] the setting up of sub-committees or Boards, s/he has no function in regulating their composition, or numbers.[22] However, the number of members cannot exceed twelve if it is to remain a statutory sub-committee.

The Minister has pointed out that "no person employed for the purposes of the school shall be a member of the Board of the School" and clearly C/L No. 73/74 was correct at the time.

4.6 Disqualification

The Vocational Education (Amendment) Act 1947 provides that a person convicted of an offence which involves making or allowing to be made a false statement for the purpose of obtaining a payment shall thereafter be disqualified from being elected or being a member of a VEC or a VEC sub-committee and also be disqualified from holding an office or employment under a VEC.

This disqualification seems to be in the nature of an additional punishment and similar to the disqualification that would result from conviction of a scheduled offence under the Offences Against the State Act 1939 and, as such, can operate to frustrate the sentencing policy of a court which has convicted but exercised leniency in applying the Probation of Offenders Act 1907. The factors to be considered in exercising leniency may be those in *Clarke v. CIE* UD 1104/1978 where the Employment Appeals Tribunal, in ordering the re-instatement of Mr Clarke, stated that regard must be had to the nature of the offence, whether it was a first offence or one of a series of offences, and how such an offence though unconnected with his work, would bear on his job.

4.7 Other Bodies

A Board of Management can establish[23] two other bodies:

(a) A staff council composed of all teachers in a school under the chairmanship of the principal; and

(b) A Home/School Association composed of Board of Management, teachers, and parents of children receiving education in the school.

The function of the staff council is to consider "curricular arrangements" of the school and, if it wishes to make recommendations regarding the exten-

---

[21] Rule 8(b). Circular No. 73/74.
[22] Rule 10 (a). C/L 73/74.
[23] Rule 9 (a) and II (a) C/L 73/74.

sion of the subject range, the arranging of the time-table, and the provision of
school equipment. On request a staff council may advise the Board of any
educational problem. It may also to make submissions to the Board on any
educational matter connected with the school. The function of the Home/
School Association is (a) to discuss matters relating to the school[24] and presumably the VEC members who are officers of the Board take cognizance of
the matters discussed and implement action as a result.

4.8 Religious Worship

The Board is charged[25] with ensuring that there is religious worship and instruction[26] for pupils in the school save those whose parents[27] request the
Principal in writing[28] that they do not have such. The Board of Management
is[29] charged to ensure that there is religious worship and instruction in accordance with the pupils religion for at least two and half hours per week
during each session. It is also obliged to ensure that at all times there are
sufficient teachers in the school, appointed[30] with the approval of the competent religious authority which can inspect the religious worship and instruction by arrangement with the Board and determine if it is heretical or otherwise remiss.

4.9 Teachers of Religion

The appointment and conditions of employment of teachers of religion in
Vocational schools is a matter of some concern to the Teachers Union of
Ireland (hereinafter referred to as TUI).

In recent years the TUI has been dealing with the lack of permanency for
some teachers of religion in vocational schools. The problem is very much
due to the Bishops' concern over the protection offered to a permanent teacher
of the VEC under the 1930 Vocational Education Act.

---

[24] Rule 11 B9 C/L 73/74.
[25] Rule 10(a) C/L 73/74.
[26] The Vocational Education Act 1930 is silent as to religious worship or instruction and
   there is no statutory basis for worship. The contribution imposed by the 1889 was
   lifted in so much as it was repealed with the rest of the Act.
[27] How are the parents to know that they must inform the Principal in writing?
[28] Neither C/L 73/74 or the VEA 1930 extend such consideration.
[29] In theory one or two students of a particular religious denomination must be catered
   for, and a school could well have different religious instructors catering for the religious needs of different religious sects.
[30] Rule 10(e) C/L 73/74.

The TUI policy in this matter has been that, "A teacher of religion is entitled to the same rights as any other permanent teacher in the service". The TUI sought:

(i) Specification of qualifications for such positions.

(ii) Procedures for advertising, interviewing and appointment of (a) permanent whole-time teachers and (b) temporary whole-time teachers.

(iii The provision of a second teaching subject for such teachers.

(iv) Provision for the award of incremental credit for those teachers who cannot be made permanent, *e.g.* a priest who does not meet the qualifications set down but who would be otherwise acceptable as a teacher of religion.

(v) A method of inspection for these teachers similar to that which exists for other teachers.[31] The problem is difficult to deal with in the vocational sector, having regard to the necessity for a public inquiry under the 1930 Act if a teacher is suspended. Community Schools do not have such protection for the teacher.

Talks on the teachers of religion would only affect community schools in the event that they were constituted under the same Act. The Principal is immediately responsible for arranging religious worship and instruction, and for the attendance of pupils.[32]

Provided a teacher of religion is properly qualified and acceptable to the Bishop who has a veto, the Bishops do not appear to have any objection to permanent appointment. The usual criterion acceptable to Bishops for permanent appointment is a qualification acceptable under the terms of Memo V.7 to teach a subject other than religion. The original appointment of the person concerned should be as "Teacher of Religion and . . . some other subject)" and should the question of heresy or other impediment arise the teacher can be required to teach the second subject without loss of permanency.

Finally the Board has responsibility to set up a Home-School Association, the officers of which are to be VEC members of the Board. This subsidiary Board is to be composed of the Board of Management, the teachers and parents of children attending the school. The Board should meet to discuss school matters at regular intervals throughout the year.

---

[31] *TUI News and Views*, Vol. 1, No. 4, December 1978.
[32] Rule 10 (d) C/L 73/74.

4.10 Delegation of Powers

The maxim *delegatus non potest delegare* indicates that a primary delegate cannot sub-delegate. A statutory power must be exercised only by the body or officer in whom it has been confided, unless sub-delegation of the power is authorized by express words or necessary implication.[33] Section 21 of the Vocational Education Act 1930 provides expressly that a VEC can delegate the exercise of performance of any of its statutory powers, duties or functions. The basis for this delegation is convenience.

Boards of Management have been established under this section, being in effect sub-committees. There is no provision for sub-delegation under the Act and even if there were, the primary delegate cannot vest powers "properly exercisable only by himself".[34]

Practical convenience may be sufficient justification for entrusting power to investigate and make recommendations to a committee.[35] It is important to note that in the *Osgood* case, which involved removal from the office of Registrar of the Sheriffs' Court of the City of London, there was no delegation of lawful authority because a committee composed of its own members enquired into the complaint and reported to the Corporation. On this basis a committee of VEC members and of others is very much a sub-committee and there must be lawful delegation of authority.

In *Board of Management of Limerick Model School v. Culloo*[36] when a teacher, complained of discrimination in appointing a Principal, and obtained a recommendation in his favour, the notices of appeal against the recommendation were not valid because one was issued by an officer of the Department of Education and another was issued by the Chief State Solicitor. A meeting of the Board Of Management took place after the recommendation but they did not decide to lodge an appeal or authorise lodgement of notice of appeal. The finding of the Labour Court on this point was upheld on appeal by the High Court.

4.11 Sub-Committees

Delegation of VEC powers and duties to a Board of Management or other sub-committee is expressly provide for but then a question might be asked "Is a selection sub-committee of a Board of Management a sub-delegate"?

---

[33] Paragraph 32, Vol. 1, Halsbury.

[34] *Rathagopal v. A.G.* [1970] AC. 974.

[35] *George Osgood v. Thomas James Nelson* (1872) L.R. 5 H.L. 636. The report of the committee conducting the investigation must be such as to enable the deciding body to decide: *Jeffs v. New Zealand Dairy Production and Marketing Board* [1967] L.A.C. 551 [1966] 3 A.U.E.R. 546.

[36] High Court, unreported, 11 May 1989.

Because sub-delegation of the powers and duties of a VEC is not expressly authorized, because of the facility with which a VEC can use section 21 to create sub-committees, sub delegation would not be authorized by implication.

On this account it is suggested that care be taken to ensure that selection sub-committees be established by the VEC and not by a Board of Management composed of some members who are not also members of the VEC. The composition of a selection board might be significantly different if selected by a VEC from one selected by a Board of Management. A local authority can revoke the appointment of an individual committee member. It need not disband a whole committee.[37]

4.12 Worker Participation

The Worker Participation (State Enterprises) Act 1977 provides for the election by workers of one third of the members of the boards of seven semi-state companies.[38] In practice this means four out of a board of twelve. The Green Paper, "Education for a Changing World", 1992, proposes that Boards of Management of Secondary Schools should have two members elected by the teachers in the school.

---

[37] *Manton v. Brighton Corporation* [1951] 2 K.B. 393 [1951] 2 All E.R.101.
[38] Section 23, Worker Participation (State Enterprises) Act 1977.

CHAPTER 5

Recruitment

The best means of advertising is carried
on by present or former employees
who tell their friends that the firm
is a desirable place to work in.

Pigors and Myers, *Personnel Administration*, London, 1961, p. 264

Each VEC is a separate legal entity and, because of this, there is no central recruitment of vocational teachers. Each VEC must recruit and appoint it's own staff. Normally the first step in the recruitment process is the advertising that a vacancy exists for a particular type of teacher. Memo V.7 states that "every vacancy for a permanent whole-time position as a vocational teacher must "normally"[1] be advertised in the public press.[2] Exceptions to this requirement **may** be allowed as follows.

5.1 Class III Teachers

In relation to Class III teachers, section 12(i) states: that for the first post of Grade A and for posts of Grade B applicants should normally be sought from eligible **teachers within the school** concerned.

Section 12(ii) states:

Applicants for posts of Vice-Principal in schools with points rating up to 749, of Principal in schools with points rating up to 449 and Grade A posts after the first such post in any school should normally be sought from eligible **teachers within the scheme** of the Committee concerned.

Section 12(iii) states:

For all other posts of responsibility there should be general advertisement.

---

[1] There are exceptions when positions need not be advertised.
[2] The "Public press" can be a small advertisement inserted in Irish in a local newspaper. The phrase public press is not synonymous with national press.

5.2 Posts Higher than Class III

Section 2(b) provides that in teaching posts carrying remuneration higher than that for Class III teachers, in certain circumstances,[3] the Minister may not insist on it being advertised publicly,[4] provided the committee's teaching staff is notified of the vacancy and suitably qualified teachers on the Committee's staff are given the opportunity of applying.

5.3 Special Circumstances

Exception to the requirement to advertise a vacancy for any permanent whole-time post regardless of grade may be allowed by the Minister, "in other special circumstances."

No indication is given of what these circumstances are but some promotional posts, for example those agreed under new structures agreements in C/L14/79 and C/L5/82, did not have to be advertised in the public press. In November 1991 although two positions as Head of Department were advertised by Tralee RTC, the advertisement stated "One of the two appointments will be made from the holders of Lecturer II positions currently on the staff of Tralee RTC."

On the authority of *Harris v. Nickerson,*[5] an advertisement does not legally amount to an offer, the acceptance of which would constitute a legally binding agreement in the law of contract. As a result there is no contractual obligation whatsoever imposed on a VEC by virtue of merely advertising a post. They may change their minds and decide not to hold interviews or not to fill the position at all. If they do hold interviews they are not obliged to offer the position to the best candidate or to a candidate recommended by a selection committee. They are free to re-advertise the post, have further selection interviews and to accept the application of a candidate from those at the second interview.

A VEC, however, are under a statutory obligation by virtue of section 23 of the Vocational Education Act 1930 to appoint "such officers and servants as it shall from time to time think necessary for the due performance of its powers and duties under this Act." This duty was specifically referred to by McWilliam J. in *Phelan v. Co. Laois VEC and Parsons, post*[6] where he stated that once a vacancy existed there was a statutory obligation to fill it. He talked in terms of immediately doing so, in that particular case.

While the statutory obligation is not circumscribed by time in the statute it would be implied that vacancies should be filled by a VEC within a reasonable time.

---

[3] What these certain circumstances are is a matter for conjecture.
[4] Note the use of the word publicly not "public press".
[5] (1873) L.R. 8 Q.B. 286.
[6] *Irish Times*, 1 March 1977.

5.4 Advertisements

Memo V.7 states that the advertisement should be a brief one in the form of Appendix D or in other appropriate form.

If the Committee wish, the advertisement may contain a statement to the effect that canvassing will disqualify. It should state that the appointment is subject to the terms and conditions of Memo V.7.

The contents of an advertisement relating to employment are subject to statutory control by virtue of the Employment Equality Act 1977.

Section 8(1) of this Act provides:

> A person shall not publish, or cause to be published or displayed, an advertisement which relates to employment and indicates an intention to discriminate, or might reasonably be understood as indicating such an intention.

Section 8(2) provides:

> For the purposes of subsection (1), where in an advertisement a word or phrase is used defining or describing a post and the word or phrase is one which conotes a particular sex, or which, although not necessarily connoting a particular sex, is descriptive of or refers to a post or occupation of a kind previously held or carried on by members of one sex only, the advertisement shall be taken to indicate an intention to discriminate unless the advertisement contains a contrary indication.

The use of the words "teacher" or "lecturer" do not infringe subsection (1) but the use of words like "groundsman, storeman etc." would. A contrary indication referred to in subsection (2) would be a statement that the position is open to applicants of both sexes, *i.e.* "This VEC is an equal opportunities Employer" or "This position is open to Male and Female Applicants".

Section 17 of the Employment Equality Act 1977 excludes the application of the Act from posts where sex is an occupational qualification and this includes:

(a) where, on grounds of physiology (excluding physical strength or stamina) or on grounds of authenticity for the purpose of a form of entertainment, the nature of the post requires a member of a particular sex because otherwise the nature of the post would be materially different if carried out by a member of the other sex,

(b) where the duties of a post involve personal services and it is necessary to have persons of both sexes engaged in such duties,

(c) where an establishment or institution is confined (other wholly or partly) to persons of one sex requiring special care, supervision or treatment and the employment of persons of that sex is related to either the character of the establishment or institution or the type of care, supervision or treatment provided in it,

(d) where either the nature of or the duties attached to a post justify on grounds of privacy or decency the employment of persons of a particular sex,

(e) where because of the nature of the employment it is necessary to provide sleeping and sanitary accommodation for employees on a communal basis and it would be unreasonable to expect the provision of separate such accommodation or impracticable for an employer so to provide,

(f) where it is necessary that the post should be held by a member of a particular sex because it is likely to involve the performance of duties outside the State in a place where the laws of customs are such that the duties can only be performed by a member of that sex.[7]

The Equal Opportunities Commission in Northern Ireland has ruled[8] that an advertisement by Dungannon Royal School for a headmaster, although it excluded women did not constitute discrimination on the grounds of sex. The school were justified in excluding women because it was a boys school, *i.e.* a single sex institution that would have come within the ambit of the exceptions in section 17.

A job advertisement must not include a requirement of qualifications which are not essential for the job.

5.5 Short-listing

By virtue of section 23(5) of the Vocational Education Act 1930, a VEC is deemed to be a local authority within the meaning of the Local Authorities (Officers and Employees) Act 1926 and section 5 of the Local Government (Officers and Employees) Act 1983 provides that where the Principal Act (Local Authorities (Officers and Employees) Act 1926) or any provision of it is applied by or under any other Act to any particular office or employment, or in relation to any board, committee or other body, the Principal Act shall apply to such office or employment or body, with and subject to the amendments in this Act, *i.e.* the Local Authorities (Officers and Employees) Act 1983.

---

7 Section 17(c).
8 *Equal Opportunities Commission in Northern Ireland v. Dungannon Royal School* January 1985.

Section 4(b) Local Government (Officers and Employees) Act 1983 provides:

> . . . where by reason of the number of persons seeking admission to the competition and the standard of knowledge, training or experience in general of such persons, the Commissioners consider that it would be reasonable not to admit all the persons to the competition, the Commissioners may admit to the competition only such persons who appear to them to be likely, to attain a standard sufficient for selection and recommendation for appointment.

Obviously it is preferable that each candidate is informed in advance that short-listing may take place either in the advertisement or in the application documents.

An applicant for public sector employment is entitled to expect that he will not be discriminated against and that the same criteria will be applied to all applicants. If he/she applies for a position on the basis that certain qualifications are required and is not granted an interview or is not short-listed because some unknown hidden criteria have been applied to screen applicants, he/she may apply for an injunction to prevent an appointment being made, or for judicial review on the basis that his/her application has not been fairly considered and that he/she has been wrongly excluded from being interviewed. An applicant for public sector employment has a right not to be unlawfully excluded and denial of an interview could constitute unlawful exclusion.

The Northern Ireland Fair Employment Act 1976, as amended, makes discrimination in the arrangements an employer makes for determining who should be offered employment unlawful.

Damages in tort for such unlawful discrimination are awarded to compensate for loss or injury and can include compensation for expenses, loss of opportunity and loss of earnings, as well as injury to feelings. Aggravated and exemplary damages may be awarded up to a maximum of £30,000 at present.

The *Irish Times* of Wednesday, 17 June 1992, reported that Queens University Belfast denied bias but agreed to pay compensation of approximately £40,000 to two Catholics who claimed religious discrimination, while a further eight cases were pending.

Although there is no presumption of constitutionality in favour of the 1930 Act it can still be argued that all proceedings, procedures, discretions and adjudications which are permitted or prescribed by the Act are intended by the Oireachtas to be conducted in accordance with the principles of natural and constitutional justice; and that such principles require that every application be considered upon its own merits. Failure to do so may amount to negligence, breach of duty, breach of statutory duty or indeed conspiracy.

5.6 Exclusion from Interview

Exclusion from interview may be patently unfair, arbitrary or capricious and amount to an unreasonable and unjustified interference with a candidate's unenumerated constitutional right to practice a particular profession or vocation.

Vetting or short-listing can only be validly done by the interview board, *i.e.* the Selection Board, which is a sub-committee of the VEC. It cannot be lawfully done by an administrator, a clerk or a principal. See *post* regarding the composition of interview board vetting written applications.

Exclusion by short-listing is a different matter entirely from claiming exclusion by virtue of an employer allocating a position to an area in which one is not qualified. Undoubtedly an employer is entitled, in the absence of a collective agreement to the contrary, to decide the area in which a vacancy will be allocated and exclusion from interview on the grounds that a person is not qualified in that area would be legitimate.

Such a claim was, advisedly, not pursued in *Byrne v. CDVEC*[9] although the plaintiff had been granted an interim injunction. He had been interviewed on two occasions for a post which the employer then allocated to a different area and excluded him from interview on the grounds that he did not teach in the areas where they had specified the promotion should be.

5.7 Interview Procedures

> Interviewing is more than a technique. It is an art . . . every interview ought to be a satisfying experience. Whatever its specific objective, the general purpose is always to promote mutual understanding and confidence.

> Pigors and Myers, *Personnel Administration*, London, 1961

Interview procedures must not be discriminatory and questions asked of an applicant at interview having regard to the circumstances in which, and the purposes for which[10] they were asked can be indicative of prejudice.

In *Chaney v. U.C.D.*[11] questions which could not have formed part of the board's assessment of the applicants technical competence to perform the job were considered crucial by the Employment Appeals Tribunal and inferences

---

[9] High Court, unreported, *Irish Times*, 14 December 1984.

[10] *Saunders v. Richmond-upon-Thames London Borough Council* [1978] ICR. 75. EAT.

[11] EE 15/83 (1983) 1 ILT 94: See also: *O'Connor v. Southern Health Board* EE.8/1984, where appointment and compensation were recommended and *Bradley v. Eastern Health Board* EE 2/1981; *Bradley v. Quinnsworth Power Supermarkets Ltd.*, EE 1/1981; *Hayes v. McCarthy Daly Stapleton* EE.17/81; *Jennings v. H.V. White Ltd.* EE.14/1979, where compensation was awarded.

drawn regarding the purpose of asking such questions resulted in a finding that the claimant had been discriminated against.

In *Tuite v. The Coombe Hospital*,[12] at an interview for a position as a student mid-wife, the claimant was asked, how long she was married, how her husband felt about her studying again, whether there were any little Tuites, and whether she would be able to study and be a housewife at the same time. It was held that the claimant had suffered discrimination.

Remarks made by interviewers may also be indicative of prejudice. In *Kinsella v. National Building Agency*[13] a Labour Court Equality Officer found that a married woman was treated "less favourably" in an interview than other candidates because of her marital status. It was claimed that she was introduced by a member of the interview board as "the only married woman for interview today" and that this was a discriminatory remark. At a previous interview for a staff officer post in 1982 the same member of the board asked what her attitude was towards women with children continuing in employment. She was upset by the remark at the time because she had a child, but had not pursued the matter under the Employment Equality Act. In *Murray v. Midland International Ltd.*,[14] compensation was awarded for "distress" when an interviewer allegedly referred to the recent birth of the claimant's baby and asked "Had you a boy or a child?" and then enquired how many children she had and remarked that four was quite a handful. Section 4 of the English Sex Discrimination Act 1975 provides against discrimination by way of *victimisation* as distinct from discrimination on the grounds of sex or marital status.

5.8 Selection

> The personnel interview continues to be the most widely used method for selecting employees, despite the fact that it is a costly, inefficient, and usually an invalid procedure.
>
> Dunnette and Bass, *Industrial Relations*, 11 (1963) 115-130

5.9 Interview Boards

Section 21 of the Vocational Education Act 1930 permits a VEC to appoint sub-committees and the selection of teachers for appointment to a position within a vocational school or college is done by such sub-committee (interview board) which is appointed by the VEC. This involves the selection sub-committee conducting the interviews and recommending either, the appointment of a particular applicant, or the establishment of a panel in order of

---

[12] *Tuite v. The Coombe Hospital* EE 17/1985.
[13] *Evening Press*, 16 May 1985.
[14] *Irish Independent*, 4 April 1991.

merit. A VEC interview board or selection panel has power to govern its own proceedings but it cannot decide to sit with less than the specified minimum size or constitution. See C/L 29/97 previously 16/79.

If for example the Minister's representative, an Inspector takes ill, does not attend and is not replaced, the panel cannot decide to proceed with less than its full complement, as it is then not a properly constituted or authorised selection panel. Neither the Department of Education or a CEO can validly authorise it to do so, and if it does proceed, an appointment made on foot of such a recommendation would be open to challenge. Normally the full panel must meet first to consider written applications, then to interview those originally selected (the long interview) and finally to interview the candidates on the short list.

Unless a selection panel sits as constituted, subject to the proviso as to a member being replaced, it is not a selection panel and it would be improper for a VEC to act on the recommendation of such a panel.[15]

5.10 Resolutions to make Appointments

The unauthorised communication of a resolution to make an appointment arose in *Wilson v. Belfast Corporation*[16] where a resolution passed by the council was reported in the press by a reporter who could not be excluded from the meeting. It was held that the resolution was not intended as an offer, and unauthorised publication did not constitute communication.

In another case[17] it was held that knowledge of the passing of a resolution to appoint a person as head master, acquired by unauthorised communication, does not confer any rights on the candidate concerned.

The facts were that the plaintiff and two other candidates were short-listed for a position as headmaster at an English School. At a meeting of the managers on 26 March it was proposed and seconded that the plaintiff should be appointed. Three of the members voted in favour and two against. The Chairman did not vote but declared that the motion had been carried and that the plaintiff was the successful candidate. No directions were given by the meeting as to communicating the result of the voting to the plaintiff but the Hon. Sec. was requested by the Chairman to send a telegram to another candidate informing him that he had been unsuccessful.

---

[15] If a selection sub-committee does not sit as constituted, it is not the designated sub-committee. A selection sub-committee is a specific size with a specific constitution and even though it may be authorised to govern its own proceedings, it **may not delegate** performance of its functions to a limited number of its own members or to other persons who are not members. (A sub-committee of a sub-committee) *Delegatus non potest delegare*. See *Reg. v. Liverpool City Council*, 82 LGR 648.

[16] (1921) 55 ILTR 205.

[17] *Powell v. Lee* [1908] 99 L.T. 284.

Subsequently a fresh meeting of the managers to re-consider the appointment was summoned by the Chairman for 2 April. On 1 April, without any instruction to do so by the managers as a body, the Hon. Sec. sent a telegram to the plaintiff: "The . . . School Managers selected you as head master on Tuesday last. Dismore, Hon. Sec." The meeting of the managers the following day agreed to rescind the resolution passed at the first meeting appointing the plaintiff and passed a resolution appointing another candidate as head master. The plaintiff brought an action claiming breach of contract.

It was held that an unauthorised communication of intention is equivalent to no communication, that there must be proved an intention to communicate on the part of the person, or body alleged to be a party to the contract. The Hon. Sec. had not been authorised to communicate the passing of the resolution of the 26th to the plaintiff. There was no contract.

On appeal the decision was upheld. There must be communication made by the body of persons to the selected candidate. The managers had not authorised a communication to the plaintiff. The Hon. Sec. made the communication as an individual and not for the body of the managers. Mere knowledge of what happened at the meeting was not sufficient: there must be notice of acceptance from the contracting party in some way, and the mere fact that the managers did not authorise the communication, which was the usual course adopted, implied that they meant to reserve the power to reconsider the decision at which they had arrived.

The passing of the resolution without authorised communication to the plaintiff did not constitute a contract to appoint him to the post.

5.11 Confidentiality

The proceedings of an interview board should normally be confidential and the personal details of a candidate should not be revealed to parties who do not have a *bona fide* interest in the proceedings.

It is suggested that confidentiality in relation to interviews, in particular for public sector employment, is not to protect the interviewers but to protect the interviewees as well.

Any applicant is entitled to query the results of an interview and the interviewers should be able to stand over and to justify their choice. As stated elsewhere, it could be argued that a candidate for public sector employment should be notified who the successful candidate was, what his/her qualifications for the post were, and why s/he was selected. At one time it was usual to publish the names of successful applicants in the press.

The author considers that it would be absurd if confidentiality could be used as a cloak for mistakes (*e.g.* where a person not entitled to do so, votes by mistake at a VEC selection), or to cover wrongdoing by interviewers, and indeed it could be argued that where a mistake or wrongdoing has taken place there is an onus on right thinking members of an interview panel to disclose what has occurred. There is a particularly heavy onus on the Inspector representing the Minister in this regard.

In the *State (Cussen) v. Brennan*,[18] although the Local Appointments Commissioners had openly informed candidates for an office of paediatrician with the Southern Health Board that extra credit would be given to qualified and suitable candidates having a good knowledge of Irish, they were held by the Supreme Court to have acted *ultra vires* in purporting to introduce a qualification which had not been approved of or directed by the Minister for Health.

Henchy J. stated at p. 195

> The prosecutor had learned at some stage (through what appears to have been a reprehensible breach of confidentiality on the part of certain members of the interview board) that the oral Irish test was the reason . . . why another Doctor was recommended for the office in preference to the himself.

O'Higgins C.J. also referred to the lack of confidentiality in this case.

One cannot help commenting that had there not been a breach of "confidentiality" the likelihood of the prosecutor taking the action would probably have been remote, and that whoever made the disclosure may have considered it a public duty to do so.

5.12 Discovery of Confidential Information

If it is essential in the interests of justice that a confidence should be overridden, an industrial Tribunal or a Court can order the disclosure of reports, references, assessments or other documents. Disclosure should only be ordered after inspection of the document in question and may be subject to conditions as to the divulging of it.

The fact that information or opinions have been given in confidence does not in itself bring immunity from disclosure or attract privilege. The Court of Appeal have rejected the contention that there is a public interest privilege prohibiting the diclosure of confidential documents. The principle was established in *Nasse v. Science Research Council*[19] which involved a claim of alleged discrimination on the grounds of marital status and trade union activities in exclusion from interview (see 5.6 above) and in *Vyas v. Leyland Cars*[20] which involved a claim of discrimination on grounds of race. Disclosure of documents in relation to successful candidates may be necessary. Acording to Lawton L.J.:

---

[18] [1981] I.R. 181.
[19] [1978] I.R.L.R. 352.
[20] *loc. cit.*

> If amongst the defendant's documents there are some, albeit confidential ones, which will help the applicant to prove his case, he is entitled to see them.[21]

A VEC body is a body established by or under an enactment (other than the Companies Act 1963 to 1990) and is, therefore, a public body for the purposes of the Freedom of Information Act 1997. Under section 7 of this Act a request for access to records may be made to the head of that public body.

5.13 Composition of Teacher Selection Boards

Under section 125 Vocational Education Act 1930 the Minister has power to make regulations respecting the procedure of VECs in connection with the business imposed or transferred to them by the Act. On 14 February 1997 revised appointment procedures for appointment to Assistant Principal ("A" Posts) and Special Duties Teacher ("B" Posts) were issued by the Department of Education. The accompanying letter stated that the composition of the Selection Board as set out would also apply to posts of Principal, Deputy Principal and teaching posts generally in the vocational sector.

Subsequently CL 29/97 (June 1997) provided that the composition of the selection board would henceforth be:

- two VEC representatives,
- one Inspector,
- one Personnel Specialist, and
- one Educationalist.

The Chairperson would always be one of the VEC representatives. The quorum for a board is four and must include one VEC representative. The IVEA and the TUI should agree panels of Personnel Specialists and Educationalists for inclusion on selection boards for each VEC and the VEC would then nominate Board members from these panels. The selection of the actual persons to serve will be by agreement between the VEC and the branch concerned. During the summer of 1997 the IVEA and the TUI agreed on the categories of persons eligible to serve as personnel specialists and educationalists. See Appendix 3.

5.14 Selection Criteria for A/P "A" Posts and S/D "B" Posts

CL 30/97 states that the objective of the Board is to select the most suitable candidate and in making its selection the Board should adopt the following criteria and marking system when determining their order of merit for submission to the VEC:

---

[21] *loc. cit.*

Capacity of applicant to meet the needs of the school	50 marks
Service to school in Permanent Wholetime capacity	30 marks
Experience of a professional nature in the field of education and involvement in the school	20 marks

Marks for service to school in a PWT capacity should be on the basis of 100% of the available marks for the most senior candidate and *pro rata* for the other candidates.

5.15 Appeals for A/P Posts and S/D Posts

If the above criteria and marking scheme are not applied the new procedures provide that a candidate may appeal within five school days of the announcement of the VEC's decision. Such an appeal must be in writing, should state the grounds on which the appeal is being taken etc. and be delivered to the CEO within the five school days. The CEO refers the appeal to an agreed Arbitrator. The Arbitrator will be advised by a nominated advisor from both IVEA and TUI. A meeting of the Arbitrator and the advisors will be held if the Arbitrator or any of the parties to the agreement deem it necessary.

The Arbitrator may interview the parties, will make the written statements available to both parties and will normally make a decision based on the written statements. The Arbitrator will notify the VEC of his/her decision and the VEC will consider the matter at its next meeting. If the appeal is upheld the VEC shall organise a new competition. If the appeal is rejected the VEC will so inform the appellant and request the Department to sanction the appointment. The IVEA and the TUI should agree the detailed procedures to be observed in appeals including the application of time limits at various stages.

5.16 Advisers

There is no provision for advisers in the new selection boards prescribed in CL 29.97 but the present position is that where categories of persons have attended as advisers in the past (with the agreement of the local TUI branch) they may continue to attend in future where advisers are involved they should be present for the interview of all candidates for a particular post.

5.17 Voting

Only those members present at the interviewing of all candidates called and attending for interview can vote in the final selection. The Chairman of the Selection Board may exercise a casting vote in the case of a tie.

In 1984 the Minister for Education issued Circular Letter 45/84 to management authorities and principal teachers drawing attention to the code of practice of the Employment Equality Agency and suggesting that wherever possible a woman should be included among the interviewers.

5.18 Interference in Selection

A recurring accusation has been made that VECs are open to political interference and consequently candidates cannot be guaranteed an equal opportunity of success, nor indeed is there any system whereby an unsuccessful candidate can appeal on the grounds of political (or other) interference on behalf
of a competitor for the post. It is equally claimed that in certain instances
management authorities have ensured that their preferred candidate is successful, and it is claimed that this is far more commonplace. In November
1996 the TUI restated their concern pointing out that the persistence of allegations served to blemish the entire sector. The union sought defined criteria
for appointments, an appeals mechanism and a re-organisation of selection
boards to protect against "political" appointments. Following the breakdown
of talks with the IVEA in December 1996 the IVEA agreed to re-enter talks
and the TUI suspended a series of one day strikes.[22] In June 1997 revised
selection procedures were introduced by CL 29/97.

In certain circumstances the provisions of the Employment Equality Act
1977 could be invoked by an unsuccessful candidate[23] but, it is submitted that
candidates for public service employment should have a right to be informed
of the identity of the successful candidate and what his/her qualifications are.

5.19 Proof of Discrimination

While the formal burden of **proving discrimination** lies on the applicant it is
a burden which **moves very easily on to an employer** as a result of the applicant's evidence.

The EAT allowed an appeal in the case of *Humphreys v. Board of Managers of St. Georges' Church of England (Aided) Primary School*[24] and directed
that the case be re-heard, to hear the Boards explanation.

The facts were that two teachers applied for a post at a higher grade. The
successful applicant was not a graduate, but held the minimum qualification,
was still on probation when the vacancy was announced and had only fin-
ished probation at the date of interview. The unsuccessful applicant was a
Bachelor of Education and had approximately eight years experience. The
EAT held that it is only in exceptional or frivolous cases that it is not necessary for the employer to put his case. The employer must justify his selection.

---

[22] See *Irish Independent*, 12 November 1996, *Irish Times*, 18 November 1996 and *Irish Times*, 3 December 1996 and *TUI News and Views*, 3 December 1996, Vol. 19, No. 3.

[23] Where discrimination on grounds of sex or marital status occurs. See *Higgins v. Co. Laois* VEC EE 15/1996 File No. EE 15/1995. See Ch. 7.10 *post*.

[24] [1978] ICR. 546, EAT.

[25] [1980] IRLR. 193. See also Elias, Napier and Wallington, *Labour Law Cases and Materials* (Butterworths, 1980), p. 159.

This approach has since been endorsed by the Northern Ireland Court of Appeal in *Wallace v. South Belfast Education and Library Board*[25] the first successful discrimination case before this court. In it, the three judges overruled an Industrial Tribunal decision and found that Mrs. Wallace had been discriminated against when a full time job which she had occupied part time for four years, was given to a man. The Tribunal had found as fact the Mrs. Wallace had superior educational qualifications and better experience than the successful man. In both of the foregoing instances the claimants were lucky enough to find out that they had better qualifications and experience but in many instances in Ireland an applicant does not discover that he has been discriminated against until many years later.

5.20 Employment Equality

A person who believes that s/he has suffered unlawful discrimination may obtain a written explanation from the employer[26] for presentation in evidence and if the employers replies are "equivocal or evasive" the tribunal may infer that discrimination has occurred.[27] This provision was scheduled to be replaced by section 40 Employment Equality Bill, 1996 which empowered the Minister for Equality and Law Reform to prescribe forms by which a person who considers s/he had been discriminated against might seek information other than confidential information to decide whether to initiate a case or to formulate and present a case, It also provided for forms by which an employer might reply. Under section 45 if an employer failed to give information requested by questions under section 40 or supplied a false or misleading response or one which was not such as the complainant might reasonably have required. The Courts or the Director might draw such inferences as seemed appropriate.

Section 38 of the Employment Equality Bill, 1996 provided for the office of Director of Equality Investigations and section 43 obliged the Director or the Court to investigate certain cases. For the purpose of obtaining information section 58 stated that a designated officer might enter premises, require production of records, books etc. inspect and copy records, books etc. and inspect work in progress. Any person in possession of relevant information could be required to furnish it to the Director or Chairman or to attend before them for that purpose.

5.21 Suitability

It should be expressed that qualifications and experience are not the only factors to be taken into account when appointments are being made. Such

---

[26] Section 28, Employment Equality Act 1977.
[27] See Elias, Napier, Wallington, p. 760 notes and *Virdle v. ECC Quarries Ltd.* [1978] IRLR 295.

matters as suitability for the particular post, ability to teach, to control a class, to impart information lucidly and also the ability to work in a team are additional considerations.

Superior educational qualifications may be difficult to define or assess in relation to the requirements of a particular post and better experience does not necessarily mean more years.

5.22 Revised Selection Procedures

Following allegations in January 1979 that some interview boards in the vocational sector were not properly constituted[28] and that appointments made as a consequence were invalid, the Department of Education issued revised Selection Procedures in CL16/79. These new procedures stipulated that there should be a minimum of 2 VEC members and a Department of Education representative on interview panels for selection of DIT staff. Opposition politicians however still remained dissatisfied. The new composition of Selection Boards under CL 29/97 is outlined in paragraph 5.13 above and the selection criteria for A/P "A" posts and S/D "B" posts is outlined in paragraph 5.14 above.

---

[28] See *Irish Times*, 18 January 1979.

CHAPTER 6

Qualifications

> I've never been over-impressed by academic qualifications.
> I know an awful lot of people who have an armful of academic
> qualifications . . . they are wholly useless most of them.
> *They have no common sense at all.*

John Major, British Prime Minister, in TV interview, 31 March 1991.

Section 23(2) Vocational Education Act 1930 states "The numbers, **qualifications,** salaries or remuneration, and appointment of all officers shall be subject to the approval of the Minister". This gives the Minister total discretion. The qualifications of any particular "officer"[1] must be approved by the Minister, but s/he can approve any qualifications which s/he deems appropriate.[2] In appendix G of Memo V.7 dealing with eligibility for promotion to Assistant Lecturer it is provided that the terms of section 10 of Memo V.7 which deal with the qualifications specified for posts of Lecturer and Assistant Lecturer are applicable only to posts filled by publicly advertised competition and not to those filled by promotion.

No other person or body can prescribe or introduce a qualification which has not been approved of, or directed by the Minister and if they purport to do so they are acting *ultra vires*. A disadvantaged party can seek an order of *certiorari* to quash the introduction of such a qualification. In *The State (Cussen) v. Brennan*[3] the Supreme Court held that the Local Appointments Commission had acted in excess of their statutory powers in introducing an Irish test. They had usurped the functions of the Minister in that respect.

The word "qualifications" in the sense in which it is used in the Vocational Education Act 1930 according to O'Higgins C.J. in the same case:

> denotes particular conditions which must be fulfilled or observed before a candidate can be considered for appointment. If a candidate does

---

[1] The word "officer" is not defined in the Vocational Education Act 1930. "Office" means an office under a VEC section 1(1) Vocational Education (Amendment) Act 1944.

[2] "The Minister for Education had reserved the right to decide on qualifications. He/she will now do so following consultation with the TUI, the CEO's and the IVEA Qualifications are limited to the subjects taken in the degree. Existing teachers who have been recognised as teachers of subjects would continue to be so recognised", *TUI Views & News*, Vol. 3, No. 1, September 20 1974.

[3] [1981] I.R. 181.

not comply with any **one** of the conditions or qualifications declared, he cannot be appointed under any circumstances. Therefore, the *possession of* **all** the prescribed qualifications is essential.[4]

The minimum academic and technical qualifications approved by the Minister for appointment as a whole-time vocational teacher of Art, Building Trades, Commerce, Domestic Science, Educational Woodwork, Engineering, Irish, Metalwork, P.E. and Rural Science are specified in Memo V.7 which states that, whenever possible, these should be supplemented by practical experience in related business or industry.

In relation to other subjects, the Memo states that the qualifications will be specified by the Minister in approving the proposal to create the appointment. Normally the minimum requirement will be a degree of a recognised university with the subject or subjects to be taught.

The qualifications specified in Memo V.7 are the minimum qualifications but the Minister **may** accept a qualification which in his opinion is **equivalent** to any of the qualifications specified. "Equivalent qualifications" have been accepted by the Department in individual cases[5] but generally the conditions specified in Memo V.7 have to be adhered to by a VEC selection committee or the Minister's approval may be withheld.

6.1 VPT Qualifications

The qualifications needed for permanent appointment on VPT courses are specified in CL 32/92 as

1. degree or equivalent in subjects relevant to the course; **or**

2. degree and either
   (a) an appropriate qualification in an area relevant to the course. **or**
   (b) three years approved experience (including industrial and teaching experience) in the appropriate area; **or**

3. qualifications other than those at 1 or 2 above which would be acceptable for posts in the Colleges sector.

All appointments are subject to the approval of the Department.

---

[4] *Ibid.,* p. 189.

[5] Persons with lower qualifications but extensive experience may be considered equivalent to those specified in Memo V.7, on the other hand higher qualifications are often preferred or desirable. In *CERT Ltd. v. Landy* EE 20/1983 exemption was made from the need to possess qualifications concerned in the case of two applicants with part-time experience but not in respect of ten other applicants who did not possess the qualifications and had not worked part-time with the company.

6.2 Minister's Powers

There is no obligation to bring the approved qualifications for vocational teachers before the Houses of the Oireachtas or even to enshrine them in a Statutory Instrument. Even though minimum qualifications are specified in Memo V.7 this informality and the absence of Dáil control has been questioned in the past.

6.3 Irish Language and CTG

The relevance of the language qualification was referred to by Henchy J. in the *Cussen* case[6] when he stated:

> It is incontestable under the Constitution which recognises Irish as the first language (Article 8) and which empowers the State in its enactments to have due regard to differences of capacity, physical and moral, and of social function (Article 40,s.1), a law may provide that proficiency in Irish be a qualification for an office when proficiency in Irish is relevant to the discharge of the duties of that office.[7]

Circular letter 43/97[8] headed Qualifications in the Irish language for appointment as a teacher in a Community College or Vocational School[9] advised VECs of changes in the Irish requirement for second level teaching with effect from the first day of the 1997/98 school year. Section 9.2 of Memorandum V.7 was amended as follows.

> *Qualification in the Irish language*
> The Ceard Teastas Gaeilge (Oral)[10] of the Department of Education and Science or an equivalent qualification recognised by the Minister is required to satisfy the Irish requirement for appointment to a teaching position in a Community College or Vocational School.

> A candidate who does not satisfy the Irish requirement at the time of appointment, may be appointed provisionally to a teaching position subject to his/her obtaining the Ceard Teastas Gaeilge (Oral) or equivalent qualification within a period of three years.

Where no candidate (**otherwise properly qualified**) for a permanent whole-time post possesses qualifications in Irish a VEC may make a tempo-

---

6 Note 3 above.
7 *loc. cit.,* p. 194.
8 Dated Nollaig 1997.
9 Note that Comprehensive Schools are not specified although the requirement relates to second level teaching.
10 The Oral CTG only is specified. Prevrisiously both written and oral were required.

rary whole-time appointment for the academic year and subject to the approval of the Minister continue the appointment for the following academic year.

A non-national who is otherwise fully-qualified **may** be granted exemption from the CTG requirement if there is no other candidate fully-qualified for the post. A similar exemption may be granted to a person who was born and educated in Northern Ireland.[11]

6.4 Irish for VPT

In accordance with CL 16/93, a pass in the oral Irish component of the CTG examination will be regarded as an acceptable qualification in Irish for permanent wholetime appointment on VPT courses.

6.5 Irish for RTCs

Special provisions apply for appointment at Lecturer I and Assistant Lecturer grades in RTCs.[12]

6.6 Disputes

There have been at least two disputes over the requirement of a qualification in Irish, one in 1977 and another in 1979. In 1977 the Department of Education disqualified a Scottish lecturer from taking up a senior post at the new Limerick Technical College at Moylish, because he did not know Irish. The same lecturer was later re-appointed by the Limerick City VEC to the post of Senior Lecturer, Grade I subject to the sanction of the Department. The post was re-advertised without a knowledge of Irish as an essential requirement.

6.7 The *Cussen* case

Unlike the situation which obtained In *The State (Cussen) v. Brennan*[13] the Minister for Education has specified in Memo V.7 the appointments for which qualifications in the Irish language are essential and also those where preference must be given and will be given to those holding qualifications in Irish.

The facts of the *Cussen* case were that the Southern Health Board wished to fill a vacancy in the office of paediatrician to the Board and requested the Local Appointments Commissioners to recommend a suitable candidate for that office. The Commissioners informed candidates that "extra credit will

---

[11] Para B(i) Memo V.7.
[12] Lecturer Standard Qualification – Addendum after para. 5 altered to an Oral test by Circular Letter No. 28/79.
[13] [1981] I.R. 181.

be given to qualified and suitable candidates having a good knowledge of Irish". The Minister for Health, the person responsible for prescribing the qualifications for the position had made no such decision and had not prescribed that knowledge of the Irish language was one of the qualifications for the appointment. The prosecutor was interviewed but did not undergo the Irish language test. The Commissioners recommended another candidate who was appointed by the Board. In the words of O'Higgins C.J.

> It appears that subsequent to the interview the prosecutor learned from members of the interview board that the Irish test had proved crucial in the selection of the candidate to be recommended.[14]

The prosecutor applied for and was granted a conditional order of *certiorari* quashing the Commissioners recommendation (unless cause could be shown to the contrary). The Supreme Court held that the Commission had no power to apply such a new qualification as the Irish test.

The situation is totally different when a Minister has specified Irish as part of the requirements for her/his "approval" for appointment.

It is noteworthy that Memo V.7 which indicates preferential treatment for candidates with a qualification in the Irish language uses statements that preference must be given to those **otherwise properly qualified** for situations in vocational schools, and to those **otherwise suitably qualified** for positions in VEC Colleges.[15]

It is suggested that Irish Language qualifications for all appointment to all teaching positions should be the same.[16]

6.8 The *Groener* case

In 1989 the European Court of Justice held that the requirement of an Irish language qualification did not contravene the Treaty of Rome. In the case of *Groener v. The Minister for Education and the City of Dublin VEC*[17] the Irish High Court asked the European Court for a preliminary ruling being of the opinion that in the circumstances, knowledge of the Irish language was not actually necessary to carry out the relevant duties.

Miss Anita Groener, a Dutch woman, was refused a permanent appointment to lecturer in Art at the Dublin College of Marketing & Design after failing a compulsory Irish language test. The CTG or passing a special ex-

---

[14] *Ibid* p. 187.
[15] *Irish Independent*, 1 March 1979.
[16] All applicants fully qualified and holding Memo V.7 requirements and a C.T.G. have not been give preference presumably not being suitably qualified and the loose use of these terms does not help toward certainty and a definite interpretation.
[17] Case 379/87 Luxembourg, 29 May, 1989.

amination in the Irish language is required by C/L 28/79. (It is only required when there are other fully qualified candidates.)

Miss Groener sought an exemption, but this was refused by the Minister as there were other fully qualified candidates for the post. The Minister, consented to her appointment (she was part-time) provided she passed the Irish language examination. She failed the examination in Irish and challenged the refusal to appoint her before the Irish courts arguing that C/L 28/79 was incompatible with Article 48 EEC and Article 3 of Council Regulation 1612/68 on freedom of movement of workers within the Community, which prohibits discrimination against Community nationals. The ultimate aim of the requirement was to make Irish nationals learn Irish rather than to keep away non-nationals.

The European Court concluded:

> A permanent full-time post of lecturer in public vocational education institutions is a post of such a nature to justify the requirement of linguistic knowledge within the meaning of the last sub-paragraph of Article (3)1 of Council Regulation 1612/68, provided that the linguistic requirement in question is imposed as part of a policy for the promotion of the national language which is, at the same time, the first official language and provided that that requirement is applied in a proportionate and non-discriminatory manner.[18]

6.9 Age Limits

Section 6 of the Vocational Education (Amendment) Act 1944 provides:

> The Minister may declare any specified age to be the age limit for all offices or for such offices as belong to a specified class, description, or grade or for one or more specified offices.[19]

Declarations made by the Minister under this section come into force six months after the day on which they are made.

Normally,[20] on first appointment[21] as a permanent whole-time vocational teacher one must be not less than 21 and not more than 30 years of age. A person over 30 and under 40 years of age "may be appointed if the Minister is satisfied that he is a suitable person having regard to his teaching or other experience".

The Minister may, however, sanction the appointment of a person who is

---

[18] *Ibid.,* p. 3994.
[19] Section 6(1) of the Vocational Education (Amendment) Act 1944.
[20] The use of this word means that there are exceptions.
[21] Para 3 of Memo V.7.

not less than 20 years of age, and is a fully qualified teacher of Domestic Science, or of Art, or of Physical Education, or of Rural Science or of wood-work", or who is a University graduate qualified in accordance with Memo V.7 (in accordance with paragraph 8 of some versions and of paragraph 9 of other versions) A qualified person who is over 40 years of age, in special circumstances, may also be sanctioned for first appointment.

In order to ensure compliance and for pension purposes paragraph 5 of Memo V.7 requires "[e]very person **appointed** to a position of permanent whole-time teacher under a Committee" to furnish as evidence of age a certified extract from a Public Register of Births.

6.10 Age Limits and Employment Equality

Discrimination on the grounds of age was expressly prohibited in section 8 of the Employment Equality Bill, 1996. Discrimination is taken to occur under section 6 where one person was treated less favourably than another was, had been or would be treated on the grounds that (s. (2)(f)) they were of different ages, where a person was under 65 or 18 or over.

In the past upper age limits in public sector employment were challenged as being **indirect** discrimination contrary to section 2(c) of the Employment Equality Act 1977 in a number of cases.

In the *O'Broin* case,[22] Mrs. O'Broin, a clerk typist employed by the EHB in a temporary unestablished capacity complained that by refusing to establish her in a permanent capacity the EHB discriminated against her contrary to section 2(c) of the Employment Equality Act 1977. They refused to do so because she did not comply with the upper age limit for appointment to a permanent post, which was 27. It was argued on behalf of the claimant that her claim was also valid under Article 119 of the Treaty of Rome and EEC Council Directive No. 76/207 of 9 February 1976.[23]

She was 32 when first recruited by the Board. As a temporary unestablished officer, she was not on an incremental scale and not admitted to the Board's Superannuation or Sick Leave schemes. She submitted that the requirement regarding the upper age limit of 27 was not an essential requirement for the employment.

The Equality Officer at first hearing concluded that the case had similarities to that of *Price v. British Civil Service Commission*[24] where fewer women could comply with the age limit since many women were either hav-

---

[22] *Eastern Health Board v. A Worker and Local Government and Public Services Union Equality officer* 13/80 – Labour Court DEE-3-81. See also *Donegal Co. Co. v. O'Shea* EE8/1982, *Price v. Civil Service Commission* [1978] 1 All E. R. 1228 and *Huppert v. UGS & University of Cambridge, Central Office of Industrial Tribunals (Britain)* COIT 35260/84.

[23] See Caroline Fennell and Irene Lynch, *Labour Law in Ireland* (Dublin, 1993), p. 185.

[24] Note 22 above. *Price v. Civil Service Commission* [1978] I.C.R. 2.

ing or bringing up children and were, therefore, out of the labour market for several years in their twenties, thirties and forties but was different in that Mrs. O'Broin wanted a declaration that she should be automatically established with all her service treated as if she were permanent whereas Ms. Price was prepared to compete on equal terms with all applicants.

The Equality Officer found that the upper age limit was discriminatory against Mrs. O'Broin, that the limit of 27 years was not essential to the Board's administration.

Having regard to the fact that EHB employments were pensionable, a run of a minimum of 15 years would be desirable, if the pension was to be of any appreciable level, and the age limit of 50 years suggested by Mrs. O'Broin would be about right. The Equality Officer so recommended.

The Labour Court concluded that the operation of an entry age limit generally appeared to be discriminatory against married women as the proportion of that group who could comply was evidently smaller than the proportion of married or single persons of either sex. The discrimination against Mrs. O'Broin rested solely in depriving her of eligibility to compete for posts simply because of her age, she had no prior right to establishment but the necessary arrangements should be made to enable her to compete for the post in the standard manner. The Court had no means of assessing what the proper age limit might be. This reluctance may have been because of a realisation that a person over 50 years of age may also be discriminated against.

6.11 Upper Age Limit

An upper age limit of 21 years prescribed for a post as clerical officer was challenged in *O'Shea v. Donegal County Council*,[25] again on the basis that it amounted to discrimination within the meaning of section 2(c) of the Employment Equality Act 1977 and also because this Act is based on the Second Directive of the European Communities *viz.* Article 2 of the Council Directive which states:

> For the purposes of the following provisions, the principle of equal treatment shall mean that there shall be no discrimination whatsoever on grounds of sex either directly or indirectly by reference in particular to marital or family status.[26]

Mrs. O'Shea submitted that precedents for her claim had already been established by the *O'Broin*[27] and *Martyn*[28] cases and she cited a statement by the

---

[25] Note 22 above.
[26] EEC Council Directive No. 76/207, OJL 39, February 14 1976, No. L 339/40
[27] Note 22 above
[28] *North Western Health Board v. Martyn*, Supreme Court, [1985] ILRM 226

Minister for Labour and the Public Service on 5 November 1981, that the time for ending such discriminatory practices was long overdue. The Minister had stated:

> These low entry limits, where they are not essential to the proper performance of the job in question, have no justification other than the tradition of a different time in the economic and social development of this country. . . . With a view to removing low entry age limits in the public service, I will shortly be bringing the issue before the Government for decision on the required recruitment policy changes involved.[29]

She also claimed that it appeared she was being penalised for the fact that she opted to continue her education at third level and for obtaining a Diploma in Public Health after a three year course. Had she instead sought employment on leaving school at 18 the chances were that she would have successfully negotiated the upper age barrier.

The Equality Officer found that the circumstances of the claimant were in no way similar to those in the *O'Broin* or *Martyn* cases and she could not rely on them to prove her case. The specified age limit was not an essential requirement. From an analysis of the available statistics the proportion of single females aged not more than 21 was substantially higher than the proportion of married females. Mrs. O'Shea was not discriminated against, she was eligible on four occasions to compete in the years 1975-1978 inclusive, but the Minister should raise the upper age limit to an age where the proportion of single females able to comply would not be substantially higher than the proportion of married females.

On appeal, the Labour Court agreed that the upper age limit of 21 was likely to result in indirect discrimination and the fact that the claimant had not applied at an earlier date when she was under 21 was irrelevant. If an employer operated a rule prohibited by section 3(2) all persons who fell foul of the rule must be taken to be discriminated against. Therefore, there had been discrimination against Mrs. O'Shea and the Court recommended that the age limit be raised for future competitions.

In *Kennedy v. Co. Donegal VEC*[30] the Equality Officer suggested that the age limit might be raised to the maximum level allowed under the Superannuation Pension Scheme 1977, *viz.* 55 years. Ms. Kennedy had been unable to compete for the position of library assistant because of the age requirement. The requirement was held not to be essential to the job and discriminatory, in that the proportion of single females able to comply with it would be substantially higher than the proportion of married females.

Similar cases on the same grounds received a set-back following the

---

[29] EE 8/1982, EP8/1982.
[30] (EE 11/83) [1983] I ILT. 58.

High Court decision in *N. W.H.B. v. Martyn*[31] because, as Deirdre Curtin points out:[32]

> Since 1983, the nature of the evidence necessary to establish a *prima facie* case of indirect discrimination has altered markedly, in particular by requiring the production of relatively sophisticated statistical evidence.[33]

Martyn had contended successfully before the Labour Court that the refusal of the Health Board to allow her to compete for posts on the basis that an applicant should be under the age of 28 years was indirect discrimination within the meaning of section 2(c) of the Employment Equality Act 1977.

6.12 High Court

When she was awarded £3,000 compensation the Board appealed to the High Court contesting that the age qualification was discriminatory and claiming that it was unable to comply with the finding, because the age qualification was a requirement imposed by the Minister for Health under the Health Act 1970.

Mr. Justice Barron held that, while an age qualification may be discriminatory, there had been no evidence before the Labour Court to justify a finding of discrimination in this case, there was no proof of discrimination within the meaning of section 2(c) of the Act and that, accordingly, there were no grounds for awarding compensation. He stated that:

> Where candidates for employment must comply with a requirement which is not essential for that employment, **it must be established as a matter of fact** that the number of those of a particular marital status able to comply is substantially higher than the number of those of a different marital status but of the same sex able to comply.[34]

In the present case no statistical evidence was given to establish that a substantially higher number of married women would have applied without the impugned condition.

---

[31] *North Western Health Board v. Worker Equality Officer* 14/81 Labour Court DEE-1-82, [1987] I.R. 565

[32] Deirdre Curtin, *Irish Employment Equality Law* (Dublin, 1989).

[33] *Ibid.,* p. 241

[34] [1987] I.R. 565 574

6.13 Supreme Court

On appeal, the Supreme Court[35] set aside the order of the High Court thus leaving undisturbed the Labour Court conclusion that the age limit constituted discrimination, but it did so on the basis that, since both parties before the Labour Court had proceeded on what amounted to an admission of the relevant facts which would constitute discrimination, it was not open to the High Court judge to proceed on the basis that the facts of the particular case had to be proved before him. The conclusion of the Labour Court that the age limit constituted discrimination, in this case, was upheld by reason **only** of the fact that it formed an assumption of fact not contested by the respondent and the determination should not be taken as a precedent upon which a conclusion could safely be based that relatively low age limits can, and do, constitute discrimination within the meaning of section 2(c).

It appears from this decision that tribunals must provide findings of fact based on evidence which supports such findings and the inability to provide such evidence may now be a factor in the scarcity of cases under this heading.

6.14 The Constitution and Age Limits

Age limits and the right to work were considered in *Landers v. A. G.*[36] where the father of a young boy sought to have sub-sections of the Prevention of Cruelty to Children Act 1904 declared to be unconstitutional.

Section 2 of that Act created an offence of causing or procuring a boy under the age of fourteen to be in a licensed premises for the purpose of singing etc., between the hours of 9 p.m. and 6 a.m. The father and manager of Michael Landers a young singer, aged about eight at the time, were summoned and convicted under this provision. The father then took an action claiming that these provisions were repugnant to the Constitution.

The case was argued on a number of grounds including that the restriction was a discrimination and a failure to accord the infant the right to prepare for and follow a chosen career contrary to Article 40.3.1° of the Constitution, which provides "The State guarantees in its laws to respect, and as far as practicable, by its laws to defend and vindicate the personal rights of the citizen". The right to earn a living is one such personal right.[37]

Finlay J. rejected the plaintiff's contentions. He considered the real personal right relative to the issue, to be the personal right of Michael Landers to

---

[35] *North Western Health Board v. Martyn* [1985] ILRM 226.
[36] *Landers v. A.G.* [1975] 109 I.L.T.R. 4, see also *O'Brien v. Keogh* [1972] I.R. 144.
[37] *Per* Kenny J. in *Murtagh Properties Ltd v. Michael Cleary* (1972) I.R. 330 and *Moran v. Att. Gen.* (1976) 110 I.L.T.R. 85 at p. 87. See also *dictum* of Carroll J. in *Ni Bheolain v. CDVEC, Ireland and Attorney General*, unreported , High Court, January 1983, p. 30 and at p. 21 *ante*, also *Landers v. A G.* [1975] 109. I.L.T.R.

prepare for and follow a chosen career and this was guaranteed by Article
40.3.

In relation to discrimination he cited the judgment of Ó Dálaigh C.J. in
O'Brien (an Infant) v. Keogh:[38]

> As was said in the judgment of this court in the *State (Hartley) v. Governor of Mountjoy Prison* (21 December 1967) a diversity of arrangements does not effect discrimination between citizens in their legal rights.
> Their legal rights are the same in the same circumstances. This in fact
> is equality before the law and not inequality. . . . Article 40 does not
> require identical treatment of all persons without recognition of differences in relevant circumstances it only forbids invidious discrimination.[39]

Finlay J. considered that he was bound by the principle thus laid down and
that it applied to the *Landers* case.

Professor Casey[40] states:

> The implications of the right identified in the *Landers* case remain to
> be worked out. It clearly opens the way to challenging unreasonable
> restrictions on entry to a trade or profession, whether imposed by statute or by private arrangements, but no such challenges have as yet occurred.[41]

6.15 The PESP

In relation to age limits in recruitment to the Public Service, the 1991 Programme for Social and Economic Progress (P.E.S.P.) agreed between the
Government and the Social Partners provided:

> In the context of changing work patterns, the provision of job opportunities for the long-term unemployed, and the desirability of promoting
> equal access to employment, the Government commit themselves to a
> policy of substantially raising recruitment age limits throughout the
> public service. This policy will not, however, preclude the holding of
> competitions for school leavers, trainees and graduates.[42]

---

[38] *O'Brien (an Infant) v. Keogh* [1972] I.R. 144.
[39] *Ibid.*, p.156
[40] Professor James Casey, *Constitutional Law in Ireland* (London, 1987), p. 316.
[41] *Ibid.*, p. 322
[42] P.E.S.P. (Paragraph 110, Section IV, Social Policy)

6.16 The Right to Work

Equality of opportunity or access is just that. The right to earn a livelihood has been held to be one of the personal rights of the citizen under Article 40.3 of the Constitution in the case of *Murtagh Properties Ltd. v. Cleary*[43] but "It does not mean that the State must either provide work or provide for work. It seems to mean that where a person is in employment, unconstitutional means cannot be used to remove him."[44]

It is suggested that it is, in effect, of the same nature as the right to work specified in Article 23 of the Universal Declaration of Human Rights which provides:

> Everyone has the right to work, to free choice of employment, to just and favourable conditions of work and to protection against unemployment.[45]

But in *Langston v. A.U.E.W.*[46] it was stated that this was a general right, not a right to work for any particular employer or in any particular place. It is a right based upon public policy rather than contract. Neither do the rights under the Human Rights Convention guarantee a right to hold a position in public service, because in *Ahmed v. U.K.*,[47] a teacher lost his claim before the Commission that a school should arrange his time-table to facilitate his attendance at Friday prayers in a mosque. He was refused permission to attend a mosque during hours of employment and claimed that he was forced to resign in order to do so.

6.17 Health Certificate

Everyone appointed for the first time as a permanent whole-time vocational teacher **must** provide the VEC with a Certificate of Health (on Form L.A.2 or L.A.3) at his/her own expense, from a medical practitioner nominated by the VEC. A certificate of Health **may** also be required on the appointment of a person who holds or has held a whole-time post under another VEC. Such persons may be required to undergo a HIV or AIDS test and if an applicant refuses approval of his appointment could be lawfully withheld provided such testing is applied to applicants of both sexes.

---

[43] [1972] I.R. 33, See Mary Redmond, *Dismissal Law in the Republic of Ireland* (Dublin, 1982), p. 37, Reference 39.

[44] Brian Doolan, *Constitutional Law and Constitutional Rights in Ireland* (Dublin, 1984), p. 141.

[45] Reproduced in Luke Clements, *European Human Rights* (London, 1994), Appendix 2, p. 240

[46] *Langston v. A.U.E.W. (No. 2)* [1974] IC.R. 510 at 521 (NIRC).

[47] [1982] 4. E.H.R.R. 126.

CHAPTER 7

Appointments

One science only will one genius fit;
So vast is art, so narrow human wit.

Pope, *Essay on criticism*, Pt.i,1.60

The sole prerogative of making appointments as a vocational teacher is vested in vocational education committees, who are expressly given this statutory power and indeed duty to appoint staff, by section 23 of the Vocational Education Act 1930.

The filling of a teaching post involves two quite distinct stages involving two separate entities, *viz.* (1) the making of an appointment by a VEC; and (2) the approval of the appointment by the Minister (the relevant Education Board by virtue of section 59 of the Education Bill 1997). Neither the VEC or the Minister have total discretion in relation to appointments, and without both an appointment cannot take effect.

7.1 Duty of VEC

Section 23 of the 1930 Vocational Education Act clearly specifies that appointments are made by a VEC and imposes an obligation on it to make such appointments by stating:

(1) Subject to the provisions of this section, every VEC **shall appoint** a chief executive officer and such other officers and servants as it shall from time to time think necessary for the due performance of its powers and duties under this Act.

(2) The numbers, qualifications, salaries or remuneration, and **appointment** of all officers shall be subject to the approval of the Minister.

Although not expressly designated as officers in the Vocational Education Acts, whole-time vocational teachers have always been regarded as officers and the provisions of the Vocational Education Acts relating to officers have been applied to them. See the discussion on this topic, *post*.

The Minister can indicate by means of Memos and Circular Letters how it is proposed to exercise the statutory powers conferred on him/her by the Vocational Education Act 1930.

A vocational teacher may be:

(a) whole-time, permanent and pensionable,

(b) temporary whole-time,

(c) eligible part-time, *i.e.* fixed term contract,

(d) regular part -time, or

(e) hourly part-time.

Memo V.7, published by the Department of Education,[1] contains the standard conditions of appointment and service applicable to whole-time, permanent and pensionable posts as vocational teachers. This document has been significantly altered and amended and it is difficult for most persons to gain access to an up to date copy.

Once appointed, a vocational teacher holds office or employment from the VEC which appointed him or her and not from the Board of Management which manages the school.

7.2 Standard Conditions

Because all whole-time teachers employed under approved schemes of technical and continuation education would be eligible under certain conditions for superannuation or gratuity under the Local Government Act 1925 it was seen as important to ensure that Technical Instruction Committees would not be "encumbered" with indifferent officers for whose pensions the local rating authority would be responsible. The Commission on Technical Education in their report of 1926 recommended "that the Department should draft standard conditions governing the appointment and duties of whole-time officers."[2] This was duly put into effect and now Standard Forms of appointment and duties of office composed and issued by the Department are used. These Conditions of Service deal with the nature of the post, probation, salary and allowances, duties, attendance at courses, leave of absence, extern work and notice to be given. The duties of different grades of vocational teacher are specified in appendices to Memo V.7.

Teachers and members of Technical Instruction Committees complained to the Commission:

(a) that there were no fixed salary scales that similar appointments under different TICs carried different salaries,

(b) that there was no uniform policy in regard to increments. Some teachers had remained on the initial salary point for over fifteen years and in some

---

[1] Appendix C(i).
[2] Recommendation No. 92, p. 150.

cases teachers seeking increments had to solicit the support of individual members of the local committees, and

(c) that travelling expenses and subsistence allowances were far from adequate and in some cases no expenses were paid.

The Commission concluded that these grievances tended to reduce the efficiency of the teaching staffs and to deplete their numbers[3] and recommended[4] that definite salary scales and rates of travelling and subsistence expenses should be drawn up by the Department and made obligatory on local committees employing whole time teachers. In the absence of any cause for complaint on grounds of conduct, salary increments should be granted automatically on receipt of a satisfactory report from the Department's Inspector.

In general, the terms or conditions of a person's employment are not solely derived from written conditions. Other rights and obligations arise from the Constitution, from custom, from common law, from collective agreements and also from national agreements. What was contained in the job advertisement, what the employee was engaged to do and indeed what was said at the interview may also be relevant. In *Redbridge LBC v. Fishman*,[5] the EAT held that an Industrial Tribunal paid too much attention to the contractual position and concluded that what the headmaster said at the interview represented the intention of the school governors and the LEA and was binding on them.

7.3 The Old System

Under the old system, specified in Memo V.7, even a proposal by a VEC to make an appointment of a permanent[6] whole-time teacher had first to be submitted to the Minister[7] for sanction and then the Minister had to be satisfied: that the appointment was necessary, that the standard conditions of service obtained, and that the VEC resources were sufficient to enable them to contribute to the cost of the appointment.

In *Devitt v. Co. Dublin VEC and Minister for Education*[8] it was held that the Minister was entitled to exercise her statutory powers in relation to numbers in accordance with the new forms introduced in 1973 but also to reserve the right to seek justification of an appointment to a particular post. It had

---

[3] Report of the Commission on Technical Education, Dublin, 1926, Chapter XII, para. 327.
[4] *Ibid,* Recommendation 91.
[5] [1978] I.C.R. 569.
[6] The position with regard to temporary whole-time appointments is not covered by Memo V.7 but all appointments are covered by s. 23.
[7] In reality to the Department of Education. This is the equivalent of Rule 18 Rules for National Schools 1965, Rule 23 Constitution of Boards and Rules of Procedures 1975.
[8] *Devitt v. Co. Dublin VEC & The Minister for Education* [1989] I.L.R.M. 639.

been argued in Devitt that once posts were within the whole-time equivalents in FORMS 9ABCD the Minister had no power other than to query suitability.

In 1927 the Commission on Technical Education suggested that a total of less than 800 hours instruction in the academic year should not normally be regarded as sufficient to warrant the appointment of a teacher on a whole-time basis.

7.4 Memo V.7

Paragraph 1 of Memo V.7 (not observed in practice since 1973) specifies that the documents which must be sent to the Department when seeking sanction to make an appointment are:

(a) a statement explaining the need for the post.

(b) a draft copy of the conditions of appointment.[9]

(c) a draft copy of the conditions of service.[10]

7.5 The New System

The word appointment in section 23(2) is in the singular and indicates that the Ministers approval relates to each individual single appointment.

In 1973 the Minister for Education introduced FORMS 9ABCD which form the basis on which teaching staff vacancies are allocated. These forms collate details of current and projected student numbers, the utilisation of the teacher allocation, and the provision of teaching services to other institutions. The statistics then form the basis on which the annual allocation of teachers is made on whole-time teacher equivalents. Every year the Department of Education gives each VEC an allocation of class three teaching posts for second level schools. Sanction for permanent or TWT appointment is still required after selection.

7.6 Selection

Section 21 of the 1930 Act authorises a VEC to appoint as many sub-committees as it thinks proper and selection for appointment to a position as vocational teacher within a vocational school or college is by a VEC sub-committee who interview applicants and either draw up a list in order of merit or recommended that a particular applicant be appointed.

The VEC passes a resolution adopting the recommendation. Although it is most unusual, a VEC is entitled to reject the recommendation of their sub-committee and, for example, direct them to hold further interviews. The County

---

[9] Appendix B Memo V.7.
[10] Appendix C Memo V.7.

Dublin VEC considered doing so in 1988 but, in view of objections, reconsidered at a second meeting and accepted the recommendation.

In *Wilson v. Belfast Corporation*[11] a resolution passed by Belfast City Council was not an offer, the unauthorised publication of it in the press did not constitute communication and there was no right to assume that the resolution was unalterable. No contract existed.

If a candidate hears unofficially that s/he has been recommended for appointment s/he has no legal rights against the VEC or Board of Management. In the case of *Powell v. Lee*,[12] it was held that such unauthorised communication does not confer any rights on the candidate concerned even where a resolution to appoint him had been passed.

7.7 Appointment of Vocational Teachers

The appointment, the numbers, the qualifications, salaries, and remuneration of all officers are subject to the approval of the Minister under section 23(2). Fixed term contract (EPT) and part-time teachers are not officers and EPT can only be appointed with the consent of the Department while hourly part-time may be appointed without the approval of the Minister.

Section 23 of the 1930 Act provides that a VEC shall appoint a CEO and **such other officers** and servants as it thinks necessary for the proper performance of its powers and duties subject to the approval of the Minister (now of the relevant Education Board by virtue of section 59 of the Education Bill 1997

Lest it be thought that a VEC is under an arbitrary or unnecessary constraint by virtue of the Ministers power of approval under subsection (2), it should be pointed out that the exercise by the Minister of his/her discretion under section 23(2) must be in light of section 23(1) and section 30 which obliges the VEC to appoint such officers as it sees are necessary. The Minister cannot exercise his/her powers in such a way as to prevent the operation of the Vocational Education Acts and frustrate the will of Parliament.

7.8 Minister (Education Board) Cannot Appoint

Under the existing legislation the Minister cannot make an appointment. The statutory power to do so has been entrusted to the VECs. In *Devitt v. The Minister for Education,*[13] the Minister refused to approve the appointment on a permanent whole-time basis but purported to appoint as a temporary whole-time teacher. This purported appointment by the Minister was held to be invalid

---

[11] *Wilson v. Belfast Corporation* 55 I.L.T.R. 205.
[12] *Powell v. Lee* [1908] 99. L.T. 284.
[13] *Devitt v. Minister for Education, op. cit.*

and quashed. In *O'Connell v. Listowel U.D.C.,*[14] the plaintiff was entitled to be paid on a *quantum meruit* basis for work he had done under an appointment which the Minister subsequently refused to approve. The plaintiff was appointed as an engineer and town surveyor by the council and, purporting to act under that appointment, worked for the council for six months before the Minister's refusal.

On the other hand, a VEC appointment has no legal effect without the Minister's approval. In *O'Callaghan v. Co. Meath VEC,*[15] where it was held that the plaintiff had no contract of appointment to a permanent post of religious teacher in the Community College, Dunshaughlin, Co. Meath. Mr. Justice Costello stated that the fatal flaw in Mr. O'Callaghan's case was that a resolution of the VEC appointing him, or for that matter any teacher in a permanent capacity has no legal effect until it is approved by the Minister under section 23 of the Vocational Education Act 1930. A Department of Education letter to the VEC in September 1981 showed that he had not been appointed in a permanent capacity and that the Department did not regard him as qualified for such appointment.

7.9 Minister's Approval or Sanction

By virtue of section 23(2), the Minister for Education on behalf of the State, exercises a degree of control over both the numbers and qualifications of vocational teachers. This provision enabled the Minister to prevent the over-rapid expansion of the system and the creation of an unacceptable burden on the public finances.[16]

Although this power of approval is (subject to the constraints outlined above) totally at the Minister's discretion, the Minister is confined to considering the application before him/her, but is entitled to take into account, *inter alia*, the need for new teachers, the resources of the VEC, and the financial implications of the appointment.

It was stated in the *Devitt* case that the Minister is not entitled to limit the scope of the discretion entrusted to him/her under the 1930 Act, or to disable himself/herself from fully exercising this power by adopting rules and proce-

---

[14] *O'Connell v. Listowel U.D.C* [1957] Ir. Jur. Rep. 43.

[15] *O'Callaghan v. Co. Meath VEC,* unreported, High Court, 20 November 1990, Costello J., see also *Irish Press,* 21 November 1990, *Education Rules Circumvent Law—Judge* by Paul Muldowney.

[16] In *Cotter v. Ahern,* unreported, High Court 25 February 1977 Finlay P. held the appointment to be legal although no formal confirmation had been issued by the Department where Cotter had been chosen from a list of candidates previously vetted and approved by the Department.

A VEC is obliged to appoint a principal if there is such a vacancy and if it refuses to do so is in breach of statutory duty. *per* McWilliam J. *Phelan v. Co. Laois VEC and Parsons,* unreported, High Court, 28 February 1977. See also *Irish Times,* 1 March 1977.

dures. This finding was based on the principle that a public authority with a discretionary power must not fetter its discretion by adopting a binding policy to which there are no exceptions.[17] The fact that the Minister had departed in practice from the procedure she had laid down in Memo V.7 did not debar her from reverting to it. If an estoppel could be raised because of this, it could only be raised by the VEC and not by a teacher.

One of the consequences of a vocational teacher being regarded as an officer is that there is no promotion within the office held. The only way of advancement is to apply for and obtain a higher office by interview and then relinquish the old office.

The absence of the Minister's approval was also central to the decision of McWilliam J. in *Phelan v. Co. Laois VEC and Parsons*[18] where he stated that:

> In the absence of the consent of the Minister, Michael Parsons was not appointed Principal and the subterfuge of appointing him acting Principal and leaving him in that position without the consent of the Minister was wholly improper.[19]

Like *Crowley v. Ireland*,[20] the *Phelan* case involved the purported appointment of a person to the position of Principal who allegedly did not have the requisite years service.

7.10 Discrimination

Section 3(1) of the Employment Equality Act 1977 prohibits discrimination against an employer, a prospective employeee or an en employee of another:

> "In relation to –
>
> (a) access to employment,
> (b) conditions of employment,
> (c) training or experience for or in relation to employment,
> (d) promotion or re-grading, or
> (e) classification of posts."

An employer is also prohibited from having rules or instructions which would discriminate against an employee or class of employee.

---

[17] See *R. v London Borough of Bexley, ex parte* Jones [1994] Crown Office Digest 393, and *Gilheaney v. The Revenue Commissioners*, unreported, High Court, Costello J., 4 October 1995, at p. 25.

[18] Unreported, High Court, 28 February 1977, see also *Irish Times*, 1 March 1977.

[19] *Ibid.,* p.8

[20] McWilliam J, 1 December, 1977 (injunction); McMahon J, 21 July 1978 (substantive action), Supreme Court, 1 October 1979, all judgments are unreported.

By virtue of section 1 of the Employment Equality Act 1997 an employee means, *inter alia*, an officer or servant of a vocational education committee, and thus Vocational teachers come within the remit of these provisions.

Under section 2 discrimination for the purposes of this Act shall be taken to occur in any of the following cases:

(a) where by reason of his sex a person is treated less favourably than a person of the other sex,

(b) where because of his marital status a person is treated less favourably than another person of the same sex,

(c) where because of his sex or marital status a person is obliged to comply with a requirement, relating to employment or membership of a body referred to in section 5, which is not an essential requirement for such employment or membership and in respect of which the proportion of persons of the other sex (as the case may be) of a different marital status but of the same sex able to comply is substantially higher,

(d) where a person is penalised for having in good faith—

    (i) made a reference under section 19 of under section 7 of the Act of 1974, (Anti-Discrimination (Pay) Act 1974),

    (ii) opposed by lawful means an act which is unlawful under this Act or the Act of 1974,

    (iii) given evidence in any proceedings under this Act or the Act of 1974, or

    (iv) given notice of an intention to do anything referred to in subparagraphs (i) to (iii),

and cognate words shall be construed accordingly.

In the future these provisions will undoubtedly be used although it must be pointed out that equality of access which means opportunity to apply, does not confer any other right. Discrimination in interviewing is a separate matter and is dealt with elsewhere.

It may be possible for an unsuccessful candidate for a position as a vocational teacher to contest his/her non-appointment under the provisions of this Act. This happened in the case of *Board of Management of Limerick Model School v. Culloo*[21] when the defendant Culloo successfully claimed that he had been discriminated against in the appointment of a principal in the school. An equality officer, acting under the Employment Equality Act issued a recommendation in his favour. See also under Chapter 14 Memo V.7.

---

[21] *Board of Management of Limerick Model School v. Culloo,* unreported, High Court, 11 May 1989.

In *Higgins v. Co. Laois VEC*[22] an equality officer, and later the Labour Court, found that the VEC had discriminated against Ms. Higgins on grounds of her sex when it did not appoint her to an "A" post of responsibility:

> . . . the fact that the interview board failed to consider the claimant's obviously superior work experience and qualifications in their decision-making, is evidence in support of the allegation that there was discrimination against her. . . .[23]

7.11 Transfers

Normally a teacher can be transferred from one school to another or from one class of teaching to another unless his conditions of service specify that s/he is to teach a special class or in a particular school. See *Huff v. Harlan County Board of Education*.[24] VECs expressly have the right to assign a teacher to any school within their area.

Transfer, although within the competence of the person authorising it, will be actionable if done maliciously and without probable cause. In *Corless and Diggin v. Ireland*,[25] Mr. Justice Hamilton held that there could be an actionable wrong in the nature of slander by actions alone. The two plaintiffs were detective sergeants transferred out of the Garda Technical Bureau after a controversy over a fingerprint in the case of the murder of the British Ambassador. They claimed that their transfer amounted to demotion and sought damages for defamation alleged to consist of the actions of the Minister for Justice and the former Commissioner of the Garda Síochána in transferring them. It was held that, in effect, the act was privileged and not actionable at law, unless it was established that the act was done maliciously and without probable cause.

Each year at the commencement of the academic session there are complaints from second level teachers who are transferred from one vocational school within a scheme to another. The problems which arise are usually about who is to be transferred rather than whether a transfer is justified or not. The IVEA claim the right to transfer in accordance with teachers' contracts while the TUI claim that such disputes should be referred to an independent person to adjudicate on them.

Transfers may also come within the ambit of equality legislation and are capable of challenge on grounds of sex or marital status. One such case was

---

[22] EE 15/1996.
[23] *Ibid.* See p. 29, para. 5.14. The Labour Court recommended that she be offered an "A" post with effect from November 1994 and awarded her £2,500 compensation. (*See Irish Independent*, 29 April 1997.)
[24] (Ky) 408 SW 2d 457.
[25] Unreported, High Court, 23 July 1984.

Limerick VEC v. Cotter[26] where Mr. Cotter alleged discrimination against him on grounds of marital status in breach of section 3 of the Act in transferring him from Kilmallock to Abbeyfeale vocational school. The VEC claimed that the decision to transfer him was taken solely on educational grounds. Mr. Cotter was single but a more junior teacher of the same subject was married. Mr Cotter supplied written statements from four TUI representatives which indicated that his marital status was considered by the CEO when deciding the transfer.

The Equality Officer found that the CEO had discriminated against Mr. Cotter and recommended that he be transferred back to Kilmallock and paid £1,500 by way of compensation in respect of distress and injury to his feelings.

7.12 Probation

The Commission on Technical Education 1926 recommended that candidates for whole-time permanent appointments as technical teachers, should serve a two year probationary period, during which their suitability and competence might be assessed. In common with many other occupations, first-time appointees as vocational teachers must now serve a one-year probationary period.[27]

On completion of probation, an appointment may (a) be confirmed, (b) continued for a further period of probation, or (c) terminated, at the direction of the Minister or by a VEC with the Minister's approval.

In *The State (Daly) v. Minister for Agriculture*,[28] a veterinary inspector informed that the conditions of his probation had not been satisfied and that his appointment was terminated was successful in having the decision quashed by an absolute order of *certiorari*. It was held by Barron J. that the decision to terminate under section 7 of the Civil Service (Regulations) Act 1956 must be formed *bona fide* on a factually sustainable basis, and must not be unreasonable. It had to be presumed that the Minister's decision was not so formed, since he refused to disclose the material on which the decision had been based.

7.13 Non-application of Unfair Dismissals Act

If a vocational teacher is an officer, section 2(1) of the Unfair Dismissals Act 1977 as amended does not apply to him/her, whether whole-time or temporary-whole-time.

Section 2(1) states:

This Act shall not apply in relation to any of the following persons:

---

[26] EE11/1989.
[27] Paragraph 7 Memo V.7.
[28] Unreported, High Court, Barron J., 14 February 1987.

(j) officers of a health board (other than temporary officers), or a vocational education committee established by the Vocational Education Act 1930.[29]

The provisions of the Unfair Dismissals Acts do, however, apply to employees and to EPT or hourly part-time vocational teachers, neither of whom are officers of a VEC.

The Unfair Dismissals Act 1977 section 3(1) states that the Act does not apply in relation to a dismissal during probation or training (a) if the contract is in writing, the duration of the probation or training is one year or less and is specified in the contract.

Two decisions of the EAT are germane to dismissal of teachers during probation or training. Firstly in the case of *Marsh v. U.C.D.*,[30] a university lecturer employed for a temporary period to expire on 30 September 1974, had his appointment renewed in May 1974 for the academic session 1 October 1974 to 30 September 1975 and subsequently for a further year. The respondents decided not to grant him tenure and his employment was terminated on 30 September 1977. The EAT held:

(1) That his employment was not excluded from the Unfair Dismissals Act.

(2) That the respondents complaints against the Appellant did not amount to substantial grounds justifying the dismissal.

(3) That the appropriate redress was re-instatement.

In *Stevenson v. Dalton Secondary Preparatory Schools (1976) Ltd.*[31] the claimant worked as a teacher for a probationary period from 1 October 1975 until 31 July 1976. In April 1976 he was told that his employment would continue for a further probationary period until 31 July 1977 on which date he was dismissed. It was held that renewal of the contract, whether on the basis of an extension of the probationary period or not, had the effect of extending the period of the claimant's employment to a greater period than one year referred to in section 3(1)(b) and the dismissal did not take place within one year of the "commencement of the employment" which was 1 October 1975. His claim was not excluded from the Act. The dismissal was deemed to be unfair and the appropriate remedy was re-instatement.

---

[29] Section 3 of the Unfair Dismissals (Amendment) Act 1993 amends section 2 by the substitution of a new paragraph (j). The effect of the amendment is to insert the words "other than temporary officers" thus extending the protection of the Act to temporary officers in Health Boards.

[30] UD 27/ 1977. As to when dismissal is effective see *Gunton v. London Borough of Richmond Upon Thames* [1980] 3.W.L.R. 7145 *and Brown v. Southall & Knight* [1980] I.C.R. 617.

[31] UD 10/1978.

7.14 Absence During Probation

In the event of absence because of illness during the probationary period the appointing authority may consider the probationer's performance of his duties during a shorter period, if that period constitutes a sufficient basis of assessment.[32]

Article 32 of the Local Government (Officers) Regulations, 1943 states:

> every permanent officer shall hold office until he shall die, resign, or be removed from office.

7.15 Temporary Whole-Time Teachers

A person who is otherwise fully qualified but who lacks a Ceard Teastas Gaeilge or who does not have the requisite experience may be appointed on a Temporary Whole-time basis. Such a person may apply later in open competition for a permanent post but may not get it. Article 3 Local Government (Officers) Regulations, 1943 defines "temporary officer" as an officer appointed to hold office either (a) for a specified period; or (b) until a specific work or duty has been completed; or (c) until the appointment of another person to hold the office; or (d) as a substitute officer.

TWT vocational teachers are appointed on a renewable annual basis and their appointments, in default of re-appointment, end on 31 August following the beginning of the school year to which their appointments relate.

In *O'Sullivan v. Western Health Board*,[33] where the respondent was authorised by the Minister for Health to make a temporary appointment, the Employment Appeals Tribunal decided that a "temporary" clinical psychologist was an officer and as such excluded from the provisions of the Unfair Dismissals Act 1977. Her "temporary" employment was a "limbo-type" relationship, she not being clearly an officer nor a non-officer. She held the office on terms less favourable than had she been "made permanent" but held it, nonetheless, and that was the reality.

The following agreed differences existed between the claimant's employment and that which she would have enjoyed if she were a permanent officer.

	TEMPORARY	PERMANENT
1.	Not pensionable	Pensionable
2.	Social Insurance payable	Exempt person
3.	No increments	Increments
4.	Sick pay earned by service	Entitled to sick pay
5.	Not entered on register	Entered on register

[32] *Patrinos v. Economic and Social Committee of the European Communities,* Case C17/88 1989-11 ECR 4249.

[33] UD 131/1979.

Mr. M. Merrigan, a member of the tribunal, expressed the view that the Unfair Dismissals Act should be extended to cover such persons. They were (1) not governed by the statutory regulations afforded permanent and established officers and (2) were deemed, for the purposes of the Unfair Dismissals Act, to be outside its scope. Subsequently, section 3(a) of the Unfair Dismissals (Amendment) Act 1993 amended the Principal Act and extended its scope to temporary officers of a Health Board but not to temporary officers of a VEC.

The *O'Sullivan* decision was followed three years later by *Western Health Board v. Quigley*[34] in which Mr. Justice Barrington held that a temporary staff nurse was employed at most as a "temporary officer" and thus excluded from the Unfair Dismissals Act. The EAT had decided that she had been unfairly dismissed and this was affirmed on appeal to the Circuit court.

There was no suggestion that the procedures for appointment to permanent office were followed but it seems that Barrington J. was influenced by the idea that a psychiatric nurse must be an officer and that the appellant only had power to appoint the respondent as a temporary officer for a fixed term.

Gavan Duffy P. in *Devanny v. DBA*[35] stated:

> As to the barbarism of "quasi-permanent" nurses, I can give it the charity of silence since I have not to decide what it is supposed to mean.[36]

The plaintiff had been appointed to a post which purported to be of a temporary nature, but was not for a specified limited time for a special purpose. She was dismissed and restored to her position a year later without payment for that period. She sought declarations that she was a permanent pensionable officer, that her purported dismissal was invalid, and that she was entitled to damages.

Gavan Duffy P. commented that he approached the case:

> with all the diffidence becoming an ill-equipped explorer who penetrates *terra incognita*, as I make my painful way through the tortuous labyrinth of an unexplored administrative code[37]

and he went on to hold that her appointment must, if possible, be ascribed to a lawful exercise of the powers of the Board, that she had been appointed an officer with tenure for life, subject to age limit, resignation, or removal by lawful authority. Her purported dismissal was unlawful and she was entitled to salary during the period thereof.

---

[34] [1982] I.L.R.M. 390.
[35] [1949] 83 I.L.T.R. 113.
[36] *Ibid* at p. 122.
[37] *Ibid* at p.113

7.16 Conversion of Temporary into Permanent Appointments

Paragraph 17 of Memo V.7 provides for the conversion of temporary into permanent appointments and states:

> Notwithstanding the requirements governing permanent appointments, the Minister will be prepared to consider exceptionally a proposal from a Committee for the permanent appointment of a fully qualified teacher who is in its employment as a TWT, subject to satisfactory reports during the period of his TWT employment and to compliance with the conditions of section 1 *(within allocation)*, section 3 *(age limits)*, section 5 *(birth certificate)* and section 6 *(health certificate)* of this memorandum.

7.17 EPT Vocational Teachers

Part-time teachers may be employed on an hourly basis or, if they qualify as Eligible Part-Time, under a fixed-term, renewable annual contract (*i.e.* have worked for not less than half the hours of their equivalent permanent wholetime colleagues). EPT were created as a result of Labour Court Recommendations LVR 10395 and LC 11328. In order to come within the scope of the Unfair Dismissals Act 1977, part-time teachers are required to work at least eight hours a week under the Workers Protection (Part-time Employees) Act 1991 and have at least one year's continuous service under the Unfair Dismissals Act 1977. (See para. 7.22 Hours Worked, post).

Recourse to the Unfair Dismissals Act can be excluded in a contract for a fixed term or specific purpose of limited duration if (a) the contract is in writing and (b) the contract expressly provides that the Unfair Dismissals Act is not to apply. There are no such terms included in the EPT Contracts. Non-renewal in the absence of such terms could amount to unfair dismissal and could also ground a claim under the Redundancy Payments Acts.

In *Open University v. Triersman*[38] it was held that the relevant date to determine whether a lecturer was employed under a contract for a fixed term of two years or more within section 15(2) of the Redundancy Payments Act 1965 and paragraph 12(b) of the Schedule of the Trade Union and Labour Relations Act 1974 was the final contract of employment, irrespective of whether it was a re-engagement or renewal of a previous contract. The lecturer had been employed initially for a fixed period of eighteen months and at the end of that period for another seven months. Since the lecturer's second contract was for seven months only the employer was not entitled to rely on a clause in it excluding her right to claim redundancy or compensation for unfair dismissal.

---

[38] [1978] I.C.R. 524

Ferdinand von Prondzynski,[39] states that Barrington J. in *Western Health Board v. Quigley* appeared to have accepted the respondent's argument that the applicant's employment under a series of consecutive three month contracts brought her outside the protection of the Unfair Dismissals Act which, in the absence of clauses excluding the Unfair Dismissals Act, would be a highly doubtful conclusion.

The report of the case does not disclose whether such clauses were included. Because of the grounds on which the case was decided the present author inclines to the view that it did not contain clauses excluding the Unfair Dismissals Act and must confess to some disquiet about the rather pragmatic approach that seems to have been adopted and to the outcome which resulted.

In *Hunt v. Co. Sligo VEC*[40] it was crucial to determine if the applicant was an officer or a servant for the purposes of the Industrial Relations Acts in order for the Labour Court to have jurisdiction to hear the dispute. The Labour Court decided that the claimant, as **an eligible part-time teacher, was an officer** of the Sligo VEC, and, therefore, not a "worker" within the meaning of the Industrial Relations Acts 1946-1990 and, accordingly, was excluded from access to the Court. The Court would not hear the substantive case.

Section 23(1) of the Industrial Relations Act 1990 defines a "worker" as any person aged 15 years or more who has entered into or works under a contract with an employer . . . but does not include (b) a teacher in a secondary school, (c) a teacher in a national school, or (e) an officer of a VEC. Section 4(1) of the Industrial Relations Act 1946 excluded "an officer or servant" of a VEC and it is to be noted that "servant" was dropped from the 1990 definition. It seems clear that the intention was to exclude teachers because of the special teachers Conciliation and Arbitration scheme. It is also noteworthy that the exclusion relating to teachers in the 1990 Act relates to a teacher "in" a secondary or national school. It does not distinguish between full time, part-time or EPT teachers. It applies to all types of teachers who work in secondary or national schools and the Labour Court did not distinguish between full-time or EPT vocational teachers. It obviously considered all teachers who work in a vocational school to be officers of a VEC for the purposes of the definition of "worker" under the 1990 and other Industrial Relation Acts.

It must be remembered that the decision is a recommendation and not legally binding. It should not be taken as a legal interpretation. The court's determination that Ms. Hunt was an officer should not be construed as establishing a precedent that an EPT teacher is legally an officer of a VEC. Even in relation to the interpretation for the purposes of the Industrial Relation Acts this matter could be challenged by judicial review. The crucial factor in relation to the recommendation in the *Hunt* case is that it was an interpretation of

---

[39] *Employment Law in Ireland* (2nd ed., 1989), p. 126.
[40] 24 November 1992, Ref: CD 92333.

the definition of "officer of a VEC" in relation to the Industrial Relations Acts only.

7.18 Continuous Service

In *Sinclair v. CDVEC*,[41] Judge Gerard Clarke pointed out that Ms. Sinclair did not have 12 months' continuous employment as required under the Act even though she had worked for the Dublin VEC from 1981 to 1983 and he allowed an appeal by the VEC against an Employment Appeals Tribunal award of £2,000 compensation to Ms. Sinclair. This decision seems to be totally at variance with that of the House of Lords in *Ford v. Warwickshire County Council*[42] in 1983.

The English Employment Protection (Consolidation) Act 1978 provides that, to qualify for the right not to be unfairly dismissed, an employee must be "continuously employed" for a period of not less than 52 weeks. Our Unfair Dismissals Act provides that the Act does not apply to a dismissed employee, who at the date of dismissal, had less than one year's continuous service. Continuous service is determined by rules in the First Schedule, Minimum Notice and Terms of Employment Act 1973 as amended by section 20 of the Unfair Dismissals Act 1977.

By Schedule 13, paragraph 9(1)(b) the English Act adds:

> absent from work on account of a temporary cessation of work . . . that week shall . . . count as a period of employment.

The House of Lords held that the word "temporary" was used in the sense of transient, *i.e.* lasting only for a relatively short time and the continuity of employment for the purposes of the Act in relation to unfair dismissal and redundancy payments was not broken unless and until, looking backwards from the date of expiry of the fixed term contract, there was to be found between one fixed term contract and its immediate predecessor an interval that could not be characterised **as short relative to the combined duration of the two fixed term contracts;** and that such characterisation was a question of fact and degree and, therefore, a question primarily for an industrial tribunal.

The council having conceded that the intervals between the appellant's successive contracts could be categorised as "temporary" cessations of work, it was not necessary to remit that issue.

The Unfair Dismissals (Amendment) Act 1993 provides that, where after the expiry of a fixed term an employee is re-employed within three months in similar employment, regard may be had to whether the employer entered into the later contract wholly or partly for the purpose of avoiding liability under

---

[41] Unreported, Circuit Court, *Irish Independent*, 18 January 1987.
[42] [1983] A.C. 71.

the Act. If so, this device will not work and the employee can claim under the Act.

In *Loscher v. The Board of Management of Mount Temple Comprehensive School*, EAT, UD 47/31, 21 March 1996; [1994] ELR 84 the preliminary issue was whether the claimant was qualified to make a claim under the Unfair Dismissals Acts.

The claimant was an EPT employed by the respondent school from October 1988 until June 1992. In June 1992 a new teacher was appointed and this resulted in a re-distribution of part-time teaching hours including all of the claimant's hours.

It was submitted that the claimant did not have 52 weeks continuous service as the school was only open for 30 weeks per year but the claimant referred to section 10 of the first schedule of the Minimum Notice and Terms of Employment Act 1973 which provides that absence from work for a period of not more than 26 weeks shall count as a period of service and that the claimant took holidays as given to him by the respondent.

The Tribunal found that the claimant had one year's qualifying service for the purpose of the Unfair Dismissals Acts 1997–1991.

The claimant was dismissed due to redundancy and had not been unfairly selected for it.

7.19 Extended Probation

It must be noted that the number of teachers who have been denied confirmation of appointment in a permanent capacity on termination of a period of probation has been extremely limited. One former CEO only encountered one such case of extended probation in thirty-three years experience and ultimately that person was confirmed in appointment at termination of the extended probation.

The provisions of the Unfair Dismissals Act 1977 do not apply to officers of a vocational education committee and, as permanent and temporary whole-time vocational teachers are regarded as officers, they do come within the parameters of either the *Marsh* case[43] or the *Stevenson* case[44] in the way that EPT vocational teachers can. They may, however, be able to rely on (a) contractual entitlement to fair procedures or (b) on natural or constitutional justice or due process.

In relation to contractual entitlement, Walsh J. in *Glover v. BLN*,[45] pointed out that "once a matter is governed by the terms of a contract between the parties, it is immaterial whether the employee concerned is deemed to be a servant or an officer." He then went on to state, that it was necessarily an

---

[43] *Marsh v. UCD* (UD 27/ 1977) *op. cit.*
[44] *Stevenson v. Dalton Secondary Preparatory Schools (1976) Ltd.* UD 10/1978, *op. cit.*
[45] [1973] I.R. 388 at 427.

implied term of the contract that any inquiry and determination should be fairly conducted.

7.20 Natural Justice and Constitutional Justice

In relation to natural justice and constitutional due process under Article 40.3 of the Constitution, Walsh J. in the same case stated:

> This court in *Re Haughey*[46] held that that provision of the Constitution was a guarantee of fair procedures. It is sufficient to say that public policy and the dictates of constitutional justice require that statutes, regulations or agreements setting up machinery for taking decisions which may affect rights or impose liability should be construed as providing for fair procedures.[47]

Hogan and Morgan[48] point out that this *excursus* into the "broader reaches of constitutional justice" was *obiter* and that the passage quoted depends on the impregnation of contract law by constitutional principles. They also claim that there has been judicial reluctance, in the High court, to follow what they describe as "this innovatory approach" and they instance *Lupton v. AIB*[49] and *Farrell v. Minister for Defence*[50] as illustrating this reluctance.

In *The State (Gleeson) v. Minister for Defence*[51] Henchy J. outlined the distinction between "constitutional justice"; and "natural justice" when he stated that the expression "constitutional justice" seemed to have originated in a passage in the judgment of the Supreme court in *McDonald v. Bord na gCon*[52] and that the requirements of "constitutional justice", sometimes called "constitutional due process" covered a wider field than the two maxims, *nemo iudex in causa sua* and *audi alteram partem* encompassed by the concept of natural justice. He went on to state at p. 295:

> The necessary implementation of express or implied constitutional guarantees meant that decisive acts and procedures could be impugned for a variety of reasons including that the accused was deprived of a fair, competent and impartial jury; or the person affected received unjustifiable unequal treatment.[53]

---

[46] [1971] I.R. 217.
[47] *Ibid.*, p. 425.
[48] Hogan and Morgan *Administrative Law in Ireland* (London, 1986), p. 275.
[49] (1984) 3 JISLL 107.
[50] (1985) 4 JISLL 105.
[51] [1976] I.R. 280.
[52] [1965] I.R. 217.
[53] At p. 295

It was however, necessary for a person seeking to have a decision condemned on the grounds that it was incompatible with the constitution:

> to plead and prove, first, the application in the circumstances of a speci-fied constitutional right, either express or implied, secondly that the de-cision or decisive process in question has infringed that right; and thirdly, that he stands aggrieved by that infringement.[54]

In the *Gleeson* case, the prosecutor was unable to point to any particular right of constitutional origin which he could invoke to support his claim and the issue fell to be decided under the common law. It then rested on non-compli-ance with the rules of natural justice *audi alteram partem* and his discharge was held invalid because of the breach of the principles of natural justice.

7.21 Regular Part-time Teachers/Lecturers

This category of vocational teacher is derived from the Worker (Regular Part-Time Employees) Act 1991 which defines a regular part-time employee as one who is normally expected to work not less than 8 hours a week and who has not less than 13 weeks continuous service with the same employer. Sec-tion 3 of the Act applies relevant enactments to regular part-time employees and this includes the Unfair Dismissals Acts 1977 to 1993.

Under section 2(2) of the Employment Appeals Tribunal has discretion to consider:

(a) whether a dismissal followed by re-employment within 26 weeks, or

(b) reduction of weekly working hours

was used by the employer for the purpose of avoiding obligation under the Act and where it considers that such dismissal or reduction was so used, they are deemed not to operate so as to break the continuity or effect the computabilty of service of the employee.

Even if a contract of employment contains a clause enabling a VEC to vary hours worked, a strategy to bring a teacher's hours or the number of continu-ous weeks, below the minimum for statutory rights may amount to construc-tive dismissal, if the reduction is a very dramatic one. As to reduction of hours and constructive dismissal see *Hogg v. Dover*.[55]

---

[54] *loc. cit.*
[55] [1990] ICR 39 EAT.

7.22 Hourly Part-time Teachers

Hourly part-time teachers are those employed for less than 8 hours a week. A VEC is entitled to employ an hourly part-time teacher for as many hours as it sees fit, i.e. for 7 or 7 and a half hours and thus avoid the accrual of statutory rights by virtue to the Worker Protection (Regular Part-time Employees) Act 1991 and the creation of an EPT. A reduction in hours is, however, a totally different matter.[56] The provisions of the Unfair Dismissals Act 1997–1993 do not apply to such teachers nor do the provisions of section 7 or 8 of the Vocation Education Act 1944 because such a teacher is not an officer. Such a teacher might be entitled to pursue a claim for wrongful dismissal at common law.

7.23 Hours Worked

In relation to hours worked. The hours worked by a teacher are not confined to those during which he actually teaches. The CDVEC General Conditions of Appointment of Part-time Teachers provides that in addition to work in class, the teacher is required to set and examine homework, to make reports on the working of his/her class, and to fulfil such other duties incidental to the proper management of and the testing of the progress of his/her class, as may from time to time be required. The payments made for actual teaching hours cover these incidental duties. Teachers are also expected to arrive a reasonable time before the commencement of class. The Conditions also state "subject to these conditions all appointments terminate at the close of each session."

In one English case[57] a teacher sought to include three hours preparation of work at home, two 20 minute morning breaks, periods of 10 minutes before lessons in the morning and afternoon, and a 30 minute discussion period with her head of department, in calculating her weekly hours of employment for the purposes of a complaint of unfair dismissal. It was alleged that her weekly hours of employment normally involved less than 16 hours so that she had not been continuously employed within the terms of Schedule 13 to the Employment Protection (Consolidation) Act 1978 for the period of one year.

She was employed as a part-time teacher on the basis of 15/30ths of full time service. It was agreed that she worked for at least 14 hours and 50 minutes. There were 15 periods for teaching and a further five periods when she was available for either supervisory or free periods.

The English Employment Appeals Tribunal held:

(1) That she was not obliged to do preparatory work outside school hours in order to fulfil her contractual duties; that sufficient time was allocated for

---

[56] See para. 7.21 above.
[57] In 1987.

preparatory work within her undisputed weekly employment. *Lake v. Essex Co. Co.*[58] applied.

(2) The test to be applied to the 20 minute break periods was whether she was contractually obliged to perform any duties. She could have been required to perform supervisory or pastoral duties during the break periods and the industrial tribunal had correctly included these periods in her weekly hours of employment.

(3) It was not part of the employee's contractual duties to be present before morning assembly and afternoon lessons and she was not entitled to include that time in calculating her weekly employment.

(4) The decision of the industrial tribunal that the 30 minute meetings with her head of department were regular and necessary and normally took place weekly and should be included in her total weekly employment should be upheld. Accordingly her working week exceed 16 hours and she was entitled to bring a complaint of unfair dismissal.

7.24 Probation and Natural Justice

"It is a failure of natural justice not to communicate to a probationary teacher the gist of adverse confidential reports on him prepared by school inspectors." *per* Woolf J. in *R v. Department of Education and Science, ex parte KUMAR.*[59] In *The State (McGarrity) v. Deputy Commissioner Garda Síochána*[60] D'Arcy J. adopted the view expressed by Mr. Justice McWilliam in *Hynes* case,[61] the previous year, that the Commissioner was not bound to furnish the information which he considered in coming to his decision and held that the decision to dismiss was not arrived at otherwise than in accordance with natural justice.

7.25 Vocational Teacher an Officer

The Vocational Education Act 1930 refers to two categories of staff, officers and servants. A person can become an officer or office holder by virtue of holding an office or being appointed to an office. Whole-time vocational teachers have always been treated as officers, certainly in all of the cases which have come before the courts. Even in *Carr v. CLVEC*,[62] where it was claimed that the plaintiff was a "statutory employee", sections 7 and 8 of the Voca-

---

[58] [1979] I.C.R. 577, C.A.
[59] *The Times,* 23 November 1982. Note there is no requirement to produce the confidential report itself but merely to communicate the gist of it.
[60] [1978] ILTR. 25.
[61] *Hynes v. Garvey,* unreported, Supreme Court, 19 July 1977.
[62] Unreported, High Court, 31 July 1987, Murphy J. Note that despite the claim that Ms.

tional Education (Amendment) Act 1944 which apply only to officers was applied. Section 23 of the Vocational Education Act 1930 gives a VEC the authority to appoint officers and servants. Clerical officers and staff officers are titled as officers, while technicians, caretakers and groundspersons employed in vocational schools have been regarded as employees. The position of a vocational teacher is not designated or indicated to be an office in the vocational education Acts but if a VEC appoint a person as an officer or to hold an office, that person is an officer or the holder of an office under the VEC. If a VEC does not do this then a person employed by them is a servant or employee.

A vocational teacher, as an officer, holds an office under the Vocational Education Acts and enjoys tenure normally terminable[63] at will by the VEC and for cause by the Minister for Education.

The characteristic features of an office were stated by Kenny J. in *Glover v. B.L.N.*[64] to be;

> that it is created by Act of the National Parliament, charter, statutory regulation, articles of association of a company or of a body corporate formed under the authority of a statute, deed of trust, grant or by prescription, and that the holder of it may be removed if the instrument creating the office authorises this.[65]

Rowlatt J. in *GWR v. Bater*[66] defined an office as "a subsisting, permanent, substantive position, which has an existence independently from the person who fills it, it goes on and is filled in succession by successive holders." Rideout and Dyson state[67] that the word "permanent" is used here only in the sense of a possible succession of holders, it does not distinguish "temporary" appointments.

Standard Conditions The standard conditions issued to persons engaged by a VEC regardless of their status, contain the phrase "subject to the provisions of the Vocational Education Acts and subsequent Acts replacing or amending these Acts." This has the effect that an officer appointed to a VEC is subject to the terms of the Acts and that the provisions of the Acts apply to employees. There is no doubt that the sections which apply to officers have never been applied to employees like clerks and caretakers. An employee to

---

Carr was a "statutory employee" the Supreme Court in an *ex tempore* judgment on 17 October 1991, amended the High Court Order to declare that she was still "an officer" of the VEC.

[63] Note: the Unfair Dismissals Act 1977 applies to servants but not to officers of a VEC.

[64] [1973] I. R. 388 at 414 .

[65] *loc. cit.*

[66] [1923] K.B. 266 at 274.

[67] Rideout and Dyson, *Rideout's Principles of Labour Law* (London, 1983), p. 15.

whom the provisions of the Acts applies is called a "statutory employee". The provisions of the legislation in relation to suspension and dismissal/removal are of vital importance. The original section 27 of the 1930 Vocational Education Act applied to both servants and officers. This section, therefore, applied to vocational teachers regardless of their status. Section 23 was repealed and replaced by sections 7 and 8 of the Vocational Education (Amendment) Act 1944 which are specified as applying only to the holder of an office. In all cases, except *Carr v CLVEC*,[68] it was agreed that the vocational teachers were to be regarded as officers and the courts applied sections 7 and 8. In the *Carr* case it was agreed that the teacher was a "statutory employee" in preference to the words officer or servant, yet sections 7 and 8 were applied. In the interests of clarity it is suggested that the incorporation phrase in the standard conditions of vocational teachers should include the word "appropriate" before "provisions".

Doubts about Status   Doubts about a vocational teacher being an officer seem to be founded on the remark by *Costello J. in O'Callaghan v. Meath VEC*[69] In this case Mr. Justice Costello stated:

> Provision was made for the establishment of Vocational Education Committees by the Vocational Education Act 1930....No express provision is made for the appointment of teachers by VECs but they are empowered to appoint officers and servants and teachers are regarded as "officers" of the VEC who appoints them.[70]

Was there any significance in the use of inverted commas in relation to teachers being "officers"? It may have been used by Mr. Justice Costello to indicate the lack of a specific legal authority for the classification of vocational teachers as officers. The fact that the word officers is in inverted commas may have no other significance.

On the next page of his judgment the word "servants" is also in inverted commas. Costello J. stated:

> Now it is agreed that all teachers appointed by VECs to teach in their schools are "officers" and not "servants" of the VEC.

There appears to be no significance in his use of commas in this statement.

---

[68] Note 60 above.
[69] Unreported, High Court, 20 November 1990, Costello J.
[70] *Ibid.*, p. 1

7.26 Legislation

Doubts have also been raised because of section 112 Vocational Education Act 1930 which provides:

> The Minister may by regulations made under this Act prescribe the minimum rates of travelling and maintenance expenses payable to **teachers and officers** of vocational education committees who have to travel in the performance of their duties.

Are the words in bold print disjunctive? Do they indicate a clear distinction between vocational teachers and officers or may a person be a teacher and officer at once? It is suggested that even if the section was disjunctive and making a distinction between vocational teachers and officers of a VEC these matters were resolved by an amendment of the section by section 10 of the Vocational Education (Amendment) Act 1944 which states:

> Section 112 (which relates to travelling expenses for officers) of the Principal Act is hereby amended by the insertion of the word 'other' before the word "officers".

This amendment obviously implies that a vocational teacher is an officer. In the Dáil Debates on the Bill, the Minister had been criticised for addressing himself to teachers only, in referring to officers[71] and W. T. Cosgrave had stated "By an officer I mean a teacher or any other official employed by the committee."[72]

In the Dáil at the Committee Stage of the Vocational Education Bill, 1930[73] a number of amendments were moved in relation to the then section 109, now section 111 of the Act. One amendment suggested in subsection (1) was the insertion of the words "and officers" after the word "teachers" and the insertion of the words "or officers" after the word "teachers" in subsection (2). The Minister stated:

> Besides the teacher *the only person who in many of the schemes would come into question would be the chief executive officer* of the committee. . . . There are a few other schemes in which you may have other officials.

The Amendments were withdrawn.

---

[71] *Dáil Debates*, Vol. 93, Col. 177.
[72] *Dáil Debates*, Vol. 93, Col. 354 . See *Wavin Pipes Ltd. v. Hepworth Iron Co. Ltd*, unreported, High Court, 8 May 1981, where the Parliamentary history of the Patents Act 1964 was used as a guide to statutory interpretation. Farry M., *Education and the Constitution* (Dublin, 1996), p.19.
[73] On 29 May 1930, col. 284.

7.27 Consequence of Being an Officer

Primary and secondary teachers are not officers. An officer or office holder was a person who was often a member of a profession, traditionally had a higher status than an ordinary worker and was accorded a right to a hearing before dismissal. Hogan and Morgan[74] state:

> The office is a legal form for a "superior" post (which was in past centuries, even regarded as a property right of the holder. An office is a position to which certain important duties are attached, usually of a more or less public character, with its holder likely to be better qualified and freer from day to day control than a servant.[75]

According to Rideout and Dyson:[76]

> The classification as office holder conferred significant rights to natural justice and reinstatement to those whom the courts thought should be conceded a status above the run-of-the-mill servant.

It should be noted that it is not the courts who decide whether a particular position is an office or consequently whether the person who occupies it is an office holder. Note that, in *O'Sullivan v. EHB*,[77] the EAT held that an office existed by classification and not by job description.

Demotion or promotion of an officer is not possible. Advancement is only possible by securing a higher office by competition. The only sanction is suspension or removal from office. Different grades of vocational teacher were introduced when the Regional Colleges were established in addition to the concept of promotion from one grade to another. Appendix G of Memo V.7 dealing with eligibility for promotion to Assistant Lecturer grade provides that "A permanent whole-time Class III teacher who devotes the major portion (*i.e.* not less than 55%) of his/her teaching time to courses, the entry standard to which is the Leaving Certificate or its equivalent, is regarded as eligible for promotion to Assistant Lecturer grade." *Note that a reduction in teaching hours accompanied by a reduction in salary may constitute dismissal or constructive dismissal.*[78]

A primary or secondary teacher who refuses to accept additional pupils in a class can have part of his salary withheld for doing so,[79] and on the basis of the House of Lords decision in *Miles v. Wakefield Council*, a vocational teacher because s/he is a salaried holder of an office, may also have part of his/her

---

[74] Hogan and Morgan, *Administrative Law* (2nd. ed., London, 1991).
[75] At p. 472.
[76] Rideout and Dyson, *Rideout's Principles of Labour Law, op. cit.,* p. 15.
[77] UD 131/1979
[78] See *Hogg v. Dover College* [1990] I.C.R. 39 E.A.T.
[79] See *Royale v. Trafford Borough Council* [1984] I.R.L.R. 184.

salary withheld for being in breach of his/her statutory obligations under that office.

In 1987 the House of Lords in the *Miles* case[80] held that the Council were entitled to deduct wages for part performance of duties by an officer, that there was no great difference between the position of an employee and such an officer in relation to payment for work done. It held that, for the purpose of the appeal, there was no logical distinction between the holder of an office and an employee, the plaintiffs salary not being an *honorarium* for the mere tenure of an office. The views of the Supreme Court in *Garvey v. Ireland*,[81] see chapter 12, in particular the judgment of Kenny J. were at variance with the decision of the House of Lords, whereas the views of Parker L.J. in the Court of Appeal are similar to the Irish judgment.

In the *Garvey* case[82] the Supreme Court rejected a ruling by McWilliam J. in the High Court that the relationship between the Government and the plaintiff, who occupied the office of Commissioner of the Garda Síochána, was equivalent to that between a master and servant under a contract of employment which was intended to endure for an indefinite period, and held that the plaintiff was the holder of an office and was not employed under a contract of employment.

The Lords in the *Miles* case[83] were careful to recognise that the position involved was an office and their judgment refers specifically to payment for teaching and does not affect suspension or indeed removal from office, which was the issue in the *Garvey* case.[84] The notion of retaining the traditional concept of an office holder for the purposes of removal from office but not for other purposes, while undoubtedly attractive and administratively expedient, is extremely difficult to reconcile (see also chap. 12).

While the creation of the office of vocational teacher was not specifically authorised by the 1930 Act, it has always been accepted that permanent, whole-time vocational teachers are officers. (See section 7.25 above). They have not been regarded as employees. In the Safety Health and Welfare at Work Act 1989, which imposes obligations on employers and employees, it was necessary to specify that a VEC was an employer for the purposes of the Act. Although the Local Government (Superannuation) Act 1956 does, however, provide for reduction of pension entitlement for unsatisfactory service. See, however, *Lovett v. Minister for Education*,[85] where it was held that the right to a pension was a property right protected by the Constitution and that a provision for forfeiture of pension amounted to an unreasonable and unjustified interference with the Applicants constitutional entitlements.

---

[80] *Miles v. Wakefield Council* [1985] I.C.R. 363. See Chap. 9 *post.*
[81] [1981] I.R. 75, see Chap. 12.
[82] *Ibid.* p. 414
[83] Note 78 above
[84] Note 79 above
[85] Unreported, High Court, 11 July 1996, Kelly J.

Deductions from salary have been made in the case of teachers who are employees. In *Royale v. Tafford Borough Council*[84] a sum of 5/36ths was deducted in respect of a refusal to teach an extra five pupils with a class of 31 while in *Sim v. Rotherham Council*,[85] deductions from salaries were upheld for refusing to cover for an absent teacher.

7.28 Sanctions Against an Officer

Where an office has been created by statute the terms and grounds of removal are specified and these statutory terms are exclusive. No grounds other than those specified may be invoked but generally these grounds are widely drafted and cover a multitude. In *Carr v. CLVEC*,[86] however, Murphy J. has held that, in the case of a vocational teacher, additional terms acceptable to the parties could be introduced provided that they were not in conflict with the statutory provisions. He held that a provision for termination by three months' notice was a valid condition or term of appointment.

In the past the distinction between an officer and a servant was important in the Republic, but the adoption of the Constitution in 1937, and the constitutional guarantee of fair procedures conferring on all citizens the same right to due process has rendered the distinction of less significance than heretofore.

The concept of fair procedures is wider than *nemo iudex in causa sua* and *audi alteram partem*, the basic rules of natural justice. Dismissal of a vocational teacher without prior suspension is most unusual.[87]

7.29 Temporary Officer

In *Western Health Board v. Quigley*[88] Barrington J. held that a temporary staff nurse was employed at most as a temporary officer and thus the Employment Appeals Tribunal had no jurisdiction to deal with the case because officers of a health board are excluded from the Unfair Dismissals Act 1977. Officers of a VEC, both temporary and permanent, are similarly excluded from the scope of the Act.

On the basis of the *Quigley* decision a temporary whole-time vocational teacher would come within the ambit of the *Quigley* case and be excluded also from the Unfair Dismissals Act 1977 in accordance with the dictum of Barrington J. An hourly part-time or EPT teacher is not an officer and therefore not excluded from the protection of the Act.

---

[86] Note 74 above; *Royale v. Tafford Borough Council* (1984) I.R.L.R. 184 *op. cit.*
[87] [1986] I.C.R. 897.
[88] Note 60 above.
[89] For suspension from office, see *Hunt v. Co. Roscommon VEC*, unreported, High Court, 24 November 1982.
[90] [1982] I.L.R.M. 390.

CHAPTER 8

Disqualification from Holding Office

Education is an ornament in prosperity
and a refuge in adversity.

Aristotle (Diogenes Laertuis, Aristotle, 19)

Disqualification is a term most often associated with driving offences and with disqualification as a company director under section 150 of the Companies Act 1990. (See *Business Communications Ltd. v. Baxter and Parsons*).[1] It is also a term which applies to members of Local Authorities, Officers of Local authorities and to Members and Officers of Vocational Education Committees.

8.1 Disqualification under Vocational Education (Amendment) Act 1947

A person may be disqualified from becoming a vocational teacher by Section 6(6)(b) Vocational Education (Amendment) Act 1947, which provides:

> A person who is convicted of an offence under this section shall thereafter be disqualified from being elected or being a member of a vocational education committee or a sub-committee . . . and shall also be disqualified from holding an office or employment under a vocational education committee or such a body, council, or committee as aforesaid.

The offence in question is set out at 3(a):

> A person who knowingly makes or allows to be made a false statement for the purpose of obtaining a payment under this section for himself or another shall be guilty of an offence under this section, and shall be liable on summary conviction thereof to a fine not exceeding fifty pounds, or at the discretion of the court, to imprisonment for a term not exceeding one year.

---

[1] Unreported, High Court, 21 July 1995, Murphy J.

8.2 Disqualification under section 34 Offences Against the State Act 1939

Prior to the case of *Cox v. Ireland*,[2] a second type of disqualification could take place under section 34(3)(a) of the Offences Against the State Act 1939 which provided:

> Every person who is convicted by a Special Criminal Court of an offence which is, at the time of such conviction, a scheduled offence for the purposes of Part V of this Act, shall be disqualified – (a) for holding, within seven years after the date of such conviction, any office or employment remunerated out of the Central Fund or moneys provided by the Oireachtas or moneys raised by local taxation or in or under or as a paid member of a board or body established by or under statutory authority.

The provisions of section 34 of the Offences Against the State Act 1939 applied to vocational teachers because they were remunerated out of money provided by the Oireachtas and raised from the county rates.

The provisions regarding disqualification under the Offences Against the State Act, which were held to be unconstitutional in the *Cox* case, were less draconian than those still subsisting under the Vocational Education (Amendment) Act 1947. Disqualification under the Offences Against the State Act lasted for a period of seven years but it could be remitted in whole or in part at the absolute discretion of the Government.[3] There is no time limit on the period of disqualification under the Vocational Education (Amendment) Act 1947 and there is no provision for the removal or remission of such disqualification.

While public employment cannot be conditional on an individual surrendering his constitutional rights, the State has a legitimate concern and right to screen applicants who might advocate the overthrow of the Government by force. In the same way it has the right to screen applicants for their fitness to teach, *Ohison v. Phillips*[4] and dismissal of teachers has been upheld where statutes specifically provide for dismissal on this ground.[5]

A U.S. statute prohibiting state employment of a person who advocated or distributed material advocating the overthrow of the government by force, has been held to be unconstitutionally vague, as prohibiting advocating the doctrine in the abstract.[6] Statutes making membership of the Communist Party

---

[2] *Cox v. Ireland* [1992] 2 I.R. 503.
[3] Section 34(5) of the Offences Against the State Act 1939.
[4] (DC. Colo.) US 1081, 25 L Ed 2d 819, 90 S.Ct 1520.
[5] See *Board of Education v. Jewett*, 21 Cal. App. 2d 64, 68 P2d 404.
[6] *per* 68 Am. Jur. 2d 170 p. 504.

prima facie evidence of disqualification, have also been held to be unconstitutional by not permitting rebuttal or absence of intent to further unlawful aims.[7]

8.3 Distinction between Disqualification and Forfeiture

There is a distinction between forfeiture which normally applies to a person who is in employment remunerated out of public funds at the time of his conviction, and a disqualification which can apply to a person who, under section 6 of the 1947 Act, is convicted of knowingly making a false statement for the purpose of obtaining a payment under the section for himself or another and who is not an officer or servant of a VEC under section 6 of the 1947 Act.

Rideout and Dyson[8] cite Megarry V.C. in *McInnes v. Onslow Fane*[9] where he suggested that there were at least three categories: forfeiture cases, application cases, and an intermediate category called expectation cases. In forfeiture cases there is a decision which takes away some existing right or position, or where a member of an organisation is expelled or a licence is revoked. In application cases the decision merely refuses to grant the applicant the right or position that he seeks, such as membership of the organisation or a licence to do certain acts. The very use of the term "forfeiture" is indicative of something penal.[10] Megarry saw a substantial distinction between forfeiture cases and application cases. In forfeiture cases, there is a threat to take something away and in such cases, the right to an unbiased tribunal, the right to notice of the charges, and the right to be heard in answer to the charges were plainly apt. Whereas in the application cases, nothing is taken away, normally there are no charges, and thus there is no requirement to be heard. Instead there is the wider but less defined question of general suitability. The courts require natural justice to be observed for expulsion from a social club, but not on an application for admission to it.

The application of disqualification prevents a person, convicted of the offences specified, from obtaining employment in the semi-State or State sectors. Disqualification may be unconstitutional in the manner of its application even if it were not in itself the performance of a judicial act.[11]

---

7 See *Keyisjian v. Board of Regents*, 385 US 589, 17 L Ed 2d 629, 87 S.Ct. 675s.
8 *Rideout's Principles of Labour Law* (4th ed., London), 1983 .
9 Megarry V.C in *McInnes v. Onslow Fane* [1978] 3 All E.R. 211.
10 *per* Mr. Justice Kelly in *Lovett v. Minister for Education* [1997] 1 I.L.R.M. 89 at 98.
11 *Conroy v. Attorney General and another* [1965] I. R. 441.

8.4 The *Cox* case

In the *Cox* case[12] the Supreme court decided that the provisions of section 34 when it became applicable potentially constitued

> ". . . an attack, firstly, on the unenumerated constitutional right of that person to earn a living and, secondly, on certain property rights protected by the constitution, such as the right to a pension, gratuity or other emolument already earned, or the right to the advantage of a subsisting contract of employment.[13]

Significantly, the judgment also referred to the inability of a person convicted in the manner of Cox not only to continue in his pre-conviction employment but to take up employment in any of the other categories of employment coming within the provisions of section 34. This was a major curtailment of such persons' earning capacity. The court also referred to the fact that, if a citizen charged with one of the less serious offences scheduled at the time, and convicted by the Special Criminal Court, happened to be the holder of an office or employment funded by the State, he had no protection against the mandatory imposition of the forfeiture provisions contained in section 34. The ultimate factor triggering the operation of section 34 was the venue of the trial, primarily selected by the fact that the offence was scheduled, and could only be avoided by a decision of the Attorney General or of the Director of Public Prosecutions, in respect of which the accused person had no right of representation.

Unlike section 34 of the Offences Against the State Act 1939, section 6 of the 1947 Act does not provide for forfeiture of pension, gratuity or other emolument already earned, but disqualification by virtue of section 6 could affect the right to the advantages of a subsisting contract of employment and, like section 34, could also be a major curtailment of a person's earning capacity. Similarly an office holder or employee of a VEC has no protection against the mandatory imposition of the disqualification under section 6 which is triggered by the nature of the offence for which s/he is convicted.

The Supreme Court in *Cox v. Ireland*[14] stated that it was:

> satisfied that the State is entitled, for the protection of public peace and order, and for the maintenance and stability of its own authority, by its laws to provide onerous and far-reaching penalties and forfeitures imposed as a major deterrent to the commission of crimes threatening

---

[12] *Cox v. Ireland* [1992] 2 I.R. 503.

[13] *Ibid.,* p. 522. In 1984, I had written that, in my opinion, section 34 of the Offences Against the State Act 1939, was unconstitutional. See Farry M., *The Structure and the Law of Vocational Education in Ireland*, unpublished M.Litt. thesis T.C.D.

[14] Note 11 above

such peace and order and State authority, and is entitled to ensure as far as practicable that amongst those involved in the carrying out of the functions of the State, there is not included persons who commit such crimes.[15]

The Judgment then continues:

The State must in its laws, as far as practicable, in pursuing these objectives, continue to protect the constitutional rights of the citizens.

Article 40.3.1.° of the Constitution provides:

The State guarantees in its laws to respect, and as far as practicable, by its laws to defend and vindicate the personal rights of the citizen.

The final issue in the *Cox* case was whether the provisions of section 34, when read in conjunction with the other relevant provisions of the Act of 1939, were established to the satisfaction of the Court as constituting a failure of such protection not warranted by the objectives which it sought to secure

It was established to the Court's satisfaction that the provisions of section 34 failed, as far as practicable to protect the constitutional rights of the citizen and accordingly were invalid having regard to the Constitution. If it were established that section 6 of the 1947 Act failed in a similar manner, then it too would be unconstitutional.

The *Cox* case ended in the High court on 30 April 1993 with a consent agreement whereby the Department of Education agreed to Mr. Cox re-commencing work at his school from the beginning on the next academic year on 1 August. He accepted that he broke his contract as a result of his unavailability for teaching and was not entitled to salary between February, 1988 and 1 August 1993. He gave an undertaking to desist from any subversive activities or teaching any subversive doctrines. He agreed to uphold the Constitution, not to engage in any criminal activities and to attend a refresher course at his own expense.

8.5 Forfeiture of Pension

In *Lovett v. Minister for Education*,[16] the Principal of a Community school pleaded guilty to three charges of dishonesty and received a suspended sentence of two year's imprisonment. During the proceedings he applied for early retirement on grounds of disability and this was approved. The Minis-

---

[15] *Ibid.,* pp. 522-523.
[16] Unreported, High Court, 11 July 1996.

ter for Education sought to impose forfeiture of his pension as provided for in paragraph 8(1) of the Secondary Teachers' Superannuation (Amendment) Scheme 1935[17] and the plaintiff challenged the validity of the forfeiture and of paragraph 8(1) of the scheme. Mr. Justice Kelly stated that the provisions of paragraph 8(1) of the scheme went far beyond the principles and policies contained in the Teachers Superannuation Act 1928 which did not have anything to do with deterring the commission of criminal offences, whether by teachers or retired teachers.[18] The very use of the term "forfeiture" was indicative of something penal and paragraph 8(1) was *ultra vires* the powers of the Minister, null and void and of no effect.

Dealing with the constitutionality of the forfeiture, Kelly J. referred to *Cox v. Ireland*[19] above and held that the applicant's right to a pension constituted a property right which was protected by the constitution. Paragraph 8(1) of the Scheme amounted to an unreasonable and unjustified interference with the applicant's constitutional entitlements and was not warranted by the objectives which it sought to achieve. It did not, as far as practicable, protect the constitutional rights of the applicant.[20]

---

[17] SR & O 1935 No. 48.
[18] See page 11 of judgment.
[19] Note 11 above.
[20] See obligation on the State under Article 40.3.1.° "as far as practicable to defend and vindicate the personal rights of the citizen". See also Farry, *Education and the Constitution* (Dublin, 1996), Chap. 15, Constitutional Proportionality.

CHAPTER 9

Suspension

Qui pergit ea quae vult dicere, ea quae non vult audiet.

Terence

Section 7(1) of the Vocational Education (Amendment) Act 1944 provides:

> Whenever in respect of the holder of an office under a vocational educa-
> tion committee there is, in the opinion[1] of such committee or of the
> Minister, reason to believe[2] that such holder has failed to perform satis-
> factorily the duties of such office or has misconducted himself in rela-
> tion to such office[3] or is otherwise unfit to hold such office, such com-
> mittee or the Minister (as the case may be) may suspend such holder
> from performance of the duties of such office while such alleged fail-
> ure, misconduct or unfitness is being inquired into and the disciplinary
> action (if any) to be taken in regard thereto is being determined and
> such inquiry shall be held as soon as conveniently may be after the date
> of the suspension.

The suspension procedures agreed between the TUI and the IVEA in respect
of "probationary" teachers are set out in Appendix 1.

In 1982 the Supreme Court, in *The State (Lynch) v. Cooney*[4] in relation to
"where the Minister for Posts and Telegraphs "is of opinion" contained in
section 31(1) of the Broadcasting Authority Act 1960 held that the opinion
mentioned in that subsection must be held *bona fide* and be factually sustainable and not unreasonable. It also held hat the High Court had jurisdiction to
review an order made pursuant to the power conferred. *In re Ó Laighléis was
not applied.*[5]

---

[1] In earlier judgments the Courts were not entitled to review the Ministers "opinion", *cf.
The State (Burke) v. Lennon* [1940] I.R. 136 and in *Re Ó Laighléis* [1960] I.R. 93 and
J.M. Kelly, *Fundamental Rights in the Irish Law and Constitution* (Dublin, 1967), p.
217 but these do not reflect current judicial orthodoxy. When the staff subcommittee of
the Corporation met it was right that they were exercising a quasi-judicial function.
Widgery L.J. in *Hannam v. Bradford Corporation,* 1970 Sol. J. 414.
[2] An office means an office under a VEC: section (1) of the Vocational Education (Amendment) Act 1944.
[3] The three grounds are specified in section 7(1) of the Vocational Education (Amendment) Act 1944.
[4] [1982] I.R. 337.
[5] [1960] I.R. 93.

9.1 Need for Suspension Provision

This provision was introduced to cater for situations where urgent action is needed and to facilitate fuller investigation and consideration. It is clearly specified as being an interim step. In the wording of the section "while such alleged failure, misconduct or unfitness is being enquired into and the disciplinary action (if any) to be taken is being determined."

The principle of this section is taken from section 11 of the Local Authorities (Officers and Employees) Act 1926. Without this provision dismissal would be the only course open to a VEC whereas suspension is in the nature of a temporary expedient and is either lifted or leads to removal from office. (*i.e.* removal from office by the Minister under section 8 Vocational Education (Amendment) Act 1944 without a statutory local inquiry) (see Chap. 11).

If a charge against an officer proves "to be without foundation he can be re-instated, if the charge is substantiated, he has been deprived of any opportunity to do any further injury."[6] The author would put it more strongly and suggests that if the charges prove to be without foundation the officer must be reinstated.

9.2 Suspension by VEC or Minister

The power of suspension was given to the VEC to avoid the delay in obtaining Ministerial sanction. The power was given to the Minister in case a VEC were slow to take such action. Committees were not anxious to take disciplinary measures against their officers.

The grounds specified for suspension need not in fact exist but the VEC or the Minister must have a *bona fide* opinion that there is reason to believe that the specified grounds do exist. In the case of *Coras Iompair Éireann v. Bennett*[7] the EAT stated:

> . . . the question of guilt or innocence of the [employee] does not arise. What the Tribunal has to decide, is if the employer had a reasonable belief, founded on the result of a reasonable investigation, that it [*sic*] could no longer place total confidence in the [employee's] integrity.[8]

A dismissal was not unfair by virtue of the employee being acquitted of theft, (for which he was dismissed) in criminal proceedings. A *bona fide* opinion could only be based on reasonable grounds. Suspension is only envisaged for good reason, *e.g.:*

(a) that money is unaccounted for, or

(b) that the auditor has reported serious discrepancies in the accounts.

---

6   Minister for Local Government, *Dáil Debates*, 19 May 1926, 1818-1819.
7   *Coras Iompair Eireann v. Bennett* UD 449/1982.
8   *loc. cit.*

9.3 Failure to Perform Duties Satisfactorily

The first ground for suspension is that the holder of an office has failed to perform satisfactorily the duties of such office. This is also the first part of the grounds under section 8(3) for which the Minister may remove an officer from office without holding a local inquiry. Such failure may be wilful or non-wilful. Persistent refusal in the absence of mistake or misunderstanding relates to conduct and is obviously wilful, whereas lack of capability or competence may be caused by illness, lack of aptitude or skill, or physical or mental handicap. Satisfactory performance of duties relates to *competence*, the lack of which may justify dismissal of primary or secondary teachers under section 6(4)(a) of the Unfair Dismissals Act 1977. A teacher is expected to have a degree of competence such as can be expected from a normal member of the profession.

In the case of a vocational teacher, failure to perform satisfactorily may mean:

(a) inefficiency in teaching,

(b) inefficiency in teaching after inspection,

(c) unexplained repeated absences without permission,

(d) refusal to co-operate in keeping school registers,

(e) refusal to assist with stock-taking,

(f) refusal to keep classroom properly,

(g) refusal to co-operate in setting class examinations,

(h) excessive absences caused by illness, even where certified.

Where there is a contractual right to require an officer to undergo a medical examination a refusal may constitute a breach of contract. Alcoholism, HIV infection or AIDS could be a reason for certified absence although HIV infection of itself would not justify removal from office.

9.4 Duties

The extent of such failure to perform satisfactorily in the case of a vocational teacher must be extremely grave. The word "duties" indicates that the failure must relate to more than one duty. The failure to perform satisfactorily must amount to a breach which constitutes a repudiation, not just a failure to carry out one particular function, and such repudiation must be accepted. In the case of a vocational teacher the duties must also be duties of his office within the conditions of service as agreed from time to time.

A mere misunderstanding as to the duties to be carried out will not be sufficient,[9] and it would be a question of fact whether the introduction of new methods and techniques altered the nature of the duties to such a degree that they were no longer the duties which the officer had agreed to perform under the conditions of his appointment.[10] See also section 12(2)(a) RTC Act 1992 under which an officer in an RTC shall be bound to perform duties allocated to him on a redistribution or rearrangement by the college without his agreement.

In modern times where the failure relates to not carrying out a task because of a trade union directive, or decision, or dispute, the practice has been not to regard such, as a ground for suspension. According to Parker L.J. in *Miles v. Wakefield Council*:[11]

> in the absence of a breach amounting to a repudiation accepted by dismissal or a specific right to suspend, there appear to me strong grounds for saying there is no right to withhold payment and take the benefit of all work in fact done during the period in which the refusal to perform a particular function was operative.[12]

In suggesting this, Parker L. J. obviously had in mind a withholding of total payment. On appeal, the House of Lords held[13] that a proportionate deduction of remuneration for non-performance of part of the duties of office was permissible, and Lords Brightman and Templeman stated that where industrial action takes the form of "going slow" a worker cannot claim that s/he is entitled to his/her wages . . . but s/he will be entitled to be paid on a *quantum meruit* basis for the amount and value of the reduced work performed and accepted.

With a great flourish of egalitarianism Lord Templeman remarked:

> A judge and an usher on strike should arguably be treated in the same manner . . . middle class morality must not be allowed to place Mr. Dolittle in an inferior position in this respect.[14]

It must be noted that "going slow" is not the same thing as "a work to rule". In *Creswell & Ors. v. Board of Inland Revenue*,[15] the Revenue did not terminate the plaintiffs' contracts, or suspend them, or take any disciplinary action. It was willing to pay, if they returned to work, but refused to pay while they

---

[9] See *Attorney General v. Coopers Co.* (1812) 19 Ves. 187.

[10] See *Cresswell v. Board of Inland Revenue* [1984] I.C.R. 508; *Miles v. Wakefield Council* [1985] ICR 363 and chapter 7.

[11] [1985] I.C.R. 363

[12] *Ibid.,* p. 373.

[13] *Ibid.,* House of Lords [1987] I.C.R. 368.

[14] *Ibid.,* p. 387.

[15] Note 8 above.

refused to work the computerisation of PAYE. By implication, neglect of duty is involved in failure to perform satisfactorily, not just inefficiency or medical incapacity but wilful neglect.

9.5 Unjustified Absence

In *Curran v. CIÉ*[16] the claimant absented himself from work without permission, and was found drinking in a local bar and in *Evans v. CIÉ*[17] the claimant failed to cash in his waybill and receipts and did not report for work for six days after a certified period of absence. Both were not unfairly dismissed, while in *Duffy v. J. Hourihan Ltd.*,[18] another employee who absented himself from work was presumed to have voluntarily terminated his employment by his conduct.

It was argued in *Ridge v. Baldwin*[19] that "neglect of duty" must involve more than inefficiency. Neglect is nearly always involved in cases of inefficiency, but this type of *simple inefficiency would not constitute* the "neglect of duty" which constitutes this ground.

9.6 Misconduct

The second ground for suspension is where an officer has "misconducted himself in relation to such office."

The misconduct must be specifically referable to the office. Misconduct unrelated to the office is outside the scope of this section, nonetheless it is a wider ground than misconduct in office within section 8(1) which is a ground for removal. It is usually less significant than misconduct in office. Misbehaviour which includes bribery, corruption or acting fraudulently in public office is also a common law offence.[20]

If a deficiency or loss has been incurred by a VEC by reason of misconduct of an officer, or a sum of money which ought to have[21] been brought into account by him was not, then, depending on the circumstances, such conduct could constitute either: (a) failure to perform satisfactorily the duties of the office, if done without intent to defraud; or (b) misconduct, if done with intent to defraud. In *R. v. Browne*[22] Lord O'Brien L.C.J. of Ireland) stated that mere imprudence or want of judgment or even a grave error of judgment cannot be called misconduct, there must be some element of moral culpability.[23]

---

[16] UD 82/1979.
[17] UD 304/1982.
[18] M456/1987.
[19] [1964] A.C. 40 (H.L.).
[20] *R. v. Lewellyn Jones* [1967] 3 All E.R. 225.
[21] Section 39 of the Vocational Education Regulations 1931.
[22] [1907] 2 I.R. 505.
[23] *Halsburys Laws of England*, Vol. 28, para. 1306.

Misappropriation of school money has been held to justify dismissal in the U.S., on grounds of immorality as well as incompetence in *Re Flannery's Appeal*,[24] but there must be proof of embezzlement or wrongdoing. In the U.S. it has also been held that an innocent mistake would not amount to justification.[25]

It is suggested that the misconduct in question must be wilful misconduct such as deliberately doing something which is wrong, knowing it to be wrong or with reckless indifference as to whether it is wrong or not, as was defined in *Graham v. Teesdale*.[26]

"Wilful" as generally used according to Bowen L.J. in *Re Young and Harston's Contract*,[27] implies nothing blameworthy but merely that the person is a free agent and that what has been done arises from the spontaneous action of his will. That he knows what he is doing, and intends what he is doing, and is a free agent.

9.7 Falsification of Accounts

Falsification of accounts, for example, or ordering goods or work without specific authority, could constitute misconduct in office. Orders for goods or work to be done, can only be placed by an officer without specific[28] authority from the VEC in cases of urgency. The falsification (destruction, alteration, mutilation or falsification) of any book, paper, writing, valuable security or account which belongs to or is in the possession of an employer with intent to defraud, would constitute misconduct as would any false entry with a similar intent or to omit or alter or by concurring to omitting or altering any material particular form or in such book, document or account. In *Board of Education v. Weiland*,[29] the dismissal of a teacher who falsified class attendance records in order to show a continuing need for her services was upheld on the ground of immoral conduct.

9.8 Delay in Prosecuting

In *D.P.P. v. Fleming*[30] the vice-principal of a vocational school was acquitted of nine charges including the making of false entries in the school register and in a teachers' allocation school form. Delay in prosecuting the case was the factor which led to the dismissal. The legal maxim that "justice delayed is justice denied" was applied.

---

[24] 406 Pa. 515, 178 A2d. 751.
[25] In an Alabama case.
[26] [1983] 81 L.G.R. 117.
[27] (1885) 31 Ch. D 168 at 174.
[28] Section 25 of the Vocational Education Regulations, 1931.
[29] 179 Cal. App. 2nd 808, 4 Cal. Reptr. 286 (see 68 Am. Jur. 2nd page 512.
[30] Unreported, but see *Irish Independent*, 3 February 1984 and *Irish Times*, 1 February 1984.

9.9 Delay in Holding Inquiry

When a prison officer was suspended pending the holding of an inquiry in *Farrell v. Minister for Justice*[31] from May 1990 until December 1991 without an inquiry being held, the High Court ordered that the suspension be lifted.

9.10 Delay in Carrying Out Duties

Delay by a vocational teacher in carrying out his/her duties does not necessarily constitute wilful misconduct, nor indeed may unreasonable delay in doing so.

Section 6 Vocational Education (Accounts, Audit and Procedure) Regulations 1931 states:

> "The several duties assigned by these regulations to an officer of a committee shall be punctually discharged by such officer in accordance with these regulations.

The CEO is charged with reporting the failure of other officers to punctually discharge their duties the VEC but there the matter ends. There is no sequel provided for.

In *Graham v. Teesdale & Another*[32] it was alleged that the pattern of conduct was so deliberate that it could not be explained by accident, negligence or incompetence and, if it did not amount to dishonesty, it amounted to misconduct. It was also claimed that the appellant had misused his position as chairman and treasurer of the committee and benefited reasonably therefrom, that he had caused substantive payments to be made to himself, failed to ensure that they were properly recorded, documented and authorized, and that he failed to declare primary interests and to comply with the Council's Standing Orders.

Delay in carrying out the duties of an office can be caused by mistake, by negligence or even by incompetence, but delay so caused is not wilful.[33] It is not the result of a deliberate decision not to do something and, therefore, would not amount to the misconduct specified.

9.11 Unfitness

The third ground for suspension is "being otherwise unfit to hold such office"

Unfitness and misconduct are dealt with later under statutory grounds for removal from office in Chapter 10, *post*.

---

[31] Uunreported, High Court, 17 December 1991.
[32] (QBD) [1983] 81 L.G.R. 117 *op. cit.*
[33] *Haynes v. G.W.R.* 41. L.T. (N.S.) 436.

9.12 Suspension under section 7

Section 7(1) of the Vocational Education (Amendment) Act 1944 provides:

> . . . such Committee or the Minister may suspend a vocational teacher from the performance of the duties of such office while such alleged failure, misconduct, or unfitness is being enquired into and disciplinary action if any determined and such inquiry shall be held as soon as conveniently may be.

See Appendix 1, Suspension Procedures in respect of "probationary" teachers.

The word "may" indicates that the power to suspend vested in both the VEC and The Minister is a discretionary power available if needed. Alleged failure, misconduct or unfitness can, of course, be enquired into without suspending the officer involved, but there may be circumstances where it is desirable to remove an officer from, *e.g.* handling money.

Significantly, the section provides for suspension from the performance of the duties. This is not the same thing as suspension from office. The author contends that, were it not for the provisions of subsection (5), this section might allow a vocational teacher to be suspended with pay. O'Hanlon J. in *Co. Donegal VEC v. The Minister for Education*[34] commented:

> I think it is a great pity that the Act does not empower a VEC or the Minister to suspend with pay, if they think fit to do so, having regard to the length of time which may be absorbed in the conduct of an inquiry, and an amendment of the Act along these lines would ameliorate the hardship which may be unnecessarily and unjustifiably caused to some office-holders.[35]

It would be clearly iniquitous, not to mention wasteful, to suspend an officer from the performance of his duties for longer than was absolutely necessary. Thus, the provision that the suspension may be while the offence is being enquired into, clearly limits the time during which suspension is permitted, and any suspension outside this period would be unlawful. O'Hanlon J. in the *Co. Donegal* case[36] stated:

> It is by no means clear to me, from reading the provisions of section 7 of the Act of 1944, that the Minister may not terminate the suspension yet proceed with an inquiry, while having restored the teacher to his teaching duties, and I prefer to reserve my decision on this point.[37]

---

[34] [1985] I.R. 56.
[35] *Ibid.,* pp. 66-67.
[36] Note 32 above.
[37] *loc. cit.,* p. 66.

Once a suspension takes place it seems an inquiry must be held.

9.13 Inquiry — "is being inquired into"

In *Collins v. Co. Cork VEC*[38] Murphy J. rejected the suggestion that the inquiry in question could be carried out by either the VEC or the Minister and held that only the Minister had the duty to hold the statutory inquiry. It must be noted that this is not the same as the local inquiry which must be held before removal from office by the Minister under section 8, because the inquiry is a less formal one.

The obligation on the Minister to hold an inquiry, was affirmed in the judgment of the Supreme Court, when the case was appealed,[39] and in the course of that judgment Finlay P. gave the following helpful exposition of the combined effect of the different provisions of the relevant statutes, taking into account section 105 of the 1930 Act and sections 7 and 8 of the 1944 Act.

> I am satisfied that the combined legal effect of the provisions of these statutes which must be read together, is as follows:
>
> 1.   There is an obligation on a VEC, whenever it has suspended the holder of an office from his office, to report forthwith the fact of the suspension and the reasons therefor.
>
> 2   There is an obligation on the Minister upon such report being made to him to inquire into the alleged grounds of the suspension. That obligation is to do so as soon as conveniently maybe after the date of the suspension.
>
> 3.   There is not an obligation on the Minister to make that inquiry in any particular way and he may either make inquiries through his servants or agents in the ordinary way or he may exercise the powers conferred on him by section 105 of the Act of 1930 and direct a local inquiry, commonly called a sworn inquiry.
>
> 4.   If the Minister as the result of either form of inquiry is satisfied that no disciplinary action is necessary or that disciplinary action less than removal from office is necessary, he can accordingly direct.
>
> 5.   If the Minister after an inquiry other than a local inquiry is of the opinion that the holder of an office has failed to perform satisfactorily the duties of such office and that he is unfit to hold such office, he may follow the procedure provided for in section 8(3) of the Act of 1944.

---

[38] Unreported, High Court, 12 March 1982 and 27 May 1982.
[39] Unreported, Supreme Court, 18 March 1983.

6. Where the Minister has directed a local inquiry and is satisfied as
    the result of that, that any of the statutory grounds for removal from
    office exists as regards the holder of an office, he may by order
    remove him.

7. There does not appear to me to be any inhibition contained in these
    statutory provisions upon the holding by the Minister in the first
    instance after a suspension of inquiries other than a local inquiry
    and a further decision to hold a local inquiry.[40]

9.14 "As soon as conveniently may be"

The inquiry must be held "as soon as conveniently may be" after the date of
suspension[41] and the VEC is obliged to report the reasons for it to the Minister forthwith."[42] *In Rederij Kennemerland BV v. The Attorney General*[43] where
an application was required to be made "as soon as may be" to the District
Court, it was held by the Supreme Court affirming the High Court decision,
that a delay of over 24 hours constituted a failure to comply with this require-

---

[40] *Ibid.,* pp. 22-24.

[41] The provision that "the inquiry should be held as soon as conveniently may be, after the
date of suspension must be interpreted as imposing a duty to hold an inquiry as quickly
as possible because no money can be paid to the person suspended. It cannot be construed as meaning that the convenience of the Minister or the convenience of the VEC
can delay the inquiry through the convenience of the person suspended could delay it" –
per Carroll J. *in Ni Bheolain v. CDVEC and Ors,* 28 January 1983. It was not possible to
define the time precisely in the Act because a suspension could be brought about by an
auditor's report, or a special audit might be necessary. It is principal of natural justice
that an accused person should know the exact charges which he is to face and that such
charges be brought forward and formulated in the shortest possible time. Justice delayed
is justice denied. Long delays are unfair to the defendant. For delay in the administration
of justice see *Browne v. Donegal Co. Co.,* 9 February 1979 and *Gorse v. Durham Co.
Co.* [1971] 1 W.L.R. 775 [1971] 2 All E.R. 666 where a teacher was entitled to salary
during temporary suspension. *Éire Continental Trading Company Limited v. Clonmel
Foods Ltd* [1955] I.R. 170.

[42] Section 7(2) of the Vocational Education (Amendment) Act 1944. A letter from the city
of Dublin VEC to the Minister which gave "failure to perform satisfactorily the duties of
the office and misconduct in relation thereto" as provided in section 7(1) was held by
Carroll J. in *Ni Bheolain v. CDVEC* not to set out the reasons required by section 7(2).
As to the Ministers duty to hold an inquiry see also *Co. Donegal VEC v. Minister for
Education* [1985] I.R. 56. In *Donegal VEC v. Minister for Education,* notice of the
decision to suspend was accompanied by a bulky file containing 79 documents. The
Minister was not satisfied that the reasons were stated with sufficient precision either to
enable her to enquire into their validity, or to be satisfied that the suspended teacher
knew the case he had to meet. O'Hanlon J. in the High Court stated that the documents
disclosed many grounds which could be regarded as justifying the committees decision
to seek a Ministerial inquiry.

[43] [1989] ILRM 821.

ment. The VEA contains the additional words "as conveniently" and these words connote somewhat less urgency; nonetheless, in *Corcoran v. Minister for Education*,[44] leave to seek Judicial Review was granted to a teacher suspended for six months. At the hearing on 10 February 1988, the State consented to an order terminating the suspension and agreed to consider a suggestion from the bench that two months should be adequate time in which to initiate an inquiry.

9.15 Delay in Holding Inquiry

The fifth ground of appeal to the Supreme Court in *Collins v. Co. Cork VEC*,[45] was the failure of the Minister to hold an enquiry into the causes of the suspension "as soon as conveniently may be" after the suspension was notified. The judgment of the court was that there was no such failure on the part of the Minister. Finlay P. stated:

> It is quite clear that, from the very commencement of the period after the making of this order of suspension, the Appellant's attitude and contention was that it was invalid and of no legal effect and he had not got any interest in, nor did he at any time seek the holding of any enquiry whether by way of formal local enquiry or otherwise on the part of the Minister for Education. As soon as he had instituted his proceedings there must be a considerable doubt as to whether it would have been proper for the Minister to hold an enquiry on a matter which had become "*sub judice*.[46]

Whether the holding of such an enquiry would have been an impropriety or not (and one can well conceive it being restrained by order of the court on the application of the appellant) certainly it was reasonable for the Minister to comply with the request, made on behalf of the appellant. (His Solicitor had written to the Minister on 15 May 1978, requesting him to suspend the local enquiry.)

It should be pointed out that the Minister has the absolute power under section 7(3) to terminate a suspension under this section and, it was thought, by so doing to decide whether or not there should be an inquiry, but, patently in the light of the Collins decision, the suspension may only be lifted after an inquiry of some sort by the Minister.

---

[44] 326 JR 11987, High Court motion, 18 November 1987
[45] Unreported, Supreme Court, 18 March 1983.
[46] *Ibid.,* p. 27

9.16 Account of Inquiry

In *Carr v. CLVEC*[47] the Chief Justice referred to a massive injustice and commented on the fact that the plaintiff had never obtained any account of what the inquiry was, from the Minister, nor had anyone written to her to give her any indication of what the result was, other than the removal of the suspension.

9.17 Cases on Suspension

In *Collins v. Co. Cork VEC*[48] the plaintiff claimed that his suspension was invalid because a member of the VEC was a disqualified person in that he was a teacher holding a paid office. Disqualification of such persons had, however, been removed by section 24(b) Local Elections (Petitions and Disqualifications) Act 1974 and the plaintiff's plea was unsuccessful. See *Furnell v. Whengarel High Schools Board*[49] in relation to whether a teacher has a right to be heard before being suspended.

In *Co. Donegal VEC v. The Minister of Education*[50] where the Minister terminated the suspension of a metal work teacher without inquiring into the charges, the Minister contended that she had a discretion under the Act whether to hold an enquiry or not. If she took the view that the charge did not warrant a disciplinary inquiry, or that it had been mounted and prepared in such a way that there was a considerable risk of total failure, she could drop the charge. This contention was rejected by O'Hanlon J. who cited Murphy J. in *Collins v. Co. Cork VEC*[51] and the affirming decision of Finlay C.J. in the Supreme Court,[52] as well as Carroll J. in *Ni Bheolain v. CDVEC*,[53] and held that the Minister had failed in her statutory duty. The VEC had suspended the teacher in order that the Minister be obliged to hold an inquiry into his alleged failure, misconduct or unfitness to hold office. It should be noted that, once a suspension occurs, the VEC has no power to re-instate the suspended officer, this may only be done by the Minister.

9.18 Minister's Power to Terminate a Suspension

Subsection (3) of the 1944 Act provides:

> The Minister may terminate a suspension under this section and every such suspension shall continue until so terminated.

---

[47] *Ex tempore*, Supreme Court, 17 October 1991.
[48] Note 44 above.
[49] [1973] 1400 D.C.
[50] Note 32 above. See also, *Irish Times*, 13 October 1984.
[51] Note 37 above.
[52] Unreported, Supreme Court, 18 March 1983.
[53] Unreported, High Court, 28 January 1983.

The power to lift a suspension was given to the Minister:

(a) on the basis that if s/he had the power to suspend s/he should also have the power to lift a suspension; and

(b) because it was feared that frivolous charges might be made against a particular officer, and that, out of spite or some other reason, a VEC might suspend an officer.

The proviso that a suspension under the section could only be terminated by the Minister was introduced because there had been incidents in local government where county managers revoked suspensions and accepted resignations. There were also cases where officers were suspended by the Minister after acceptance of resignation but before the date of resignation. In the former instance the revocation was treated as null and void while in the latter case it was not affected by the suspension. Street[54] argues that possibly the better view would be that section 27(2) was not intended to deprive the Manager of a *locus poenitentiae* (an opportunity to undo what had been done, *i.e.* the suspension) which must be implicit in any managerial office and that acceptance of resignation, which operates only from the date of resignation, has no effect on status prior to that date, so as to enable an officer to neglect duty in the interim period regardless of consequences.

9.19 Consequences of Suspension

Subsection (4) provides:

> Whenever the holder of an office under a VEC is suspended under this section, he shall forthwith hand over to such committee all books, deeds, contracts, accounts, vouchers, maps, plans and other documents in his possession, custody, or control which relate to such office.[55]

9.20 Suspension Without Pay

Subsection (5) states that he[56] is not paid[57] any remuneration in respect of such office during his suspension and on the termination of his suspension the

---

[54] H.A. Street, *Local Government in Ireland*, at p. 271.

[55] There is no penalty imposed for failure. If, however, an officer requested to hand over records and he refuses to do so this would constitute wilful disobedience of the reasonable orders of his employers and amount to misconduct within the second statutory ground for removal from office, see *Kenealy v. The Mayor of Kilkenny and others* [1905] 2 I.R. 167.

[56] "The holder of an office"

[57] The withholding of pay from a suspended officer is an action which it is suggested could be challenged. See *Gorse v. Durham Co. Co.* [1971] 1 WLR 775.

remuneration which he would have been paid shall be wholly or partly forfeited, or paid to him, or otherwise disposed of, as the Minister shall direct. This prohibition of payment does not apply to services rendered before suspension. Street states[58] that any forfeiture must be *strictissimi juris* and cannot in equity be retrospective, unless in a case of defalcation.

In the English case of *Gorse v. Durham Co. Co.*[59] a term of the teacher's contract provided that there should be no loss of salary if suspension was followed by re-instatement and that it was only in cases where the teacher was not re-instated, that it was at the discretion of the Council or Committee either to pay or withhold salary for the period of suspension. On the face of it, a more equitable provision than subsection (5). There are few persons to whom similar provisions apply in the Republic.

It should be borne in mind that while few, if any, VECs would suspend without holding a fairly detailed investigation of an alleged irregularity and asking for an explanation, an office holder when suspended *ab officio et beneficio* may not have had a formal hearing.

9.21 Judges' Opinions

In *Carr v. CLVEC*[60] Mr. Justice Murphy stated:

> The concept of suspension and in particular suspension without pay for a protracted period is in itself an appalling one. However, in addition to the injustice which it may cause to the suspended officer it necessarily prevents any meaningful analysis of events occurring within the period of suspension until after it has been lifted.[61]

Constitutional aspects of suspension without pay were touched on by Carroll J. in *Ni Bheolain v. City of Dublin Vocational Education Committee, Ireland and the Attorney General*[62] here she stated, *obiter*, that suspension "involves an immediate interference with the plaintiff's constitutional rights."

O'Hanlon J. in *Co. Donegal VEC v. Minister for Education*[63] did not go quite so far, merely suggesting that it was a pity that the Act did not empower suspension with pay and that an amendment of the Act would relieve the hardship caused. The subsection is similar to section 11(3) of the pre -Constitution Local Authorities (Officers and Employees) Act 1926.

---

[58] Street, *op. cit.* at p. 271.
[59] [1971] 1 W.L.R. 775 *op. cit.*
[60] Unreported, High Court, 3 July 1987.
[61] *Ibid.,* p.9.
[62] Note 52, above at p. 30.
[63] Note 33 above.

9.22 Suspension with Pay

In December 1991, Mr Fergus Black, the Education Correspondent of the *Irish Independent*, reported[64] that the Minister for Education had announced that he would be including an amendment to the Colleges Bills to allow suspended VEC teachers to be paid pending disciplinary hearings. In 1992 the anomaly whereby suspension had always to be without pay, was removed for vocational teachers by section 21 of the Regional Technical Colleges Act 1992 which provides:

> Notwithstanding the provisions of subsection (5) of section 7 of the Vocational Education (Amendment) Act 1944, whenever an officer of a VEC is suspended under section 7 of that Act the committee may, if it thinks fit, make with the consent of the Minister payments *ex gratia* to the suspended officer in lieu of the remuneration which, but for that suspension would have been payable to that officer.

A few points worthy of note in relation to this provision are: firstly, this is discretionary; secondly, it is subject to the Minister's consent; and thirdly, it is *ex gratia*: there is no entitlement to it.

Subsection (2) provides that any sum paid under section 1 is repayable to the VEC and may be deducted from any monies payable by the committee to that officer. Subsection (3) provides that any such payment shall not be reckoned as salary or emolument for pension purposes.

Some vocational teachers regard this section as a minimalist response and claim that it clearly contemplates the suspension being justified and reinstatement not being ordered. It may, however, be sufficient to stave off a constitutional challenge to the practice of suspension without pay. Subsection (4) applies section 21 to officers of a college suspended under the Regional Technical Colleges Act 1992.

9.23 Other Penalties for Misconduct

In *Reidy v. Minister for Agriculture and Food,*[65] it was held that the applicant had been guilty of certain irregularities in the manner in which he carried out his duties in relation to the Beef Premium Scheme, as a Technical Agricultural Officer. The disciplinary action taken against him was: 1) deferment of pay increment; 2) a two year ban on entering for promotion; and 3) a change of headquarters to Limerick.

9.24 Deferment of Increment

Mr Reidy's entitlement to increments was regulated in part by the conditions

---

[64] *Irish Independent,* 21 December 1991.
[65] Unreported, High Court, 9 June 1989.

of service accepted by him on taking up office, and in part by Department Circulars issued from time to time. Section 13 of C/l 9/87, which supplemented the Conditions of Service of an established position as Agricultural Officer, provided that "if a certificate of satisfactory service cannot be given, payment of the increment will be deferred for a specified period, e.g. three, six, nine, or twelve months. On the expiration of the period, the officer's performance should be reviewed and the increment may be allowed with effect from the end of the review period, provided the officer's service is satisfactory."

Under paragraph 14.1 of Memo V.7, the payment of annual increments of salary to a vocational teacher is, in every instance, dependant upon the teacher's service being satisfactory to the VEC and also to the Minister.

> In assessing service regard shall be had to the teacher's aggregate number of effective teaching hours in the appropriate year including hours expended in promoting other activities recognised by the Minister as equivalent to teaching hours.[66]

The decision taken in the *Reidy* case[67] was a simple decision not to pay the increment due, whereas the correct course would have been to defer payment for a specified period, subject to review. O'Hanlon J. held that the decision taken was invalid but he added that in his opinion it would "be lawful to withhold payment of an increment or such reasonable period as was necessary to enable" an investigation to be completed. He did not consider that the payment of the increment in error, with one instalment of pay after the relevant date, when payment of the increment had not been sanctioned, prejudiced the situation of either party. The matter had then to revert back to the Department to consider whether the increment should be paid in arrears as though it had been duly certified at the time, or whether the entitlement to receive it should be reconsidered in accordance with C/L 9/89.

In August 1996[68] it was reported that Co. Meath VEC had deferred two annual increments to a vocational teacher reprimanded following an official inquiry into sexual allegations against him by female students. The inquiry concluded that he had touched the breasts of five girls but could not conclude beyond a reasonable doubt that there had been a sexual motive. The allegations had been investigated by the Gardaí but no action was taken by the DPP.

9.25 Ban on Applying for Promotion

The second disciplinary measure taken against the applicant in the *Reidy* case was a two year ban on competing for positions within or outside the Depart-

---

[66] Memo V.7, para.14.1.
[67] Note 64 above.
[68] See *Irish Independent*, 27 August 27 1996.

ment. This penalty is invalid if it is not authorised by law or by the terms of appointment or employment.

O'Hanlon J. commented:

> I can find no authority either in the Civil Service Regulation Acts, 1956 and 1958, or in any of the Circulars referring to decisions of the Minister for Finance under the powers conferred on him by section 17 of the Act of 1956, for the imposition of this penalty....This penalty is one of such significance that it cannot be regarded as one capable of being imposed independently of the disciplinary powers conferred expressly by the Acts, and the further conditions of service dealt with by Circulars emanating from the Department of Finance. Accordingly, I feel constrained to decide in favour of the Applicant that the penalty imposed was invalid and not authorised by law or by any terms of the Applicant's employment.[69]

A similar situation exists in relation to vocational teachers.

9.26 Demotion

Because of the complication of a vocational teacher being appointed to an office, demotion is not a sanction which is available against him or her. The holding of a post of responsibility, in addition to a teacher's office, is a different matter. On 5 December 1986, Mr. John Walshe reported in the *Irish Independent* that a strike called by the TUI over the demotion of a teacher in the Millstreet Community School in county Cork for actions arising from the pay row earlier in the year had been averted. A split had developed between the TUI and ASTI, who indicated that its members would not go on strike. The TUI represents vocational teachers who are regarded as officers, as well as teachers in Community schools, while the ASTI represents secondary teachers who are not officers.

In September 1997 it was reported[70] that the Minister for Education had removed the principal of Athboy Vocational School, Co. meath for misconduct in relation to his office as principal but allowed him to return to his former position as a teacher.

In *Byrne v. Newbridge College*[71] a teacher appointed as Vice Principal, and later demoted after the schools seniority listing was claimed to be incorrect, instituted a High Court action claiming that the decision of the Appeal Board on posts of responsibility in secondary schools was null and void. The ground cited was that the Board refused to afford him an oral hearing, and had acted capriciously and contrary to the principles of natural justice. The Board claimed that it had adequate and definitive information in relation to the sen-

---

[69] *Ibid.,* pp.6-7.
[70] See Irish Independent, 5 September 1997.
[71] (1989). This was more accurately a case of an uncertified promotion.

iority and that it had no obligation to afford Mr. Byrne a hearing in the circumstances. The appellant's promotion was not approved.

9.27 Transfer and Change of Headquarters

The Conditions of appointment of VEC teachers contain a provision that the officer may be required to teach at any school within the VEC scheme.

In *Reidy v. Minister for Agriculture and Food*[72] disciplinary action involved changing the applicant's headquarters to Limerick. It was held that this decision was based on a *bona fide* belief that there was a danger that the applicant was tending to relax the strict requirements of the Beef Premium Scheme when dealing with farmers close to home with whom he would be acquainted personally, and that it would be preferable to relocate him from his home area. The change was made in good faith for administrative reasons and should not be regarded as a punishment or penalty imposed, although it had been referred to as a "disciplinary action" addressed to the Applicant. The decision was, however, taken by the personnel officer, and did not appear to have been ratified by the Head of Department, as envisaged by the Conditions of Service. In addition, it had not been shown that the power to make such decision was lawfully delegated to the officer who made it. On that basis only, the decision to transfer could not stand.

In all transfer cases, the welfare of the individual and his family should be a consideration as well as the requirements of the service. Transfers have often been challenged by Gardaí and Customs Officers. The Garda Síochána have an internal appeals procedure which deals with disputes about transfers. The three-member review body is composed of an independent chairman, a representative of the Commissioner and a representative of the member, usually from his staff association. A useful precedent that could be introduced into the vocational education sector.

The issue of transfers led to a dispute between the TUI and Co. Laois VEC in November 1994 when it was alleged that the decision to transfer was made without justification or prior consultation. The VEC suspended the teachers without pay and was accused by the TUI of taking a legalistic and intransigent stance.

9.28 EPT Suspension and Removal

The Department of Education advised the TUI on 11 October 1989 that suspension and removal of EPT during the term of their contracts would be in accordance with the Vocational Education Acts as they apply to officers of committees.[73]

---

[72] Note 64 above.
[73] See IVEA letter to all CEOs, 20 October 1989.

CHAPTER 10

Removal on Statutory Grounds after a Local Inquiry

Put not your son to him,
for he will come away
as very a dunce as he went.

Yelverton J. in *Watson v. Vanderlash* (1627) Het. 69

Section 8(2) of the Vocational Education (Amendment) Act 1944 provides:

Where the Minister is satisfied as a result of a local inquiry that any of the statutory grounds for removal from office exists as regards the holder of an office, the Minister may by order remove such holder from such office.

The standard conditions of employment of vocational teachers provide that whole-time permanent posts are "subject to the provisions of the Vocational Education Acts and subsequent Acts replacing or amending these Acts." This incorporates the provisions of the Acts, in particular sections 7 and 8 of the Vocational Education (Amendement) Act 1944 into a vocational teacher's conditions of employment. Prior to the 1944, Vocational Education (Amendment) Act, such conditions would have incorporated section 27 Vocational Education Act 1930 which the 1944 Act repealed.

Dismissal of an employee is the equivalent of removing an office holder from office. In the Unfair Dismissals Act 1977, "dismissal" has been defined as "the termination by his employer of the employee's contract of employment with the employer."[1]

An unusual feature in relation to the removal of a vocational teacher from office is that the removal or dismissal may be done by the Minister for Education as well as the body under which he holds office, the VEC. This is not unknown because a similar situation obtained in *Ridge v. Baldwin*.[2]

It is permissible in a contractual sense because of the incorporation of the Acts mentioned earlier into the teacher's terms of office. In any event, the Oireachtas can and does regulate conditions of employment by legislation.

---

[1] Section 1. It also includes "constructive dismissal" and contracts for a fixed term or a specified purpose.

[2] *Ridge v. Baldwin* [1964] A.C. 40.

10.1 Function of Inquiry

The "local inquiry" referred to in paragraph one does not reach any conclusion. The crucial factor is not whether a statutory ground exists or not, but whether or not the Minister **is satisfied** that it exists.

The Minister's determination that a statutory ground existed used to be a binding determination irrespective of whether it was erroneous or not. The Supreme Court has ruled in *Kerrigan v. An Bord Altranais*[3] that, when hearing an appeal from disciplinary proceedings, the High Court must itself decide contested issues of fact. The Chief Justice observed that the disciplinary procedures contained in Part V of the Nurses Act 1985 were nearly identical with those in the Medical Practitioners Act 1978.

The Chief Justice stated that no necessity for oral evidence **in the High Court** may arise in the great majority of cases in which the issues were not direct issues of fact but rather were questions of propriety, professional standards and the consequences of undisputed facts. Note the emphasis which I have placed on "in the High Court."

10.2 Determination based on Facts

In addition, the Minister's decision would have to be a *bona fide* reasonable determination based on the facts. Grounds which come to light subsequently are no longer sufficient. In *Carvill v. Irish Industrial Bank Ltd.*,[4] the Supreme Court rejected the decision in *Kenealy v. The Mayor of Kilkenny*,[5] which followed *Boston Deep Sea Fishing and Ice Co. v. Ansell*,[6] and held that it was not open to an employer to rely on an act of misconduct, as justifying dismissal, other than the act for which they purported to dismiss. O'Keeffe J. stated:

> In principle it is difficult to understand how an act can be relied upon to justify a dismissal unless it is known at the time of the dismissal.[7]

In *Genmark Pharma Ltd v. The Minister for Health*[8] it was claimed that the respondent was in breach of natural and constitutional justice when he failed to exercise independent judgment by getting advice from the NDAB. Carroll J held that the respondent Minister was entitled to seek advice but was not entitled to rely on advice in the form of conclusions without reference to the

---

3 [1990] I.T.L.R., 30 July.
4 [1968] I.R. 325.
5 [1905] 2 I.R. 167.
6 (1888) 39 Ch.D. 339.
7 Note 4 above at 345.
8 [1997] I.L.T.R., 13 October.

basic material on which those conclusions were based, as decided in *Flanagan v. UCD*[9] and in *Jeffs v. NZ Dairy Produce and Market Board*.[10] The respondent had to be in a position to make his own evaluation of the advice based on the relevant documentation submitted.

The Medical Preparations (Licensing, Advertisement and Sale) Regulations 1984 designated the respondent as the authority for the grant of product authorisations.

10.3 Reasonableness of Minister's action

The Minister does not have an uncontrolled discretion as to what constitutes misconduct even when acting *bona fide*. The unfitness or misconduct must be such as would legally justify an individual employer in dismissing an employee without notice and the Minister must act reasonably or the decision may be impugned. See *British Leyland v. Swift*[11] and *Barrett v. Sandwell Borough Council*.[12] The difficulty of defining misconduct which justified immediate dismissal (dismissal without notice) was adverted to by Kenny J. in the *Glover* case[13] where he quoted the Privy Council in *Clouston & Co. Ltd. v. Corry*[14] to the effect: "There is no fixed rule of law defining the degree of misconduct which will justify dismissal" (but see under Misconduct in office).

In ordering a removal from office, the Minister is required to act judicially and the order may be challenged by way of *Certiorari* or judicial review. See *The State (Curtin) v. Minister for Health*.[15]

10.4 "Is Satisfied"

The phrase "is satisfied", which occurs twice in section 8 of the Vocational Education (Amendment) Act 1944, was also used in section 55(1) of the Offences Against the State Act 1939 and was the vital element in that section being declared to be unconstitutional. Mr. Justice Gavin Duffy so held in *The State (Bourke) v. Lennon and A.G.*[16] on the grounds that the Minister in being **satisfied** was exercising a judicial function which was not a limited function and it was in a criminal matter.

The requirement of a Minister "being satisfied" implies an objective test reviewable by the courts whereas the requirement that the Minister is "of

---

[9] [1988] I.R. 724.
[10] [1967] 1 A.C. 551.
[11] (1981) I.R.L.R. 91.
[12] Case 2599/84.
[13] *Glover v. BLN* [1973] I.R. 388.
[14] [1906] A.C. 122.
[15] [1953] I.R. 93.
[16] [1940] I.R. 136.

opinion" is a subjective criteria which is not so reviewable although it would have to be *bona fide*.[17]

In *the State (Bourke) v. Lennon*,[18] an order of *habeas corpus* was granted by Gavan Duffy J. who held that section 55 of the Offences Against the State Act 1939 was unconstitutional. The State appealed to the Supreme Court which held that an appeal did not lie.

Section 55 provided that:

> Whenever a Minister of State **is satisfied** that any particular person is engaged in activities calculated to prejudice the preservation of the peace, order, or security of the State such Minister may by warrant under his hand order the arrest and detention of such person under this section.

According to Gavan Duffy J.:

> The word "satisfied" may or may not imply something in the nature of a judicial inquiry; its implication depends on the context. And if the section erects the Minister into a tribunal, is he a judicial or so-called administrative tribunal?

> A **judicial tribunal**, besides acting judicially, administers justice, determining rights and liabilities according to law, upon the ascertainment of the relevant facts. An **administrative tribunal** is sometimes required to act judicially; more often it is not; but whether or not it acts judicially it does not claim to administer justice. Such is not its function; normally its characteristic function is to administer policy as it sees best in the public interest.[19]

Gavan Duffy J. concluded that the decisions of such an administrative tribunal could, therefore, properly be influenced by subjective standards; it generally had the widest discretion, a very much wider power of acting on personal opinion than is involved in the limited judicial discretion familiar to a court of law. That was why an appeal to the Courts from an administrative tribunal so frequently failed.

He described a judicial act as an act done by competent authority (not necessarily a judge or legal tribunal) upon consideration of facts and circumstances and imposing liability or affecting the rights of others.

As regards the need of the Minister to be satisfied: first, the Minister had to be satisfied that the person concerned was in fact engaged in specific ac-

---

[17] See J.M. Kelly, *Fundamental Rights in the Irish Law and Constitution* (Dublin, 1967), p. 217.

[18] Note 13 above.

[19] *Ibid.* at 147.

tivities. This was an issue of fact. Second, if he found against the man on that issue of fact the Minister had to consider whether those activities were calculated to prejudice the peace, order or security of the State and be satisfied that they were. This depended on opinion but was not a matter of discretion, but essentially a matter of fact to be determined with due regard to the evidence; the Minister had to be satisfied as a matter of fact. Sometimes a strong opinion might inevitably affect the Minister's judgment upon this kind of fact, but it remained a matter of fact. Gavan Duffy J. then opined that the Minister in this weighting of the evidence had been acting judicially and he added:

> . . . the Minister must be satisfied on the evidence that his present activities are calculated to prejudice the State. . . . If I am right in holding that, the Minister is acting judicially in his essential enquiry, in finding "the grounds" for internment. I cannot hold that the essential character of his duty under the section is altered by his discretion (if any, for it is not clear that he has a discretion) as to proceeding to apply the statutory sanction, if he does not prosecute. Now many civil servants are called upon in divers directions to act judicially, without thereby administering justice or acting merely in an administrative capacity, but the test is useful because it goes a long way towards ascertaining the essential character of this particular statutory function.[20]

Criminal justice is exercisable only by a judge under the Constitution and in this case the Minister's powers were an invasion of the judicial domain and as such, repugnant to the Constitution. Gavan Duffy J. considered that the nature of the duty imposed on the Minister was the best guide to the meaning of the word "satisfied" in the section. Part VI of the Act was its own best dictionary, and the grave duty which the section imposed did not suggest any loose use of the word "satisfied" but in his opinion clearly suggested a serious inquiry resulting in a serious finding of "satisfied" or "not satisfied", as the case might be.

Subsequent to this decision the phrase "Whenever a Minister **is of opinion**" was used in the Offences Against the State Amendment Act 1940.

It is significant that this phrase was not used some four years later in section 8 of the Vocational Education (Amendment) Act 1944 although the requirement for suspension under section 7 is one of "opinion". The intention of the legislature therefore was to place a more onerous responsibility on the Minister in removal cases.

The power to strike a solicitor off the roll has been held by the Supreme Court in *Re Solicitors Act 1954*[21] to be an administration of justice and not

---

[20] *Ibid.* at 15.
[21] In *Re Solicitors Act 1954* and in *Re O'Farrell and O'Gorman* [1960] I.R. 239.

merely the exercise of limited power of a judicial nature within Article 37.
As a result this function has to be performed by the Courts.

10.5 Statutes Governing Discipline

In statutes, grounds of dismissal or removal from office are often phrased in
broad general terms and the wording of the particular statute is crucial because the body exercising the power is limited to the grounds specified. *Spencer v. Laconia School Dist.*[22] and *School Dist. v. Bear.*[23] A statute providing
for dismissal only for cause cannot be circumvented by including a power to
dismiss without cause in the individual's contract.[24] In addition, the power
granted by statute is subject to constitutional restraint and may not be exercised in an unconstitutional, discriminatory or arbitrary manner.[25]

The Constitutional limitation imposed by Article 37 of the Constitution
in confining the exercise of powers of a judicial nature, in matters other than
criminal matters, to limited functions led to the Courts holding (in the *Farrell*
and *O'Gorman* case) that the Incorporated Law Society could not strike a
solicitor off the roll and prevent him from practising. It was a function appropriate to the Courts.

It has been suggested that:

> The *Solicitors Act* case leaves many questions unanswered, the princi-
> pal being — what is the position of the statutes governing discipline in
> other professions? . . . a recent High Court decision points the way out
> of any constitutional difficulties that may arise in regard to such (disci-
> plinary) bodies.[26]

Professor Casey cites *M. v. Medical Council*[27] where a Fitness to Practice
Committee enquired into allegations of (*inter alia*) professional misconduct.
The Committee then reported to the Council who could decide that the practitioner's name be erased from the register. The practitioner was entitled to
apply to the High Court within 21 days to cancel the decision. If no such
application was made, the Council could apply to the High Court for confirmation of the decision, and, unless it saw good reason to the contrary, the
High Court was to confirm it. Finlay P. (as he then was) pointed out that
neither the Committee or the Council had any power to erase a practitioner's

---

[22] 107 N.H 125, 218 A2d 437.
[23] 106 Okla. 172, 233 p 427, 38 ALR 1413. Note that in *Carr v. CLVEC*, unreported High
    Court 31 July 1987 it was accepted that the statutory provisions (ss.7 and 8 of the
    Vocational Education (Amendment) Act 1944) dealt solely with unfitness and miscon-
    duct and that the parties themselves were free to agree other terms for termination.
[24] *Thompson v. Gibbs*, 97 Tenn. 489, 37 Sw 277.
[25] 68 Am. Jur. 2d. 161.
[26] Professor James Casey, *Constitutional Law in Ireland* (London, 1987), at p. 209.
[27] *M. v. Medical Council* [1984] I.R. 485.

name from the register, to suspend him from practice, to make him pay compensation or to award costs against him. The only power vested in them was to initiate proceedings in the High Court.

According to Professor Casey, disciplinary provisions of this type may be somewhat cumbersome, but a degree of cumbrousness seems preferable to a shadow of possible unconstitutionality.

As Chief Justice Finlay in *Kerrigan v. An Bord Altranais*[28] stated:

> The essence of.the procedure contained in the Act for the regulation of the registration and disciplining of members of the nursing profession was that it was in the High Court that the decision effective to lead to an erasure or suspension of the operation of registration must be made.[29]

The necessity for that procedure to vest the power unequivocally in the Court, arose, in his view, from the constitutional frailty that would attach to the delegation of any such power to a body which was not a court established under the Constitution, having regard to the decision in *In re the Solicitors Act 1954*.

In the recent case of *Geoghegan v. The Institute of Chartered Accountants*[30] it was decided that the power of the institute in matters of professional discipline was not tantamount to the exercise of the judicial power of the State. There was a distinction between solicitors, doctors[31] and nurses[32] on the one hand and accountants on the other. The distinction according to O'Flaherty J. (Blaney J. concurring) was that "the procedure in each of these cases has been set up by Act of the Oireachtas and in each of these cases there is a right of review by the High Court."

There is no specific provision in the Vocational Education Acts for review of disciplinary powers which they contain by the High Court.

It is suggested by the author that in new legislation the provisions in the Nurses Act 1985 or the Dentists Act 1985 could serve as a model for the teaching council proposed in chapter 6, paragraph 8 of the 1992 Green Paper.

In relation to the liability of public authorities and their duty when exercising statutory powers Brian Doolan comments:[33]

> Where there has been a delegation by statute to a designated person of a power to make decisions affecting others, unless the statute provides

---

[28] Note 3 above.
[29] *Ibid.*
[30] Unreported, Supreme Court, 16 November 1995.
[31] *Re M. v. Medical Council* [1984] I.R. 485.
[32] Above n. 3.
[33] Brian Doolan, *Principles of Irish Law* (3rd ed., Dublin, 1991).

otherwise, an action for damages by a person adversely affected by an *ultra vires* decision does not lie against the decision-maker unless he or she acted negligently, or with malice, or in the knowledge that the decision was in excess of authorised power. This was decided by the Supreme Court in *Pine Valley Developments Ltd. v. Minister for the Environment*,[34] where planning permission granted by the Minister was later found to be *ultra vires*. In reaching his decision, the Minister had acted *bona fide* on the advice given by the department's senior legal adviser.[35]

10.6 Information to be Provided before Special Inquiry

In *Hogan v. Minister for Justice*,[36] Mr. Justice Hamilton considered the plaintiff should have been given:

(1) full notice of the grounds upon which he was considered unfit,
(2) full notice of the essential facts and findings alleged to constitute the reason for so considering, and
(3) particulars of the alleged breach of discipline

before the special inquiry proceeded and before the plaintiff was required to advance reasons against his proposed dismissal.

The plaintiff Garda Sergeant was, however, the holder of an office, as was an enlisted Army private in the *State (Gleeson) v. Minister for Defence*.[37] The distinction would appear to based on the fact that where an office holder is involved there is a purported infringement of a legal right.

10.7 "A" Local Inquiry

Section 8(2) of the Vocational Education (Amendment) Act 1944 is significantly different in drafting to section 25(2) of the Local Government Act 1941 in one respect, namely that whereas the Vocational Education Act states "where the Minister is satisfied as a result of **a** local inquiry", the LGA states "is satisfied as a result of **any** local inquiry."

This means that the local inquiry in the case of a vocational teacher would have to be one held specifically to inquire into his/her case.

In the case of a local government officer the inquiry may be into something else or someone else, *e.g.* in *The State (Curtin) v. Minister for Health*,[38] Curtin was not formally charged with any misconduct in the sense that he received any written document alleging that he had done something wrong

---

[34] [1987] I.R. 23.
[35] Doolan, *Principles of Irish Law*, at p. 199.
[36] Unreported, High Court, 8 September 1976.
[37] [1976] I.R. 286.
[38] [1953] I.R. 93.

or that his conduct was specifically made one of the subjects of the inquiry.

The inquiry was into the circumstances connected with a patient at Ennis Mental Hospital sustaining a fracture of the left femur and into the conduct and condition of a doctor at the hospital. A witness gave sworn evidence that Curtin asked her to "go back on", a statement which she made prior to the inquiry. Curtin volunteered to give evidence and denied the allegation but was subsequently dismissed by order of the Minister.

10.8 Removal from Office under section 8 of the Vocational Education (Amendment) Act 1944

Section 8 of the Vocational Education (Amendment) Act 1944 replaces section 27 of the Vocational Education Act 1930 which provided that, after a local inquiry, the Minister could by order remove from office or employment any paid officer or servant whom he considered unfit, or incompetent to perform his duties, or who at any time refuses or wilfully neglects to perform his duties. The 1930 Act had given servants the same treatment as an officer. The new section 8 does not deal with servants who can be dismissed without a local enquiry.

10.9 Statutory Grounds for Removal under section 8

Section 8(1) sets out the statutory grounds for removal from office for the purpose of this section as:

(a) **unfitness** of such holder **for such office**;

(b) the fact that such holder has **refused to obey or carry into effect any order lawfully given to him** as the holder of such office; or

(c) has **otherwise misconducted himself in such office**.

10.10 Unfitness

Unfitness, the third statutory ground for suspension, is the first statutory ground for removal from office. The Act does not specify what unfitness for office consists of, but it is likely that this unfitness is not that covered by subsection (3) which relates to teaching ability.

In the wide general sense, unfitness relates to suitability. A person can be unfit for a particular occupation by virtue of temperament, by virtue of attitude, philosophy, political ideology, sexual perversion, behaviour, *e.g.* using drugs or alcohol during work, inability to control students, inability of a Principal to manage teachers, etc.

A teacher whose qualifications are sufficient may none the less be **unfit** because of continual insubordination, or refusal to obey school rules which impairs discipline in the institution. In *R. v. London Co. Co. Education Staff Sub-Committee, ex parte Schonfeld* [39] the Governors sought the removal of the headmaster because they alleged he was too strict a disciplinarian and that his punishments were unreasonable.

In the Local Government (Superannuation) Act 1956, unfitness does not include unfitness due to infirmity of mind or body or old age but section 10 refers to absence from the place where the officer's duties are performed and refraining from performing those duties, such absence or refraining being deliberate and unauthorised.

It is not necessary to hold a public inquiry in relation to unfitness based on teaching because of the power given to the Minister by section 8(3). The unfitness in question, therefore, stems from causes other than teaching ability.

In *Cox v. Minster for Education* [40] it was submitted for the Minister "that an employer is entitled to dictate the terms on which he can hold a person was no longer suitable for employment". Mr. Justice Barr stated:

> The State has a right to impose conditions of employment by statute, even outside the public sector, in the interests of the common good, *e.g.* as to maximum daily working hours or annual holiday entitlement. But these must apply to every employee or to all within specific categories and intervention by the State into the relationship of master and servant must be fair and even handed. The provisions of section 34 (Offences Against The State Act 1939) do not satisfy that test. [41]

His Lordship then went on to find that section 34 in its entirety was unconstitutional and void.

There is little doubt, however, that the legislature considered persons convicted in accordance with section 34 as being unfit to hold office and it would probably be open to the State to remove persons who are members of illegal organisations or who have committed certain offences as being unfit to hold office under section 8(1)(a).

In *Director of Public Prosecutions v. Flanagan*, [42] Mrs. Justice Denham held that the word "unfit" in relation to a driving offence had a more limited meaning than "incapable" The words were not synonymous. "unfit" connoted not suitable or not qualified, but this decision was overruled by the Supreme Court.

In *Ridge v. Baldwin* [43] Lord Morris stated;

---

[39] [1956] 1 W.L.R. 430.
[40] [1992] 2 I.R. 503.
[41] *Ibid.*, p. 511.
[42] Unreported, High Court, but see *Irish Independent*, 19 December 1991.
[43] [1964] A.C. 41.

I consider that in the context, the word 'otherwise' denotes that there may be dismissal of a constable if the watch Committee considers that he is *unfit for the discharge of his duties* even though he may not have been negligent in their discharge. In the section it seems to me that the words 'unfit for the same' were designed to cover situations where apart from any misconduct or lack of care and even apart from any physical or health condition, a constable was thought to be unfit for the discharge of his duty.[44]

It would be useful if vocational teachers were provided with guide-lines similar to those for Gardaí.[45] (See also chapter 9 in relation to suspension and chapter 11 where unfitness is discussed in relation to the Minister's power to remove from office without holding a statutory local inquiry.)

In an American case *Board of Education v. Swan*,[46] it has been held that continual insubordination, refusal to recognise constituted authority and teaching lessons other than those prescribed, rendered a teacher unfit, even though his qualifications were sufficient.

10.11 Refusing to Obey any Order Lawfully given

The second statutory ground for removal from office is that the officer **has refused to obey or carry into effect any order lawfully given.** An order to do an unlawful act is an order which is not lawfully given, *e.g.* in *Thornton v. Coolock Foods Ltd.*[47] where a person who refused to work in contravention of statute law was unfairly dismissed and in *Morrish v. Henly's (Folkestone) Ltd.*[48] a worker was unfairly dismissed when he refused to falsify records to cover a discrepancy. See also *Martin v. Wheelan.*[49]

An order may also be unlawful in the sense that, although the thing being ordered to be done is within the law, the person giving the order does not have the lawful authority to give it. It may be outside the ambit of the duties which the officer or employee is obliged to carry out. The Fourth edition of *Rideout's Principles of Labour Law* states:

A servant is certainly under no duty to obey unlawful orders, *Gregory v. Ford*,[50] but it is submitted that this is merely an extreme example of

---

[44] *Ibid.,* p. 109.
[45] Schedule to Garda Síochána (Discipline) Regulations, 1971, S.I. No. 316 of 1971.
[46] 41 Cal 2d 546 347 US 937, 74 S Ct. 627.
[47] UD 638/1987.
[48] [1973] 2 All E.R.
[49] UD 30/1978, July 1978, No. 41 Selected EAT Cases ,1978, when a barman terminated his contract of employment summarily after refusing to serve measures smaller than regular size.
[50] [1951] 1 All E.R. 121.

an order outside the scope of his contract. Even if the contract appeared
to encompass unlawful work the term conveying such appearance would
presumably be void.[51]

A vocational teacher's duties are part of his/her Conditions of Service which
contain a term "to teach for as many hours and over such periods and to be
otherwise available for duties, in accordance with agreements which are arrived at from time to time, and authorised by the Minister for Education." If
a duty is not within the ambit of such an agreement and authorised by the
Minister, then an order to perform it may not be lawfully given. As far back
as *Price v. Mouat*[52] a person employed to buy lace was held to be entitled to
refuse to work putting it on cards.

   A Principal is normally entitled to require a teacher to do work other
than that for which s/he has been engaged provided that the request is reasonable. What is reasonable will depend on the circumstances and will vary
from time to time and place to place, amongst other things bearing in mind
the particular duties which the teacher was engaged to undertake. See *Redbridge LBC v. Fishman*.[53] If a teacher has undertaken duties other than those
s/he was engaged to do such action has a significant effect on the application
of "refusal to obey" provisions.

10.12 The "All Rounder"

In the Irish case of *Waters v. Kentredder (Ireland) Ltd.*,[54] the claimant's only
function under the initial terms of his contract of employment was re-tredding
tyres but for most of his time in their employment he kept no line of demarca-
tion and applied himself to three other processes as well. When a dispute
arose he said that henceforth he would only work at re-tredding in accordance with the terms of his original contract and he was dismissed. The EAT
were satisfied that whatever his original terms were, he had become an "all
rounder" and his dismissal for not carrying out the other functions was not
unfair.

   In *Kenealy v. Mayor of Kilkenny & Others*[55] the refusal to hand back to
the Corporation their public records when they were asked for, in the judgment of Lord O'Brien L.C.J., afforded abundant ground to warrant dismissal.
The facts were that Kenealy claimed that he was wrongfully dismissed from
his position as Town Clerk of Kilkenny Corporation and deprived of his entitlement to a superannuation allowance or gratuity under the Local Govern-

---

[51] Rideout and Dyson, *Rideout's Principles of Labour Law*, p. 93.
[52] (1862) 11 C.B. (n.s.) 508.
[53] [1978] I.C.R. 569.
[54] UD3/1977.
[55] [1905] 2. I.R. 167.

ment (Ireland) Act 1898. The Corporation claimed that his dismissal was justified, that he was guilty of misconduct because he had wilfully disobeyed their **reasonable orders.** He would not give the Corporation an account of his remuneration, his salary and emoluments, and he refused to provide particulars of goods ordered, despite a resolution by the Corporation to circulate the particulars of the goods. It was held that his wilful disobedience of the reasonable orders of his superiors, amounted to misconduct justifying his dismissal, and disentitled him to the superannuation allowance, gratuity or pension under section 116 of the Local Government (Ireland) Act 1892.

There are occasions when a teacher may be justified in refusing to obey an order. In *Leclerc v. Perigord School District No. 850, Board of Trustees*[56] it was held that a teacher is justified in refusing to obey an order of a school board to suspend a pupil if he knows of no reason why the pupil should be suspended or expelled and has received no complaint against the pupil.

Another such case is *Perse v. Sunderland Corporation*[57] where it was held that teachers were entitled to refuse to obey an order to collect money for school meals. This was not a duty which could be imposed on teachers under the Education Act 1944 and it was not within the defendant's statutory powers to dismiss the plaintiffs for such a reason. The defendant corporation was acting *ultra vires.*

Wilful refusal to obey **lawful and proper orders** is the term used in America,[58] where the refusal of a PE instructor to perform coaching duties,[59] a refusal of a teacher to stop advising students to oppose the school rules,[60] to return to his classroom from a student walk-out in protest of a rumour of the discharge of another teacher, when requested by the Principal,[61] and refusing to carry out instructions concerning the financial records of a vocational school[62] have been held to constitute grounds for dismissal.

10.13 Warning

Refusal to obey a **lawful and reasonable** instruction is the term used by the British EAT in *Steels v. Goldsmith Garage Ltd.*,[63] where it was held that a failure to warn an employee that disobedience may lead to dismissal can make the dismissal unfair. Depending on the circumstances such disobedience can amount to misconduct. In applying a statute referring to **refusal to**

---

[56] (1925) 3. D.L.R. 578.
[57] (1956) 1 W.L.R. 1253.
[58] *Crownover v. Alread School Dist.*, 211 Ark. 449, 200 SW2d 809.
[59] *Granaposki's Appeal*, 332 Pa. 550, 2 A2d 742, 119 ALR 815.
[60] *Vance v. Board of Education*, 2 ill. App 3d 745, 277 NEE2d 337.
[61] *Petition of Davenport* (Vt.) 283 A2d 452.
[62] *Board of Education v. Chattin* (Ky) 376 SW2d 693.
[63] 17/3/88 EAT 467/87.

obey motivation by an insubordinate attitude is relevant. *Midway School Dist. v. Griffeath.*[64]

10.14 Lawful Order

A vocational teacher as holder of an office under a VEC is bound to carry out the VEC's instructions in so far as they are acting within the authority delegated to them. They would not be lawful instructions if the VEC were acting outside their authority (*ultra vires*). Garner[65] states "*A fortiori,* an officer is not obliged, nor indeed entitled to act simply on the instructions of an individual member of a committee, or even of the Chairman." In *Price v. Sunderland Corpn.,*[66] when the defendant council acted *ultra vires* and passed a resolution that teachers who refused to collect money for school meals, should have their employment by the council terminated it was held that this was a duty which could not be imposed by the council and the plaintiffs could not be validly dismissed for refusal to obey it.

In *Collins v. Co. Cork VEC*[67] where the appellant, a headmaster who was subsequently suspended, refused to hold a meeting with senior staff on the 13 October 1977, and to place a number of matters on the agenda as directed by the CEO in a registered letter, Finlay P. decided that the order to attend the meeting was a lawful order emanating from the Committee and the CEO.

Rideout and Dyson[68] state that:

> Refusal without justification, to obey a reasonable order within the scope of the contract of service is a breach of that contract, although, as in all other classes of breach, the refusal may not be so fundamental a rejection of the contract as to justify rescission by way of dismissal.[69]

They also point out that an employee is not obliged to be accommodating and helpful,[67] and that he is entitled to construe the terms of his contract strictly and to refuse to move outside that construction.[71]

It has been found that refusal to obey an employer's instructions in the following instances did not constitute grounds which justified a dismissal and made it fair. Refusing to use a machine without being trained to use it,[72]

---

[64] 29 Cal. 2d 13, 1172 p2d. 857.
[65] Garner, *Administrative Law* (6th ed., London, 1985), p. 356.
[66] [1956] 3 All E.R. 153.
[67] Unreported, High Court, 12 March 1982 and 27 May 1982 *op. cit.*
[68] Rideout and Dyson, *Rideout's Principles of Labour Law* (London, 1983).
[69] At p. 93.
[70] *Sec. of State v. ASLEF* [1972] 2 Q.B. 443.
[71] Note 49 above.
[72] *O'Farrell v. Recommendation of the Rights Commissioner,* UD 120/3/1978 November 1978.

refusing to sit for an examination when it was not part of the contract of employment.[73]

If a vocational teacher were ordered to take a class in a subject which s/he did not normally teach without being given sufficient notice or opportunity to prepare, it is possible that such refusal could be justifiable. The reasonableness of the employer's instruction may be of vital importance.[74]

In the case of *Gorse and Anor v. Durham Co. Co.,*[75] the plaintiff teachers, members of the NUT, withdrew from the duty to supervise meals on union instructions and refused to obey instructions to do so, even though their conditions of employment incorporated regulations which obliged them to do such supervision. It was held that, although this refusal was conduct which amounted to a repudiation of their contracts, since the defendants had merely regarded them as being temporarily suspended, the repudiation was not accepted and the teachers were entitled to be paid their salaries for the period they were excluded from the school.

Ferdinand von Prondzynski[76] takes the view that:

> The employee's duty of obedience . . . still probably exists in some form, and yet a literal approach to it cannot really be squared with the more participative view of the employment relationship now generally favoured; the duty of obedience should, therefore, perhaps now be described as Hepple and O'Higgins suggest, as the "duty of co-operation". The obligations listed in cases decided as recently as *Lister v. Romford Ice*[77] . . . tend at least to some extent to portray, the relationship as an authoritarian or paternalistic one, and cannot, therefore, be reliable guides today.[78]

"Refusal to obey or carry out any lawful order given to him." was the basis of the judgment of Finlay P. in *Collins v. Co. Cork VEC*[79] where he refers to a lawful order rather than an order lawfully given. It is suggested that the section be amended in this regard.

In the USA where statutes refer to *persistent refusal to obey school laws*, the motivation of the teacher has been considered relevant, in particular

---

[73] *Ruder and Byrne v. Irish Lights Commissioners,* UD 81/1977, June 1978. An employee can refuse to take further examinations if it is not part of his contract of employment. A requirement to sit for an examination can only be imposed after the contract is made when it becomes strictly necessary and when adequate opportunity to sit it is given.

[74] See *B. Stamp v. A. N. Stamp Ltd.,* UD 11/1978, June 1978.

[75] [1971] I W.L.R. 775.

[76] *Employment Law in Ireland* (2nd. ed., London, 1989), p. 46.

[77] [1957] A.C. 555.

[78] von Prondzynski, *Employment Law in Ireland*, p. 46.

[79] Unreported, High Court, 12 March 1982 and 27 May 1982 *op. cit.*

whether the motivation was because of an insubordinate attitude.[80] Unjustified refusal to accept a particular assignment justified dismissal in *Board of Education v. Swan*[81] but a refusal to comply with an unreasonable or dangerous assignment did not.[82]

10.15 "Otherwise Misconduct" in Office

The third statutory ground for removal is where the holder of an office has "**otherwise** misconducted himself in such office."

This is preceded by the word **or** which indicated that it is an alternative to the second ground. "Otherwise" clearly indicates that the misconduct which constitutes this ground does not result from refusal to obey or to carry into effect any order lawfully given. This is confirmed by the judgment of Lord Morris of Borth-y-Gest in *Ridge v. Baldwin*[83] where he found that the word "otherwise" in a similar context precluded the ground which preceded it.

The facts of the case were that section 191 of the Municipal Corporations Act 1882 empowered a watch committee to dismiss any borough constable whom they thought "negligent in the discharge of his duty, or **otherwise** unfit for the same."

A relevant example is the case of *Gorse v. Durham Co. Co.,*[84] where it was stated *obiter* by Cusack J. that if the behaviour of the plaintiffs was such that it amounted to a repudiation of their contracts then that must be misconduct. But refusal to obey in similar circumstances under the Irish legislation could not be construed as misconduct because this third statutory ground is specifically indicated as being an alternative and exclusive ground from the two which precede it.

10.16 Misconduct Justifying Dismissal

Misconduct depends upon the context of the employee's act and not just its consequences to the employer. In *Snia Ireland Ltd. v. Connolly*[85] the EAT stated:

> The reasons for the act have to be evaluated and put into the context of his employment and responsibility. An act of an employee can cause damage or risk to the employer but it need not be misconduct. An act minor in one situation, can be gross misconduct in another.[86]

---

[80] *See Midway School Dist. v. Griffeath*, 29 Cal. 2d 13, 172 p2d 857.
[81] 41 Cal. 2d 546.
[82] *Abraham v. Sims,* 2 Cal. 2d 698
[83] Note 2 above.
[84] Note 65 above at 785.
[85] UD 1194/1983.
[86] *Ibid.*

In the *Stamp* case[87] *supra* the EAT held that a dismissal was not unfair by virtue of an employee's misconduct in refusing to obey his employer's reasonable instruction to continue working until 5 p.m., the usual finishing time, and insisting that he was entitled to travelling time. While failing to attend for work constitutes a breach of the contract of employment, failing to attend after being refused a day off does not constitute "misconduct" within the meaning of the Minimum Notice and Terms of Employment Act so as to justify dismissal without notice.[88]

Matters which have been held to constitute misconduct include; speaking abusively to other employees and assaulting another employee,[89] assaulting a superior,[90] or a student,[91] failing to supply medical certificates in breach of contract and of a companies rule book,[92] using a company's van for personal purposes after a warning not to,[93] being drunk and in possession of alcohol on duty,[94] setting up in business in direct competition to an employer while still employed by him,[95] possession of heroin at work,[96] immoral conduct at work,[97] a teacher borrowing money from a pupil, abuse of sick leave[98] kissing a student in a dark room,[99] and encouraging students to indulge in indecent behaviour in class.[100]

In 1985 a lecturer at Warwick University was dismissed because of his alleged sexual harassment of a female student. The student said that he asked her for a hug, which she gave him, and he then made a sexual proposition to her. The lecturer denied the student's version of events.[101]

The principal of a County Meath Vocational Schhol was removed from his office for misconduct after an inquiry by an Inspector found that personation involving his sons took place during the Leaving Certificate English examination in June 1997.[102]

---

[87] *B. Stamp v. A. Stamp Ltd,* UD11/1978, June, 1978, *op. cit.,* page 5.

[88] *Kinnerk v. R. Healy T/A The Black Bar,* M 91/1978, May 1978.

[89] *Shiels v. Bonner Engineering Limited,* UD 67/1977, May 1978.

[90] *Murray v. Meath County Council,* UD 43/1978, July 1978.

[91] *Haire v. Moran,* unreported, District Court, but see *Irish Press,* 6 July 1984.

[92] *Corrigan v. Rowntree Mackintosh (Ireland) Ltd.,* UD 37/1978, August 1978.

[93] *Hillard v. Johnston Mc Inerney Ltd.,* M 194/1978, August 1978.

[94] *Redlands Purple Ltd. v. O'Sullivan,* UD 51/1978, May 1978.

[95] *Cox v. Genfitt Ltd.,* M 46/1978 May 1978.

[96] *Shiels v. Williams Transport (Ireland) Ltd., Irish Independent,* 10 July 1984.

[97] *Brennan v. Batchelors Ltd.,* UD 643/1981.

[98] *Lynch v. P.V. Doyle Hotels Ltd.,* UD 89/1989; (Working elsewhere while on sick leave.) *Murphy v. Tesco Stores Ireland Ltd.,* UD 1242/1983; (On holiday while on sick leave.)

[99] G.R. Barrell, *Teachers and the Law* (London, 1976), p. 122 refers *Jones v. University of London* (1922) *The Times,* 22 March.

[100] G.R. Barrell, *op. cit.* p. 121; *Newligin v. Lancashire Co. Co.* (1973) *Daily Mail,* 14 November.

[101] Times HES, 31 May 1985.

[102] See para. 9.29 and 9.30 above.

10.17 Fraud and Negligence

Misconduct would include fraud and negligence[103] and section 39 of the Vocational Education (Accounts, Audit and Procedure) Regulations 1931 refers to the possibility of a deficiency or loss being incurred "by the negligence or misconduct of any member or officer of a committee or that any sum which ought to have been brought into account by such officer was not so brought into account." The procedure in this regard seems to be that if the sums of money are reimbursed there would be no deficiency or loss and because the difference between negligence and misconduct is one of intent which is difficult to prove, the matter is usually dropped.

In May, 1985[104] the *Evening Press* carried a report that the Dáil Committee on Public Accounts were told that more than £33,000 of Co. Meath VEC funds were misappropriated, because of defects in the committee's internal control system and that criminal proceedings were underway. The committee was also told that two academic staff at Cork RTC had kept more than £6,000 paid to them for private work carried out on college equipment in college time. Full compensation was paid and the pair were disciplined.

In the *Glover* case[105] Kenny J. stated:

> It is impossible to define the misconduct which justifies immediate dismissal. In giving the advice of the Privy Council in *Clouston & Co. Ltd. v. Corry*[106] Lord James of Hereford said "There is no fixed rule of law defining the degree of misconduct in a servant which will justify dismissal. . . . What is or is not misconduct must be decided in each case with the assistance of a definition or a general rule. Similarly, all one can say is that it is misconduct which the court regards as being grave and deliberate." And the standards to be applied in deciding the matter are those of men and not of angels.[107]

In re Accessories Ltd.[108] telling a superior to "f... off" in the course of an argument was held not to amount to gross misconduct warranting dismissal.

10.18 Employers' Fault

In *Killian v. Carr*[109] the EAT refused to hold that allegations of misconduct against a claimant could be justified, being at least in part attributable to lack of supervision and training on the part of the employer.

---

[103] *In re Solicitors Act 1954* and in Re *O'Farrell and O'Gorman* [1960] I.R. 239.
[104] *Evening Press*, 3 May 1985.
[105] *Glover v. BLN* [1973] I.R. 388
[106] [1906] A.C. 122.
[107] Note 84 above at 405.
[108] *King v. Motorway Tyres & Accessories* [1975] IRLR 51.
[109] UD 242/1979.

10.19 Notification of Grounds for Removal from Office

If a decision can only be taken on a limited number of alternative grounds, which have been fixed by law, there is authority for holding that the decision must indicate which of the grounds forms the basis for the decision and in accordance with *Framington School, ex parte Ward*:[110]

> Where trustees have power to displace a schoolmaster upon any neglect or misbehaviour in such schoolmaster, and they, upon legitimate materials which might possibly have satisfied a reasonable man desirous of doing justice, come to a certain conclusion upon a point of fact as to such neglect or misbehaviour, it is not the office of the court to interfere with it.[111]

10.20 Notification of Reasons

In general there is no obligation to state the reasons for administrative or judicial decisions and in addition a statement of reasons is not required to be given by the rules of natural justice.[112]

In England the Tribunals and Inquiries Act 1971 imposes a duty to state the reasons for decisions on Ministers and on a number of statutory tribunals after the holding of a statutory inquiry.[113] The statement of the reasons may be written or oral but may be refused for a number of reasons on grounds of national security. Neither the Tribunals of Inquiry (Evidence) Act 1921 or the Tribunals of Inquiry (Evidence) (Amendment) Act 1979 impose a similar duty in Ireland. A voluntary statement of reasons may be given.[114]

In *Mooney v. An Post*[115] Keane J. stated *obiter* :

> Under Irish law, a person holding office at the pleasure of the Government may still be entitled to be informed of the reasons for his removal from office and to be afforded the opportunity of making representations.[116]

In *McCormack v. Garda Síochána Complaints Board*[117] an order was sought directing the Board to state its reasons for its decisions and it was submitted

---

[110] (1847) 9 L.T.O.S.

[111] *Ibid*

[112] *Fountaine v. Chesterton*, The *Times*, 20 August 1968; *R. v. Gaming Board for Great Britain* [1970] 2 Q.B. 417.

[113] For the details required see *Re Poyser and Mills Arbitration* [1964] 2 Q.B. 467 at p. 478.

[114] See *Modern Law Review*, Vol. 33, 1970, p. 159.

[115] Unreported, High Court, 11 February 1994, Keane J.

[116] See *Garvey v. Ireland* [1981] I.R. 75.

[117] Unreported, High Court, 28 January 1997.

that the Board's failure to do so justified the court in quashing it by an order of *Certiorari*. Alternatively it was claimed that the Court should order the Board to state its reasons by granting an order of *mandamus*.[118] Costello J held that the reasons for the decision were self-evident, it followed from the opinion the Board had reached and there was no need for the Board to say so.

Costello P. stated:

> It has been held that a Minister who decides to dismiss a Civil Servant should be required to give reasons. . . .[119]

The Minister's statutory function is central to this issue. In the *Lynch* case[120] it was a quasi-judicial function and a failure to state reasons might render ineffectual or prejudice a right to apply to the courts for an order of *Certiorari* or *Mandamus*.[121]

In the *McCormack* case[122] the board was not carrying out a quasi-judicial function and the issue could largely be determined by considering whether some detriment was suffered by the applicant by the failure to give reasons. The Board's reasons were not required to make effective any statutory right of appeal.

---

[118] See p. 16 of the judgment.
[119] See *The State (Lynch) v. Cooney* [1982] I.R. 337 and at p. 23 of the judgment.
[120] Above, n.119.
[121] See para. 10.3 above and *The State (Curtin) v. Minister for Health* [1953] I.R. 93 and *Maigueside Communications Ltd v. IRTC*, I.L.T.R. 6 October 1997, High Court, McGuinness J.
[122] See n. 117 above.

Removal by Minister without a Statutory Local Inquiry

> The village master taught his little school
> A man severe he was, and stern to view
> I knew him well, and every truant knew:
> Well had the boding tremblers learned to trace
> The day's disasters in his morning face.
>
> Oliver Goldsmith

The Minister for Education may remove an officer by order without holding a local inquiry in two circumstances, *viz.* under section 8(3) and section 8(4) of the Vocational Education (Amendment) Act 1944.

Section 8 (3) states "Where the Minister **is satisfied** that the holder of an office has failed to perform **satisfactorily** the **duties** of such office **and** is **of opinion** that he is **unfit** to hold such office, the Minister may . . . by order remove such holder from such office." This power would be exercisable after suspension under section 7 of the Vocational Education (Amendment) Act 1944 for failure to perform satisfactorily the duties of office referred to in chapter 9.

11.1 Failure to Perform Teaching Duties Satisfactorily

The failure to perform satisfactorily relates to **duties** (plural), not just to one duty. Unlike the repealed section 27 of the 1930 Act, section 8 of the 1944 Act does not include the words "or any of them" and the opinion of unfitness must be conjunctive with the failure. Both are required.

11.2 Illness and Sick Leave

Failure to perform satisfactorily may be due to illness and absence caused by illness.

11.3 Illness

There is no reference to sickness, injury or sick pay in the Standard Conditions of Service of vocational teachers although the Terms of Employment

(Information) Act 1994[1] requires employers to furnish new employees with a written statement of the terms of employment containing terms relating to incapacity for work due to sickness or injury and sick pay. It is suggested that this omission might be remedied in future versions of the Standard Conditions.

11.4 Sick Leave

The *TUI Diary and Handbook* states[2] that permanent whole-time teachers **are** entitled to full salary during absence due to illness for a period of up to one year. Memo V.7 uses the word **may**. Technically the use of the word may means that there is no entitlement and that payment of salary during illness is a concession, albeit one which might normally be expected to be granted.

Paragraph 21.2 of Memo V.7 states:

(i) Sick leave **may** be granted to a permanent whole-time teacher **only** where there is a reasonable expectation that the teacher will be able to resume duty.

(ii) A permanent whole-time teacher may be allowed full salary during absence due to illness for a period or periods **which in aggregate do not exceed twelve months (365 days) in any four consecutive years.** In reckoning such aggregate of twelve months, periods of annual leave for which full salary is allowed occurring in the course of the teacher's absence owing to illness must be reckoned as part of that absence. A period of annual leave for which a teacher who has been absent on sick leave produces a certificate from a duly qualified medical practitioner that the teacher is fit to resume his duties is **not to be reckoned as sick leave**.

But when does the four year period commence or end? Is it the four years immediately preceding the illness? If the ill teacher returns for a day after the twelve months aggregated period is up, is he then entitled to another twelve months? The answer would appear to be no. The twelve months is in **any** four consecutive years. If he returned for a day he would then only merit additional leave for the difference between 365 days and his previous total for the three preceding years.

11.5 Tuberculosis

(iii) A committee may grant six months on full pay, followed by six months on three-quarters pay, followed by six months on half pay to a

---

[1] Section 3(1)(k)(i).
[2] *TUI Diary & Handbook*, 1996/1997, para. 27.

permanent whole-time teacher suffering from tuberculosis subject to the condition that:

(a) the officer concerned is certified to be undergoing any treatment (*e.g.*) sanatorium treatment recommended by his medical adviser and

(b) this concession will be given only once and that subsequent sick absences even from the same cause will be in accordance with the normal sick leave conditions.

(iv) Payment of full salary may be made, **at the discretion of the Committee**, in respect of absences occasioned by minor indispositions **not exceeding seven days in a year** or **three days in any one instance**. In the case of an absence exceeding three days, payment of salary **shall** be made **only on the production of a certificate** from a duly qualified medical practitioner covering the full period of such absence. The first such certificate must be furnished not later than the fourth day of sick leave.

(v) Absences through illness — without medical certification — for which salary has been paid shall be reckoned for the purpose of calculating the maximum period ranking for sick pay under paragraph 21.2(ii) above, but any such absences for which salary has not been allowed, shall not be so reckoned.

The illness in question may or may not be causing the teacher to be absent from work.

Although the Unfair Dismissals Acts 1977 to 1993 do not apply to officers of a vocational education committee and may not apply to vocational teachers, nonetheless an examination of the criteria found acceptable under this Act may provide useful guide-lines as to how absence because of illness may be regarded.

Clause 6.2 of Memo V.7 provides:

The Minister may at any time if **he considers**

(a) that the **circumstances warrant** such a course **require** a teacher
(b) as **a condition** of continued employment —

(1) to Furnish a medical certificate (which shall include such details as the Minister may require) that he is free from any physical or medical defect likely to impair his usefulness as a teacher, **or**

(2) to present himself for medical examination by a Doctor selected by the Minister, and the Minister may declare such teacher ineligible for further employment as a vocational teacher or he may deem the teacher to have retired. if he fails to comply with the Minister's requirements or

if the medical report under (ii) shows that the teacher is mentally or physically unable to carry out his duties as a teacher."

The Minister could only reach a conclusion that the circumstances warranted such a course on the basis of evidence supplied to him by the VEC and obviously relating to illness or absences.

11.6 Abuse of Sick Leave

In *Lynch v. P. V. Doyle Hotels Ltd.*,[3] a dismissal was held not to be unfair, where the claimant while on sick leave was alleged to be working in another restaurant. In *Murphy v. Tesco Stores Ireland Ltd.*,[4] the claimant furnished medical certificates that she was unfit for work while the respondent alleged she was abroad on holidays. The dismissal was held not to be unfair.

11.7 Absence due to Illness

It seems that absence due to illness may fall into two categories: a) **absence** due to **one continuing problem**; or b) **a series** of persistent short **absences due to different problems**. The steps to be taken by an employer depend on which type of absence occurs.

Absence due to one continuing problem   Dismissals in this category are most often made on the ground of incapacity and the principles set out in *Spencer v. Paragon Wallpapers*[5] and *East Lindsey District Council v. Daubney*[6] apply. These were referred to in *Mooney v. Rowntree Mackintosh*[7] as follows:

> Faced with the problem of prolonged absence due to illness, the Tribunal considered that an employer must seek to (a) **obtain a medical report** on the employee's condition in order that he may (b) **evaluate** the likelihood of the employee returning to work in the reasonable future or of (c) **his ability** of ever being able **to perform the work** which he is employed to do. In any event having acquainted himself with the true medical position at the particular time, he would be in a position to (d) **relate the needs of his business** with the employee's **need to recover** from his illness and make an assessment whether he can any longer keep the employee's position open for him.[8]

---

[3] UD 89/1989.
[4] UD 90/1983.
[5] [1976] I.R.L.R. 373.
[6] [1977] I.R.L.R. 181.
[7] UD 473-476, 478/1980, 4 May 1981.
[8] *Ibid.*

In the *Spencer* case,[9] the EAT held that the Industrial Tribunal had correctly approached the matter by taking into account, the **nature of the illness, the likely length of the continuing absence**, the **employer's need to have the employee's work done** and **the circumstances** of the case.[10]

In *Bevan v. Day Dream Ltd.*,[11] an employee who was refused time off to convalesce, and whose skills were essential to production, only attended for 13 weeks in the 17 weeks prior to dismissal. It was held that the dismissal was not unfair.

Persistent Short Absences In *International Sports Company Ltd. v. Thomson*[12] the EAT held:

> When an employee has an unacceptable level of intermittent absences
> due to minor ailments, what is required is: firstly that there should be a
> (a) **fair review** by the employer of the attendance record and the rea-
> sons for it, and, secondly (b) **appropriate warnings**, after the employee
> has been given an (c) **opportunity to make representations**. If there is
> then (d) **no adequate improvement** in the attendance record, in most
> cases the employer will be justified in treating the persistent absences as
> a sufficient reason for dismissing the employee.[13]

Persistent absence/alcoholism In *Pfizer Chemicals Corporation v. Carroll*,[14] the claimant was employed from 21 March 1977 until 4 December 1980. In 1978 he was absent from work on 53 occasions, in 1979 on 41 occasions and up to October 1980 on 43 occasions certified and uncertified. He was given numerous warnings. The claimant's absences on the evidence before the company were unrelated to one continuing problem whereas he told the tribunal he had a drink problem and that all his unauthorised leave was due to alcohol but this only accounted for 15% of his total absences.

It was held that the dismissal was not unfair. The Tribunal referred to *International Sports Company v. Thompson* above.[15]

11.8 Certified Absence

In *Mooney and Others v. Rowntree Mackintosh Ltd.*,[16] the attendance record of each of the four claimants showed intermittent absences in percentage terms

---

9 Note 5 above.
10 Madden D. and Kerr T., *Unfair Dismissal-Cases and Commentary*, FIE Dublin, 1990.
11 UD 31/1978.
12 [1980] I.R.L.R. 340.
13 *Ibid.*
14 UD 749/1980.
15 Note 12 above.
16 UD 473, 474, 475, 478/1980.

as follows; 1-26.9%; 2-21%; 3-21.9%; 4-31.5% over a four year period. They were each written to on a number of occasions.

Faced with the problem of prolonged absence due to illness, the Tribunal considered that an employer must seek to obtain a medical report on the employee's condition in order that he may evaluate the likelihood of the employee returning to work in the reasonable future or of his ability of ever being able to perform the work which he is employed to do.

Employees, by their records of absence on medical grounds, can show a general debility or proneness to illness. In such cases, absence of an employer's knowledge of the medical condition is less important as the employee might be quite fit at the time his continuing employment is being reviewed. The Tribunal were concerned that the company had not sought medical reports but had relied on their attendance records. The management knew that the absences were on medically certified grounds, and felt that they were aware of the medical position of each claimant.

In the view of the Tribunal they were entitled to consider that the continuance of this level of absenteeism of each claimant was unacceptable. There was substantial grounds justifying the dismissals which were not unfair.

11.9 Liability of Employer

An employer has a liability for illness contacted by an employee during the course of his employment at common law as well as under the Safety, Health and Welfare at Work Act 1989 which imposes a duty (*inter alia*) on an employer to provide systems of work that are planned, organised, performed and maintained so as to be, so far as is reasonably practicable, safe and without risk to health.

Health would include physical and mental aspects and the Barrington Report which preceded the Safety, Health and Welfare at Work Act 1989 states:[17]

> ... technology, working time and payments systems should not be such as would expose the worker to undesirable physical or mental strain.

Teachers having to cope continuously with large members of disruptive and troublesome pupils could be a factor causing mental ill health. In May, 1995 an employer was found liable in the case of *Walker v. Northumberland Co. Co.*[18] for nervous injuries flowing from overwork of a social worker.

---

[17] Recommendation No.2,The Report of the Commission of Inquiry on Safety Health and Welfare at Work, Stationery Office, Dublin, 14 July 1983, p. 95.
[18] [1995] 1 All E.R. 737.

The risk to health from passive smoking in staff rooms appears to be one of the risks that must be guarded against by an employer. Recently, an English asthma sufferer won a ruling that she suffered personal injury to her lungs after office colleagues lit and smoked cigarettes in the room where she worked. The British Social Security Commissioner upheld her claim that the deterioration of her lungs had been caused by an industrial accident and she intends to claim disablement benefit under the Industrial Injuries Act.

On 20 December 1990, a Garda who got hepatitis A, following an altercation in a Garda station with a prisoner who had AIDS, was awarded £51,550 in the High Court. The incident took place in August 1989, the Garda had ensuing sickness in September and hepatitis was confirmed in October. The Garda had a "very minuscule peril" of getting AIDS.[19]

As regards the taking of drugs or alcohol at work, see *Griffin v. Beamish and Crawford.*[20] In *Kavanagh v. Carrick on Suir U.D.C.*[21] where the claimant was found drinking in a public house during working hours, his dismissal was held unfair — it was hasty and impulsive.

In section 26 of the Vocational Education Act 1930, the Minister originally had power to remove from office, by order, any paid officer or servant whom he **considered unfit or incompetent** to perform his duties or "who at any time **refuses or wilfully neglects** to perform his duties or any of them." *Note that duties is now solely plural under section 8 of the Vocational Education (Amendment) Act 1944.* The Minister was given this power in case a VEC was slow to move against an unsatisfactory teacher. Professor O'Sullivan, defending the original power stated:

> I think the Minister should be empowered to act without getting a complaint from the local vocational authority, because he may be dissatisfied with the authority.[22]

In relation to teachers, the failure to perform satisfactorily here would relate solely to teaching.

It was felt that this power should be given to the Minister in a case of inefficiency, where after inspection, inspection by a senior inspector and a second report by a senior inspector (three inspections) a committee refused to remove a teacher, the Minister would be left with no alternative but to hold a public enquiry, although no new facts would be brought to light by doing so.

In all cases where the unfitness or incapacity arose, other than from teaching, it was intended to hold a public inquiry.

---

[19] See *Irish Independent*, 21 December 1990.

[20] UD/1983.

[21] UD 505/1982. See also Madden & Kerr, *Unfair Dismissal, Cases and Commentary* (Dublin, 1990), p. 228.

[22] *Dáil Debates*, 29 May 1930. 253.

11.10 Inquiry

Although there is no requirement to hold a local inquiry, a private investigation must take place. In the Dáil Debate on the 1930 Bill,[23] Professor O'Sullivan in reply to Deputy Fahy offered to bring section 26 into touch with section 103;

> which lays down the condition of the inquiry, and that the Minister should not act in this apparently arbitrary fashion without inquiry of the kind set out under section 103; that he should have power to act if the conduct of the officer was reported as very bad, even though the committee might be prepared to stand over the officer.[24]

The Minister agreed to have the section re-drafted to bring it into line with section 103.

The Minister must be "satisfied" that the officer has failed to perform satisfactorily the duties of the office and in addition be of the opinion that he is **unfit** to hold the office.

The legal implications of being "satisfied" and the fact that it may involve acting judicially have been discussed earlier in relation to section 8(2) removal from office after a local inquiry.

11.11 Minister's Opinion that Officer is Unfit

It was pointed out in the debate on the 1930 Bill that the unfitness need not even be proved. "Unfitness" was a very difficult term to define. No proof was required. The Minister just had to consider that an officer was unfit.[25] The advent of the 1937 Constitution and the guarantees it contains in Article 40.3 can now prevent dismissal without due process.

The Offences Against The State (Amendment) Bill 1940 was referred to the Supreme Court by the President under Article 26 of the Constitution and the main focus of attention was section 4 which provided: "Whenever a Minister of State is of **opinion**." Sullivan C.J.[26] delivering the judgment of the court stated:

> The only essential preliminary to the exercise by a Minister of the powers contained in section 4 is that he should have formed opinions on the matters specifically mentioned in the section . . . having formed such opinions; the Minister is entitled to make an order for detention.[27]

---

[23] *loc. cit.*
[24] At 253.
[25] *Ibid.*
[26] *In re The Offences Against the State (Amendment) Bill* [1940] I.R. 470 at 479.
[27] *loc. cit.*

The judgment also stated that "The validity of such opinions is not a matter that could be questioned in any court." This view is not presently accepted as the correct position. It was followed in *Re Ó Laighléis*[28] and by O'Hanlon J. in *The State(Lynch) v. Cooney*[29] but was rejected on appeal by the Supreme Court.

In *Loftus v. Attorney General*[30] the Supreme Court had considered the power of the Registrar of Political Parties in relation to parties which applied to him for registration, and which in his **opinion** were genuine political parties and organised to contest elections and held *inter alia* that the power conferred on the registrar was not an arbitrary power. O'Higgins C.J. said:

> While he is given a discretion to register or not to register, this is not an unfettered discretion. He is bound to act fairly and judicially in accordance with the Constitution. Accordingly he must consider every application on its merits. . . . If the registrar exercised his powers capriciously, partially or in a manifestly unfair manner, it would be assumed that this could not have been contemplated or intended by the Oireachtas and his action would be restrained and corrected by the courts.[31]

In *The State(Lynch) v. Cooney*[32] the Supreme Court held:

> While the opinion of the former Supreme Court, expressed in 1940 and in 1957, reflected what was then current judicial orthodoxy, judicial thinking has since undergone a change. Decisions given in recent years show that the power of the courts to subject the exercise of administrative powers to judicial review is seen as having a wider reach than that delimited by those decisions of 1940 and 1957.
>
> In particular, it has been established by this court in *McDonald v. Bord na gCon*[33] and *East Donegal Co-Op. v. Attorney General*[34] that the correct approach in considering such questions is first of all to construe the statute. . . . It was in this manner that this court considered the effect of the word "opinion" in section 13(2) of the Electoral Act 1963 . . . in the view of the Court the tests laid down in those cases govern this matter. It is necessary to look at the general object of the legislation. The court was satisfied that the sub-section did not exclude review by the courts and that any opinion formed by the Minister there-

---

28 [1960] I.R. 93.
29 [1982] I.R. 337.
30 [1979] I.R. 221.
31 *Ibid.*, p. 241.
32 *The State(Lynch) v. Cooney* [1982] I.R. 337.
33 [1965] I.R. 217.
34 [1970] I.R. 317.

under must be one which is *bona fide* held and factually sustainable and not unreasonable.[35]

11.12 Inspector's Reports

Obviously, the inspectors reports are central to removal under such a provision as this one under section 8(3). In the *McCafferty* case,[36] the TUI drew the VEC's attention to Circular Letter 3/46 which stated that four unsatisfactory reports of Inspection must take place consecutively, before disciplinary action could be considered by the committee. O'Hanlon J. remarked that if this was a correct interpretation of some agreement agreed to by the Department of Education, "then parents of pupils can derive little solace from it" .

Whether these words prompted it or not, in December 1985 the Department issued Circular Letter No. 43/85 dealing with inspection of schools, colleges and courses under VEC's and the procedure in connection with adverse reports on VEC teachers.[37] It provides for three adverse reports and establishes an Appeal Board consisting of an agreed Chairperson, a representative of the Department, a representative of the VEC and two representatives of the teacher's union.

This is a totally new and very welcome innovation introducing a democratisation which is absent from the original legislation.

11.13 Procedure Prior to Order for Removal

Section 8(3) of the Vocational Education (Amendment) Act 1944 also provides for the procedure prior to the Minister making the order removing from office, *i.e.* that the Minister **may** send a notice to the officer stating the said **opinion** and consider representations made to him by the officer or the VEC.

The author considers that the Courts would regard the notification of the officer as obligatory rather than optional and that a statement of the opinion would not be considered adequate. The grounds would have to be stated with such a degree of certainty that the officer knows exactly what he has to answer. An amendment of this section on such lines is suggested.

O'Flynn and O'Regan v. Mid-Western Health Board and Ors.,[38] is not in point because the medical practitioner's contract expressly provided that he be notified of the reasons for the CEO's belief by registered post. He was given an outline of the complaints alleged against him but no reply was made to his request for further and better particulars. Barr J. granted orders for judicial review and held that the applicants were denied any opportunity of

---

[35] Above n. 23, pp. 360-361.
[36] *The State (Co. Donegal VEC) v. Minister for Education*, unreported, High Court, 12 October 1984.
[37] For C/L No. 43/85. See Appendix 2.
[38] [1989] I. R. 429.

making proper representations as prescribed. Accordingly the first respondent was not entitled to set in train the disciplinary procedure against the applicants and he quashed the first respondent's decision.

The Minister for Education, under section 8(3), may only order removal after consideration of the representations (if any) made to him/her by the holder of the office or the VEC, and the present writer suggests that, on the basis of the decision in *O'Flynn and O'Regan*,[39] the officer would be denied the opportunity of making proper representations if the Minister did not send a notice to him. Indeed it appears that mere notification may not be sufficient.

11.14 Removal by Minister after Conviction of an Offence

Section 8(4) of the Vocational Education (Amendment) Act 1944 gives the Minister an additional power to remove from office by order "Where the holder of an office is convicted of an offence which, in the opinion of the Minister, renders him unfit for such office."

The offence does not have to be one committed in the course of employment, *i.e.* relating to the office, although a conviction for such an offence would obviously come within the section. There is nothing unusual about such a provision. Dismissal from private sector employment on conviction of an offence is a common feature of collective agreements.[40] Convictions for offences like larceny, embezzlement, possession of drugs, indecent assault come to mind as possibly within the scope of this provision.

In the case of *Clarke v. CIÉ*[41] it was alleged that the appellant pleaded guilty to house breaking and larceny, in the Dublin Circuit Court and was given a suspended sentence. Later he was dismissed by the respondent from his job as a railway carriage cleaner. Although the offences to which he pleaded guilty were not connected with his employment, his employer argued that they were entitled to dismiss him even so, and that the company could not reasonably be expected to retain in its employment, and having access to its property and property of its customers, persons convicted of dishonesty.

Company policy was not to employ anyone so convicted and to dismiss any employees convicted of a criminal offence. This policy had existed for many years and was taken over and adapted from older companies. A Rights Commissioner found the dismissal not unfair and Mr. Clarke appealed to the Tribunal.

On behalf of the appellant it was argued that he had already paid his debt to society, that it was his first offence, that he should have been treated leniently and given an opportunity to prove that he would not fall again, and that the company, in effect, set itself up in a judicial capacity and sentenced him a

---

[39] *Ibid.*
[40] Farry & Asmal, *The Law of Collective Agreements In Ireland* (forthcoming).
[41] UD 104/1978.

second time. The Tribunal rejected the argument that he held a position of trust, before cleaners went into carriages they were searched. His job was about as menial as any job could be, and if he was in a position of trust, it was difficult to think of any job that was not.

The Employment Appeals Tribunal determined:

(1) a blanket policy of dismissal upon conviction of an offence unconnected with his employment was at variance with the wider public good. That each case must be decided on its own facts and its merits, and in the present case the conviction was not a substantial ground justifying the dismissal;

(2) the policy of automatic dismissal with the onus on the employee to appeal was contrary to the provisions and spirit of the Unfair Dismissals Act 1977.

In the course of the determination the Tribunal stated:

> This case raises a number of important issues: firstly we must consider questions of penology and the application of the criminal law. It is well known that the Courts may at times exercise leniency to a first offender if he holds steady employment and appears to be contrite about the first offence (as by pleading guilty). In deciding not to send such a first offender to prison, the Courts attach considerable weight to the fact that he holds a job. If sent to prison he would most likely lose his job, and after serving his sentence find it difficult to find a new employer willing to take him on, with the knowledge that he had been in prison. This in time would make it even more difficult for him to spend the rest of his life as a law respecting citizen.
>
> If, on the other hand, an employer dismisses such a person immediately after a court has exercised leniency because of the fact of employment, the intention of the Court might be frustrated. . . . Each case must be decided on its own merits. . . . Regard must be had to the **nature of the offence,** whether it is a **first offence** or one of a series of offences, **how such an offence** though unconnected with his work **will bear on his job**, and the **nature of the position he holds**.[42]

The Tribunal ordered his reinstatement and commented:

> We are satisfied that in the present appeal, given that the offence was not connected with his work, and that it was his first offence, and given the nature of his employment, his conviction in the Circuit Court was not a substantial ground justifying dismissal.[43]

---

[42] *Ibid.*
[43] *Ibid.*

11.15 Gaol Sentence

The Tribunal elaborated on this further, three years later in *Keane and McCarthy v. Limerick Corporation*,[44] two cases which were heard together. Each of the claimants at different times and in totally unconnected and dissimilar circumstances, was charged with assault, convicted and sent to prison. In each case the term of imprisonment was three months. The sentence of each claimant was reduced as a result of good behaviour. One was released after nine weeks and the other after seven weeks.

The Corporation claimed that there had been no dismissals at all, that under the provisions of his contract of employment each claimant was deemed to have terminated his employment when he was sent to gaol. If he had not terminated it, he was deemed to have terminated it on his own agreement. Secondly and by way of alternative, if the claimants had not terminated their contracts of employment, then the Corporation had terminated their contracts for reasonable cause. The Corporation had substantial grounds, that is to say, those mentioned above, *i.e.* that the policy was necessary to preserve the image of the Corporation. Further, it was necessary to protect the Corporation from liability to other employees or to third parties, in the event of persons known to have been sent to gaol for assault and who continued to work for the Corporation on determination of their gaol sentence, on some further occasion assaulting and possible injuring a fellow employee or a third party.

The Tribunal was not satisfied that the claimants accepted employment on the terms that if they went to goal they would thereupon be deemed to terminate their employment. In addition the Tribunal was of the opinion that it was unfair within the meaning of the Unfair Dismissals Act 1977 to dismiss an employee merely because he had received a gaol sentence unless:

(a) **his retention in employment would damage the employer in his business,** or

(b) **the offence reflected on his suitability for the position which he held**.

The Corporation had acted in the belief that it could deem each claimant to have terminated his employment and had erred in that regard. Its true position was that of an employer who had to make up its mind what it should do. In all the circumstances the Tribunal thought that the Corporation probably would not have dismissed the claimants, had it approached the problem from the correct angle.

There did *not* exist substantial grounds justifying the dismissal of the claimants and it was just and equitable that each claimant should be re-instated in his employment.

---

[44] UD 627 and 528/1980 11 May 1981.

11.16 Matters to be Considered

In *Barrett v. Warley College of Technology*,[45] where a senior lecturer with ten year's service was held to be fairly dismissed, the Governors of the College had to bear in mind: their **public duty**, the **reputation of the college**, and the fact that **their students** were many and various in number and came to the college in different ways. In relation to the Governors the Tribunal stated:

> They were concerned with what could be described as the public concern if the matter became known as they felt it was bound to do, now that the letter had been opened and the matter discovered.[46]

The facts were that letters addressed to a person named Fuller were opened by the college. It became apparent that they related to Barrett and were the result of his writing to "Contact" magazine in relation to sexual matters.

The decision to dismiss was influenced by the fact that this was not a first occurrence. The situation was made different by the fact that there had been a previous incident in 1981 when the applicant had been convicted of sending obscene literature through the post.

In *Kavanagh v. Cooney Jennings Ltd.*,[47] the claimant pleaded guilty to charges of indecent assault. He had a number of previous convictions of a similar nature and although the offences were unconnected with his work place, his employer considered that the nature of the charges were such as could interfere with, and damage the firm's relationship with its customers and reduce its acceptability to them. They decided to dismiss him.

The Tribunal considered **the nature of the business, the nature of the firms customers, the position of the employee; and the nature of the offence** and held that the dismissal was not unfair.

In *Reg. v. Powys Co. Co., ex parte Smith*,[48] an assistant teacher, active in the Welsh Language Society, sentenced to nine months imprisonment for conspiring to damage telecommunications installations, was informed by the County Council Staffing Panel that his imprisonment amounted to a repudiation of his contract. He appealed and was offered a further one-year contract by the Council's Appeal Committee. The parent of a child at the school sought to have this new contract quashed but it was held: (1) that the teacher's conduct amounted to a repudiation of his contract, which had, in effect, been accepted by the Council's Staffing Panel; and (2) the Appeals Committee, while having no jurisdiction to make any appointments of teachers, did have jurisdiction to vary the decision of the Staffing Panel and this is what had

---

[45] Industrial Tribunal Case No. 22599/84.
[46] *Ibid.*
[47] UD 175/83.
[48] [1982] 81 L.G.R. 342.

happened. The Appeals Committee had thus been acting within its power in varying the decision of the Staffing Panel even though the effect of the variation was to create a new contract.[49]

11.17 The Minister's *Bona Fides*

While successive Ministers for Education have acted *bona fide* (in good faith), and at times with great forbearance, the parameters of the legal constraints on the exercise of Ministerial powers must be examined in relation to the good faith required by law.

In *Listowel Urban District Council v. McDonagh*,[50] the Supreme Court held:

> (a) that there was no principle which would prevent the Circuit Court from deciding as a preliminary issue, the question raised by the defendant that he was entitled to put in issue the *bona fides* of the sanitary authority in making the order it made; and

> (b) that the exercise of a discretionary statutory power, if effected in bad faith, can be condemned as invalid.

In August 1964 the Council had made an order prohibiting the erection or retention of any temporary dwelling on Greenville Road, Listowel, being of the **opinion** that any such erection or retention thereof would be prejudicial to public health. It was argued that the Court was entitled to enquire into:

(1) what transpired at the meeting at which the order was made,

(2) what views were expressed by the members and officials, and

(3) whether or not the opinion arrived at was *bona fide*.

Ó Dálaigh C.J., delivering the judgment, stated that a discretionary statutory power, if exercised in bad faith, could be condemned as invalid and that *mala fides* was a well recognised ground of challenge. The answer to the principal question put in the case stated, "whether the Court in deciding the appeal was entitled to enquire into whether or not the said opinion was arrived at *bona fide*" was, therefore, yes.[51]

Prior to the Supreme Court decision in *The State (Lynch) v. Cooney*[52] a determination on a question of fact could not be appealed, the courts however, would examine the evidence on which a decision was reached to see if it was *bona fide*.

---

[49] *Cumings v. Birkenhead Corp.* [1971] C.L.Y. 3831 approved.
[50] [1968] I.R. 312.
[51] *Ibid*, p. 318.
[52] [1982] I.R. 337.

In the words of O'Hanlon J. in the High Court:

> not for the purpose of substituting their own decision for the decision
> impugned, but for the purpose of confirming that there were grounds
> which could reasonably support the decision which has actually been
> made.[53]

In *Edwin Barrett v. Sandwell Metropolitan Borough Council*,[54] an English
Industrial Tribunal said;

> It is not for us to substitute our opinion for that of the authorities. We
> have to decide whether they acted reasonably. It is said in the case of
> *British Leyland v. Swift*[55] that there is a range of reasonable responses
> where one employer might decide to dismiss and another employer might
> decide to extend further clemency; they could both be right, or indeed,
> of course, they could both be wrong. **A tribunal** such as this, it is stated,
> **should not interfere unless the decision taken is outside the range of
> those reasonable responses**.[56]

As already pointed out, as a consequence of the Supreme Court decision in
Kerrigan v. An Bord Altranais,[57] when hearing an appeal from disciplinary
proceedings, the High Court, must itself decide contested issues of fact.

11.18 Existence of Facts

Lord Wilberforce in *Secretary of State for Education v. Metropolitan Borough of Thameside*,[58] some six years before the *Cooney* case, had, I think,
gone further along the line toward the Kerrigan decision when he examined
the phrase "if the Secretary of State is satisfied" and commented:

> If a judgment requires, before it can be made, the existence of some
> facts, then although the evaluation of those facts is for the Secretary of
> State alone, the Court must enquire whether those facts exist and have
> been taken into account, whether the judgment has been made on a proper
> self-direction as to those facts, whether the judgment has not been made
> on other facts which ought not to have been taken into account. If these

---

[53] Above n.21 at p. 347.
[54] Case No. 22599/84.
[55] [1981] I.R.L.R. 91.
[56] Above n. 54.
[57] [1990] I.T.L.R. 30 July.
[58] [1976] 3 All E.R. 665, at pp. 681-682.

requirements are not met then the exercise of judgment, however *bona fide* it may be, becomes capable of challenge.[59]

11.19 Consequences of Imprisonment

If a vocational teacher is convicted of a criminal offence and sentenced to a period of imprisonment what are the legal consequences? It appears that such an event would not amount to frustration despite the decision in *Chakki v. United Yeast Co. Ltd.*,[60] wherein it was held to be a potentially frustrating event. According to Von Prondynski:[61]

> . . . frustration can only occur if both parties are innocent in relation to the frustrating event. If the event was caused by either side, it will not amount to frustration. In one case the British E.A.T. has, therefore, held that imprisonment for a criminal offence, since it is caused by the employee committing an offence, cannot frustrate the employment contract. *Norris v. Southampton City Council* [1982] I.C.R. 177.[62]

Frustration can only occur where accident or illness prevent a vocational teacher from performing his duties although:

> Mere absence from work, even for a long time, will not automatically constitute frustration (*Maxwell v. Walter Howard Designs Ltd.*) but if it is clear from the medical evidence that an employee is unlikely to return to work for a considerable time, there must come a point at which the employer is entitled to decide that the employee will not be returning to work and consequently treat the contract as repudiated.[63]

It would seem that imprisonment amounts to repudiatory conduct which may entitle an employer to regard the employment contract as repudiated. The British EAT, in *Norris v. Southampton City Council*,[64] held that imprisonment for a criminal offence caused by an employee committing an offence made it impossible for him to perform his part of the contract, but did not amount to discharge or frustration. It did amount to repudiatory conduct which entitled the employer to treat the contract as repudiated and to fairly dismiss him.

This has been confirmed by a judgment the following year in *R. v. Powys Co. Co., ex parte Smith*,[65] were a teacher sentenced to nine month's imprison-

---

[59] *Ibid.*, pp. 681-682.
[60] [1982] I.C.R.140.
[61] *Employment Law in Ireland* (2nd ed., London), 1989. p. 132.
[62] *Ibid.*
[63] *Selwyn's Law of Employment* (5th ed., London, 1985), p. 233.
[64] [1982] I.C.R. 177.
[65] [1983] 81 L.G.R. 342.

ment for serious offences of arson (who also had a number of previous convictions for offences of criminal damage and obstruction) was held to have repudiated his contract.

The criteria specified in the *Chakki* case[66] were that it was necessary to consider all the circumstances, *e.g.* whether the employer would be acting reasonably in employing a permanent rather than a temporary replacement, the length of time the imprisonment would last, the employees job and the firm's needs.

---

[66] Note 60 above.

CHAPTER 12

Removal by a Vocational Education Committee

Quis custodiet ipsos custodes?

Juvenal

Section 23 of the 1930 Act states:

> (4) A VEC may dismiss any servant of such committee and with the approval of the Minister remove any officer of such committee.

The approval of the Minister required by this section has the same legal significance as the approval of the Minister required under section 23 for appointment as a vocational teacher. Just as an appointment has no legal effect until the Minister approves, a purported removal from office by a VEC has no effect without the approval of the Minister.

12.1 Approval of Minister

In *O'Mahony v. Arklow Urban District Council*,[1] the Supreme Court held that a verbal application to the Minister for his consent was sufficient, where the consent of the Minister was required by a local authority to removal of an officer, and the regulations did not require a written application. In September, 1959, the plaintiff who was Town Clerk of Arklow U.D.C. allegedly committed an irregularity when he made an overpayment of salary to himself out of council funds. In February 1961 he paid his salary by issuing a paying order without authority. On the 6 February 1961 the Wicklow County Manager who was also the Manager of Arklow U.D.C. suspended the plaintiff by an order which stated that since he had absented himself without leave and failed to perform satisfactorily the duties of his office:

> it is hereby decided that he be suspended from the performance of the duties of the office of Town Clerk, while his failure to perform satisfactorily his duties is being enquired into and disciplinary action in regard thereto is being determined.[2]

---

[1] [1965] I.R. 710.
[2] *Ibid.*, p. 714.

Under article 31 of the Local Government (Officers) Regulations 1943 (iii) the application to the Minister for his consent shall state the reasons for the application. The plaintiff was notified that an application was being made to the Minister under section 26 of the Local Government Act 1941 and the Local Government (Officers) Regulations 1943, but in fact no written application was ever made. A copy of the order was sent to the Secretary of the Department. On 3 November 1961 the Minister made an order terminating the plaintiff's suspension and consenting to his removal from office and forfeiture of his salary for the period of his suspension. The plaintiff then applied to the High Court seeking, *inter alia*, a declaration that he had never been validly removed from office and that he was still the holder of it. The court held, however, that the form of application to the Minister for his consent was not invalid. While the Regulations required that written notice be given to the plaintiff, they did not require a written application to the Minister for his consent. The plaintiff was validly removed from office.

The failure of the VEC to seek and obtain the approval of the Minister to the removal of the plaintiff, led to the Supreme Court deciding that the plaintiff in *Carr v. CLVEC*[3] was still an officer of the VEC. Sections 7 and 8 of the Vocational Education (Amendment) Act 1944 relate to the Minister's power to remove, but it could also be argued that they also seem to apply to situations where misconduct, failure to obey, or unfitness are in issue.

12.2 No Grounds Specified

No grounds are specified for removal under section 23(4) but under subsection (5) a VEC is deemed to be a local authority within the meaning of the Local Authorities (Officers and Employees) Act 1926. Under section 23(4) not alone are no grounds specified, there is no procedure or conditions laid down, no pre-condition in the section that an inquiry be held. Yet the Minister's *fiat* is needed. It is in effect removal by the Minister at one remove. This provision seems to indicate that the office is one held at will or pleasure subject only to the application of the principles of natural justice and the approval of the Minister. Significantly a VEC has no authority to remove one of its officers solely on its own. Even though there is a statutory power to remove from office, the Courts will ensure that this power is exercised in a lawful manner.[4]

The significance of a VEC being deemed to be a local authority by virtue of subsection (5) is that section 11(1) of the Local Authorities (Officers and Employees) Act 1926 provides for the suspension of officers and servants by a local authority or the Minister on the grounds of failure to perform satisfactorily[5] (see section 7 Vocational Education (Amendment) Act 1944) and un-

---

[3] Supreme Court, *ex tempore*, 17 October 1991.
[4] *Osgood v. Nelson* [1872] L.R. 5 H.L. 636, Chap. 4 above.

fitness. Section 2(1)(b) provides that in the Act the expression "office to which this Act applies" means and includes the chief executive officer under every local authority, and every office and every employment (not being an office or employment as a teacher) under a local authority, the qualifications for which are wholly or in part professional or technical.

12.3 Background to Section

In the Dáil Debate on the Committee Stage of the Vocational Education Bill 1930, Professor Thrift said[6] that he thought it would be a good thing, even though a dismissal could only take place with the approval of the Minister:

> that some regulations should be laid down for the security of those who are engaged — that a form of procedure must be gone through in any case of dismissal."

He suggested that this might be covered by regulations, rather than appear in the Act. He thought that it should not be possible that a dismissal could take place without due notice or that the person who was threatened with dismissal should not be given an opportunity of defending himself. It would be possible under the strict letter of sub-section (4) at any meeting of the council without any notice whatever, — it might be a snap meeting, to dismiss any particular servant or officer and the only safeguard was that it could only be done "with the approval of the Minister." Granted it was a very good one.

The Minister, Professor O'Sullivan, replied that what the Deputy really meant was that, without a rather elaborate procedure, for instance, a hall porter could not be dismissed. He continued:

> Take the ordinary officer or even the ordinary servant. After all, they have a certain tenure of office. They must get notice. They have their remedy if they do not. The notice varies in the different cases. Take the ordinary person who is employed subject to a month's notice. I do not know on what terms a hall porter or a person of that type may be employed. What the Deputy suggests is really to give him longer than the ordinary month's notice. It would amount in practice to that. *What is aimed at in this section is not to give rights of that particular kind. The ordinary officer has a long tenure and he has his remedy undoubtedly. I cannot see how he could be effectively dismissed without the thing being fully ventilated.*[8]

---

5 See s.7 Vocational Education (Amendment) Act 1944.
6 *Dáil Debates*, 29 May 1930, c. 243.
7 *loc. cit.*
8 Note 4, above cl. 243-244.

The Minister was asked if he thought the staff were sufficiently safeguarded and he replied that he thought so, but that he would look further into the matter if the Deputy wished. The section was then agreed to. Later while discussing section 26 Mr. Fahy stated:

> We have been considering subsection (4) of section 23 with regard to the Minister's powers, which he says are not absolute, and that taken in conjunction with section 44 of the Local Government Act 1926 gives plenty of scope for removing from office people who are unfit. Any officer removed from office cannot get compensation if removed for misconduct or incapacity.[9]

12.4 The Wording of section 23

The wording of section 23 is of crucial importance. Section 23, like section 6 of the Police Forces Amalgamation Act 1925, does provide that a VEC may remove from office without specifying any reasons for doing so. If it did not include words indicating that the office is one held at pleasure, and adopting the *dictum* of O'Higgins C.J. in *Garvey v. Ireland*,[10] the fact that such words have not been used could not be disregarded. The Oireachtas were quite cognisant of the different types of office and had specifically created offices removable at pleasure in previous legislation. In the same case Henchy J. stated:

> It must be admitted, however, that the absence from the statute of any express restriction of the Government's power to remove a Commissioner from office at any time, must be held to connote a discretion so wide that it is only limited by what the law, as it must now be interpreted in the light of the Constitution deems indispensable, and it must be deemed to be a tacit assumption of the law that it will not require the discretion to be exercised in a manner that will be inimical to the common good.[11]

12.5 Construction of section 23

O'Higgins C. J. stated in effect that the subsection should be construed *strictissimi juris* and continued:

---

[9] *Dáil Debates,* May 29 1930, cl. 253.
[10] [1981] I.R. 75. Henchy J. at p.102 felt that the absence of an express restriction connoted a wide discretion.
[11] At p.102.

nor do I think that one can imply, from the words that are used, a meaning which would abrogate principles of law or rights which would otherwise apply. So to construe the sub-section would be contrary to settled principles of construction of statutes.[12]

The office was not one tenable merely at pleasure and **the rules of natural justice applied when it was proposed to exercise the power conferred by the sub-section to remove the holder from such office**. In the event the Supreme Court held that the guarantee of fair procedures provided by Article 40.3 of the Constitution applied to the exercise by the Government of the power of removal conferred by section 6, subsection 2 of the Act of 1925.

It could be suggested that if the office of a vocational teacher was one removable at pleasure there would have been no need to specify statutory grounds for removal from office. But the statutory grounds only apply for removal by the Minister.

It is suggested that **cause** for removal under section 23 of the Vocational Education Act 1930 might arise after suspension and non-local inquiry under section 7 of the 1944 Act, in cases where serious misconduct, failure, unfitness or refusal, have been admitted or where it transpires that a teacher does not have the qualifications which he was required to have for appointment.

12.6 Redundancy

In the English case of *Pearce v. University of Aston (No. 2)*,[13] **the only ground for dismissal provided by the statute was "good cause"**; no provision was made for dismissal on the ground of redundancy. The statute was expressly incorporated into the lecturer's contracts of employment and they enjoyed membership of the university by virtue of being employed as full time teaching staff.

If the notices of redundancy were effective to terminate their status as full-time teaching staff they would also cease to be members of the university. This would remove their security of tenure in a way which was not permitted by dismissal for "good cause only" under the statute. There was, therefore, no power to terminate the contracts of employment, assuming their independence existence, because this would be a breach of the University's domestic law (statutes).

Under the English Education Reform Act 1988, university statutes must now provide for dismissal of academic staff for "good cause" or for "redundancy".

Under the Vocational Education Act 1930 "good cause" is **not** the only ground for removal from office. Section 23 does not specify any grounds

---

[12] *Ibid.* p. 96.
[13] [1991] 2 All E.R. 499.

whatever and, therefore, could encompass this ground. According to Finlay C.J. in *Carr v. CLVEC*[14] if there was no vacancy which could be offered to the plaintiff in accordance with the terms of her contract, the legal situation quite clearly was that, provided the VEC could satisfy the Minister of that fact and that it was proper and reasonable for them to take up that situation, they could have obtained his authority to make her redundant. "But no attempt was made to negotiate with this lady so as to change her contract."

These remarks, although stated *obiter*, imply that subject to negotiation (and presumably agreement) redundancy may be a ground for removal under section 23.

12.7 Board of Management Recommendations

A recommendation by a school Board of Management for the re-instatement of a suspended teacher would not preclude the VEC from considering whether to remove him/her.[15]

A VEC alone, with the approval of the Minister is responsible for removal under section 23 and while it may act on the recommendation of a Board of Management, consideration of the recommendation must be by way of re-hearing. A VEC could not merely consider whether or not the Board's decision could reasonably be up-held.[16] In America teachers have been held to be validly dismissed for engaging in subversive activity and for making seditious utterances.[17]

Commenting on a similar provision under section 26(2) of the Local Government Act 1941, Street[18] points out:

> it would appear on the wording of this section that the grounds on which the Minister may authorise the local authority to remove are not confined to those specified in s.25 *supra*,

(*viz.* the statutory grounds of unfitness, refusal to obey, or misconduct) he also queries whether the legislature intended to confer on the Minister:

> the power to do *per alium* what he could not do *per se*, and without limit.[19]

---

[14] *Ex tempore* judgment, Supreme Court, 17 October 1991.

[15] *Honeyford v. Bradford Metropolitan City Council, The Times,* 14 November, 1985.

[16] *R. v. Governors of Litherland High School, The Times*, 4 December 1982, C.A.

[17] *Board of Education v. Jewett*, 21 Cal. App. 2d. 64 and *Re Albert's Appeal*, 372 Pa. 13, 92 A2d. 663.

[18] Street H.A., *Local Government* (Dublin, 1955), p. 270.

[19] *Ibid.*, p. 270.

12.8 Composition of VEC

A meeting of a VEC at which a proposal to remove a vocational teacher from office is considered or passed, must not be attended by persons who are managers or members of the Board of Management of the school in which the teacher involved works. If they were to do so, any resolution could be quashed because of the possibility of bias. No man can be a judge in his own case. (*Nemo iudex in causa sua.*)

In *Hannam v. Bradford City Council*,[20] it was held that such a decision would be quashed despite the fact that the members in question had not attended the Board of Management meeting. The Governors of a school did not cease to be an integral part of the body whose action was being impugned and it made no difference that they did not personally attend the meeting of the School Governors at which a decision to remove was initially taken.

12.9 Removal Only in Accordance with Law

The parameters of the power under section 23 are not as extensive as at first might appear. Removal can only be for genuine or legitimate reason and cannot be arbitrary or capricious.

Article 40.3.1° provides:

> The State guarantees in its laws to respect, and, as far as practicable, by its laws to defend and vindicate the personal rights of the citizen.

Article 40.3.2° provides:

> The State shall, in particular, by its laws protect as best it may from unjust attack and, in the case of injustice done, vindicate the life, person, good name, and property rights of every citizen.

The Supreme Court in *Garvey v. Ireland*,[21] (above) held that the guarantee of fair procedures provided by Article 40.3 applied to the exercise by the Government of the power of removal from office of the Garda Commissioner conferred by section 6(2) of the Police Forces Amalgamation Act 1925. This subsection stated "every Commissioner . . . may at any time be removed by the Executive Council"

The guarantees in this Article apply equally to the removal of a VEC officer by a VEC under section 23 of the 1930 Act.

In *Devanney v. Dublin Board of Assistance*,[22] Gavan Duffy J. commented:

---

[20] [1970] 2 All E.R. 690.
[21] Note 8 above.
[22] [1949] 83 I.L.T.R. 113.

. . . Article 31 Local Government (Officers Regulations) Order 1943 would empower the Board, with the consent of the Minister, to remove from office the holder of an office, but whereas the Minister himself can remove an officer only on the statutory grounds laid down in section 25 of the Act of 1941, Article 31 is silent as to the grounds which will justify a local authority in resorting to the extremely grave measure of throwing an officer out of the service-to the uninitiated an amazing omission — not that the officer is left unprotected, but that the protection is left too uncertain, in view of the most express restrictions on the Minister's own powers of removal.[23]

(*Note*: This judgment did not refer to Article 40.3.1° or 2° of the Constitution.)

In 1929 when the Vocational Education Act was being drafted, section 15 of the draft submitted to the Department of Finance[24] stated that section 11 of the Local Authorities (Officers and Employees) Act 1926 would be interpreted to refer to and to include every officer and servant of a committee.

During discussions, the Department of Education stated that they were advised that officers included executives, and teaching staff. The legal advisor to the Department of Local Government, commented that he did not like the section. The intention seemed to be in effect to give the Minister power to remove officers, and it would be better to do so expressly. The first portion of the section he commented:

is unnecessary. These committees will clearly be local authorities within the Local Authorities (Officers and Employees) Act 1926 and section 11 of that Act will, therefore, apply to them in any case. The meaning of the Minister "discontinuing the recognition" of an officer is obscure.

The Department of Education agreed to the omission of this section.[25]

12.10 Demotion and Re-assignment

Demotion from a position which involves a substantial reduction in salary, in effect, constitutes removal from office. Being moved from one position to another, does not constitute removal from office, unless the teacher is required to teach subjects for which he is not qualified, or required to undergo training at his own expense, and there is a reduction in salary.

---

[23] *Ibid.,* p. 118.
[24] S84/133/29.
[25] Department of Finance Memo, 7 October 1929.

12.11 Level of Teaching

In general, a Board of Management has power, within reasonable limits, to change the assignment of a permanent teacher so long as the work assigned is of an equivalent grade to that for which he was permanently appointed and it is in a subject area in which the teacher is qualified and was appointed to teach. Level of Teaching may be important in relation to promotion, *e.g.* the TUI in the past have negotiated promotion posts for those on College Teacher grade based on more than 40% of teaching time at third level as specified in paragraph 1.4(a) of Agreed Report 5/82.

Appendix G of Memo V.7 deals with eligibility for promotion of Class III teachers, who devote not less than 55% of their teaching time to courses the entry standard to which is the Leaving Certificate or its equivalent.

On the other hand a number of Primary teachers have claimed discrimination in relation to the level of teaching to which they have been assigned. See *Board of Management, Old Bawn Community School v. Le Lu,*[26] where it was claimed, unsuccessfully that a school management discriminated in contravention of the Employment Equality Act 1977, in that it omitted to afford certain experience, which the applicant considered relevant for promotion purposes, and failed also to appoint her to an "A" post of responsibility. See also *Mc Guinness v. St. Brigid's National School, Foxrock*[27] and *Moran v. St. Catherine's N.S. Bishopstown Ave, Cork.*[28]

12.12 Right to Grade

The right to continue in the same teaching grade as that appointed to, has been recognised in the American courts where the appointment has been made under a tenure law. See *Kennedy v. Board of Education*[29] and *Rosenthal v. Orleans Parish School Board.*[30] A Board of Management does not have the power to unilaterally vary, or make a fresh contract after a vocational teacher has tenure.

12.13 Transfer

The courts may order that a transfer be rescinded, even where there has been no reduction in pay or grade. In *Finot v. Pasadena City Board of Education,*[31] a re-assignment made solely because the teacher insisted on wearing a

---

[26] E.E. 4/1986.
[27] E.E. 3/1979.
[28] E.E. 12/1980.
[29] 82 Cal. 483 22P 1042.
[30] La. App. 214 S0 2nd 203.
[31] 250 Cal. App 2d 189 58 Cal. Reptr. 520.

beard while teaching, was rescinded by the courts (see also chapter 7, on Transfers).

12.14 Dismissal on Notice

In *Carr v. CLVEC*[32] the question arose whether the provisions of sections 7 and 8 of the 1944 Act of themselves, not merely raised the implication of an office enduring throughout the working life of the office-holder, but also prohibited by implication, the incorporation in **"a contract of employment"** of provisions, permitting the termination of the relationship otherwise than on statutory grounds and in accordance with the statutory procedures.

The case argued for the plaintiff was that she was employed by the VEC under a contract dated 20 December 1971 and that this contract was for life or until pensionable age.

Mr. Justice Murphy questioned how the plaintiff could contend that she was entitled to be employed for life when she, in fact, relied on a contract containing a provision "The appointment is terminable by three months notice in writing on either side."

The plaintiff sought to overcome this obvious problem by asking rhetorically, why the 1944 Act:

> should provide for removal in special events established by special, and frequently costly procedures, if in fact the employment might be terminated by the giving of an appropriate period of notice and without any suggestion of misconduct less still the establishment of such misconduct.[33]

It was contended that sections 7 and 8 provided an exhaustive code for the termination of the employment of office-holders. Against that, it was argued that the statutory provisions dealt only with misconduct and unfitness and that there was nothing to prevent the parties themselves, agreeing upon terms providing for the cessation of the engagement by the giving of a period of notice acceptable to both of them.

Mr. Justice Murphy thought that: "it might also be said that the statutory provisions related to the removal of an officer by the Minister rather than the termination of the relationship by either *the employer or employee* and he believed "that this agreement is well founded".[34] In his view it was impossible to conclude that it was *ultra vires* the parties to the contract, to incorporate a provision for the termination thereof by three months notice in writing

---

[32] Unreported, High Court, 22 May 1987.
[33] *Ibid.*
[34] *Ibid.*, p. 7.

by either of them. He did not advert to the power of removal by a VEC under section 23(4).

12.15 Author's View

von Prondzynski states:

> It is not entirely easy to define an office-holder. He may work under a contract of employment, but the legal basis of his position is something else, or at any rate something additional.[35]

To some commentators, there is nothing ambivalent about the status of a vocational teacher. He/she is an officer removable at will by the VEC and for cause by the Minister. Many do not subscribe to the duality theory (*i.e.* that one can be an officer and an employee at the same time in relation to the same functions) and others argue that in the light of the Supreme court decision in *Glover v. BLN*,[36] (*post*) the court was correct to have regard to the "contract" or conditions of service. If a vocational teacher is a statutory employee to whom the provisions of the VE Acts are applied there is no such duality involved.

There is a significant difference between the holder of an office as in the *Glover* case and the holder of a statutory office as in the *Carr* case, and the present author is of the opinion that this difference must be taken into account when considering "conditions of service or office" and that the conditions or "contract" in the case of a statutory office cannot be considered in isolation.

The description of the relationship as "a contract of employment" does less than justice to the statutory basis of a vocational teacher's employment as an officer, although it was central to the "statutory employee" basis on which the Carr case was decided in the High Court.[37] Vocational teachers are appointed by virtue of statutory powers. Their salaries are determined by the approval of the Minister under statutory authority. The provisions of the Vocational Education Acts applicable to officers are applied to them. They are treated as officers of a public local authority who may be removed by virtue of statutory powers and also on statutory grounds. There is also provision under section 105(1) of the Vocational Education Act 1930 that a local inquiry may be held in relation to the performance by an officer of his/her duties as such officer. None of these matters arise from contract in the case of an officer.

Nor, indeed, would I agree that sections 7 and 8 of the 1944 Act provide

---

[35] *Employment Law in Ireland* (London, 1989) at p. 41.
[36] Note 42 below.
[37] Note 31 above.

an exhaustive code for the termination of office, tempting as it is to do so, because of the VEC power of removal under section 23 of the 1930 Act.

12.16 Contract

A significant difference between Irish and British law in this area is that British tenure statutes generally incorporate, the terms or conditions of appointment, while the Vocational Education Act 1930 does not.

In *Regina v. Hull University Visitor,*[38] the statute provided:

> **Subject to** the terms of his appointment no member . . . shall be removed from office save upon the grounds specified in clause 2 of this section.[39]

The Court of Appeal held that this showed clearly that the section of the statute contemplated that individual contracts of employment would contain provisions for termination in circumstances other than those set out in the statute. (In the Irish context it could be suggested that section 23 Vocational Education Act 1930 has the like effect.)

The conjoint effect of the universities' statutes, and the letter of appointment was that either the University or Mr. Page could terminate his tenure of office on giving three months notice and that in addition the university could terminate for "good cause".

It is submitted that non-incorporation of terms or conditions of appointment in Ireland has a vital consequence that the contents of such terms or conditions must therefore accord with the primary source, *viz.* the incepting statute.

In *Thomas v. University of Bradford,*[40] the plaintiff was appointed a lecturer in sociology and thus became an employee under a contract of service, the holder of an office in the membership of the university, and a corporator. The contract of employment included a term that her employment and her status as a member of the university were co-terminous.

In *Gilheaney v. The Revenue Commissioners,*[41] Costello J. decided that the legal basis for the applicant's appointment to the civil service was an administrative act made by the exercise of statutory powers and was not contractual. In the absence of evidence of a clear intention, the Minister in making the applicant's appointment had no intention of entering into a contractual relationship with him.

---

[38] [1992] I.C.R 67.

[39] *Ibid.,* p. 77.

[40] [1987] ICR 245.

[41] Unreported, High Court, October 4 1995. The absence of intention to contract was also central in *R. v. Civil Service Appeal Board* [1988] 3 All E.R. 686.

12.17 Conditions of Service

The term "conditions of service" is not defined but it bears a **superficial resemblance** to "conditions of employment".[42] In *McClelland v. N.I. General Health Services Board*,[43] where there was a contract of service, it was held that the employment had not been validly terminated because it was terminable only as provided in her conditions of service, which were exhaustive in that respect and accordingly, a power to terminate her employment by reasonable notice would not be implied.

In *Garvey v. Ireland*,[44] at first instance in the High Court, McWilliam J. held that the relationship was **equivalent** to that between master and servant under a contract of employment which was intended to endure for an indefinite period, but the Supreme Court in *Glover v. BLN*,[45] decided that the issue of liability depended upon the terms of the contract between the parties, whether the plaintiff was the holder of an office or an employee. This seems to imply the prospect of discerning terms from both the statutes and conditions of appointment and considering their conjoint effect as in *Regina v. Hull*.[46] The *Carr* case was some six years after *Garvey*.

12.18 Contractual Nature of Office

Traditionally there have been two views about the nature of how a public office is held. One view was that it was an appointment under a statute; the other view that it was an appointment under a contract of employment. In *O'Connell v. Listowel UDC*,[47] it was argued that there was no contractual relationship, that the appointment was made in accordance with statutory requirements and on the Minister's *fiat*, that salary was paid under a statute and could be sued for under statute but not under contract. See *Cox v. ESB*,[48] and *The State (Minister for Local Government) v. District Mental Hospital, Ennis*.[49] It was also suggested that the officers of the Council were its servants or agents with regard to third parties, but that the relationship in fact was not contractual.[50] In the event no decision on this point was made because the case was decided on the doctrine of quasi contract.

In *Glover v. BLN*,[51] the Supreme Court held that the issue of liability

---

[42] H.A. Street, *Local Government* (Dublin, 1955), p. 256.
[43] [1957] 2 All E.R. 129.
[44] Note 8 above.
[45] [1973] I.R. 388.
[46] Note 25 above.
[47] *O'Connell v. Listowel UDC* [1957] Ir Jur. Rep. 43.
[48] [1943] I.R. 231 (SC).
[49] [1939] I.R. 258.
[50] *Doran v. Guardians of Waterford Union* [1903] 37 ILTR 158 and *Woods v. Dublin Corporation* [1931] I.R. 396.
[51] Note 43 above at p. 414.

depended upon the terms of the contract between the parties, whether the plaintiff was the holder of an office or an employee.

In the earlier High Court hearing, Mr. Justice Kenny accepted that a person who holds an office may have a contract under which he may be entitled to retain it for a fixed period and he referred to the decisions of the Supreme Court in *O'Brien v. Tipperary Board of Health*[52] and in *Carvill v. Irish Industrial Bank Ltd.*[53]

Walsh J. delivering the judgment of the Supreme Court in *Glover v. BLN*[54] on appeal stated:

> . . . unlike the present case, *Ridge v. Balwin* was not governed by the terms of a contract. In my view **once the matter is governed by the terms of a contract between the parties, it is immaterial whether the employee concerned is deemed to be a servant or an officer,** in so far as the distinction may be of relevance, depending on whether the contract is a contract for services or a contract of service. In the present case it is immaterial whether the plaintiff is an officer or a servant of his employers, and in my view the case does not fall to be decided upon that distinction but rather upon the actual terms of the contract. . . .[55]

In *Cresswell v. Inland Revenue,*[56] it is quite clear that the judge was thinking in terms of contract in relation to payment for work and he actually cited Lord Cowie in *Laurie v. B.S.C.*[57] which also treats of entitlement based on contract, despite the fact that the plaintiff was an officer, albeit a contract in which the Crown expressly reserved the right to change his conditions of service at any time. His conditions of service also acknowledged that officers held their appointments at the pleasure of the Crown and that they could not, therefore, demand a period of notice as of right, where their appointments were terminated. Nevertheless a period of notice would normally be given as specified.[58]

12.19 Tenure

Tenure is a distinct matter from conditions of service — *per* Gavan Duffy J. in *Devanney v. Dublin Board of Assistance.*[59] Tenure relates to how an office is held, conditions are the terms upon which it is held, *e.g.* remuneration,

---

[52] [1938] I.R. 761.
[53] [1968] I.R. 325.
[54] Note 43 above.
[55] *Ibid.,* pp. 427-428
[56] [1984] I.C.R. 508.
[57] Unreported, 23 February 1978.
[58] Note 55 above at p. 521.
[59] [1949] ILTR 113.

entitlements, pension rights, sickness, holidays, degree of notice to be given, etc. Meredith J., in *Cahill v Attorney General,*[60] points out that there is a difference in the prepositions used in technical descriptions. An office is said to be held by a tenure, but upon terms and conditions. Tenure of office cannot be changed. In the U.S. it has been held that some tenure laws do not secure any definite position, see *Alexander v. School District,*[61] but this is not so in relation to Irish vocational teachers.

If a vocational teacher is an officer, the office is held by the tenure in the statute which created it. Therefore, grounds for removal must come within the ambit of the grounds specified in the statute or those agreed by the parties. Conditions of service can be changed, *e.g.* remuneration or pension, but it is contended that tenure may only be changed by amending legislation.

Referring to *Cahill v. Attorney General,*[62] as an authority on conditions of service, Street comments[63] "it by no means follows that the right of an officer to tenure of an office is not a condition of his service."

12.20 The *Carr* case

If a vocational teacher holds an office, s/he does so on the terms of the statute which created the office or which regulates VECs, the authority from whom s/he holds office. In each case the Vocational Education Act 1930 as amended.

If a vocational teacher is an officer s/he is an officer removable at will although statutory grounds for suspension and removal by the Minister are provided. It is an office where removal by the Minister must be justified, and grounds, other than those which come within the ambit of the statute cannot be added as statutory grounds. The powers of a VEC and the Minister are subject to the Acts. If a vocational teacher is a statutory employee s/he is employed on the terms of the employment contract and also on the terms of the Vocational Education Acts which are incorporated into the contract.

12.21 Nature of Office

An office held at pleasure is a totally different type of office to one dismissible for cause. The holder need not have done anything wrong or need to be given a reason for removal. Perhaps this is why the *fiat* of the Minister is need by a VEC acting under section 23(4). Despite the power of removal from office by a VEC under section 23(4) the plaintiff in *Carr v. CLVEC,*[64] could only have been removed on statutory grounds or by agreement, subject

---

[60] [1925] I.R. 70 at p. 80.
[61] 84 Or. 172, 164 p. 711.
[62] [1925] 1 I.R. 70, 80.
[63] H.A. Street , *Local Government* (Dublin, 1955) at p. 257.
[64] Note 3 and 43 above.

to the rules of natural and constitutional justice. See Natural Justice and *Garvey v. Ireland,*[65] and *Mooney v. An Post*[66] where Keane J. stated that, under Irish law, a person holding office at pleasure may be entitled to be informed of the reasons for his removal from office.

Conditions of service cannot create new grounds for removal from a statutory office. If it were so it would clearly frustrate the intention of Parliament. Section 23 of the 1930 Act is, to some degree, an equivalent provision to section 26 of the Local Government Act 1941 which provides that the appropriate Minister may empower the relevant local authority to remove from office with the consent of the Minister, the holder of an office and **may** define the procedure to be adopted and the conditions to be fulfilled in relation to the exercise of the power so conferred.

12.22 Tenure

Nor is there a provision in the Vocational Education Acts that an officer shall hold office on terms specified by a VEC. There is no equivalent to section 112(2) of the British Local Government Act 1972 which states that an officer appointed under subsection (1) "shall hold office on such reasonable terms and conditions, including conditions as to remuneration, as the local authority appointing him think fit". In England the concurrence of the responsible Minister is only required for the removal of certain officers.

12.23 Conditions of Service

In the case of vocational teachers who are officers, conditions of service cannot alter or be at variance with the statutory provisions and it is suggested that they are null and void in so far as they seek to do so. Therefore, it is suggested that provisions with regard to periods of notice must be construed in accordance with the provisions of the Acts.

The conditions of service specify the minimum period of notice to be given by an officer on resigning his office and the minimum amount of notice to be given to him before removal. They do not create a power to remove from office without cause. This already exists under section 23(4). In one respect they specify the equivalent of the minimum notice required to be given to and by others under the Minimum Notice and Terms of Employment Act 1973 and Terms of Employment (Information) Act 1994.

In *Carr v. CLVEC,*[67] the Supreme Court made a declaration that the plaintiff was still an officer of the VEC, in the position of a principal of a school within their jurisdiction and entitled to payment of salary from the date on

---

[65] Note 8 above.
[66] Unreported, High Court, 11 February 1994 and Chapter 10 *supra.*
[67] Supreme Court, *ex tempore*, 17 October 1991.

which she was originally suspended less credit for payments. The court remitted the ascertainment of damages back to the High Court which ordered[68] that the net balance due to the plaintiff was £147,477.42 (£252,009.33 gross). Following the Supreme Court ruling Ms Carr had been reinstated on the VEC payroll from November 1991.

[68] Mr. Justice Barron, 11 July 1996.

CHAPTER 13

Local Inquiry

Il est plus necessaire d'etudier les hommes que les livres.

La Rochefoucauld, *Maximes Posthumes*, No. 550

Section 105(1) of the Vocational Education Act 1930 provides:

> The Minister **may** at any time cause an inquiry (in this Act referred to as a Local Inquiry) to be held in relation to the performance by a VEC of its duties under the 1930 Act, or the performance by an officer or servant of a VEC of his duties as such an officer or servant (as the case may be), and for that purpose **may** appoint **an officer of the Minister** to hold such local inquiry.

13.1 Obligation on the Minister

The word **may** in the phrase "The Minister may at any time" indicates that the Minister has a discretion with regard to holding a local inquiry because there is no indication elsewhere in the statute that it is meant to be imperative.[1] This construction was affirmed when the application of this section to the performance of duties by a vocational teacher arose in *Collins v. Co. Cork VEC.*[2] In this case, Chief Justice Finlay gave the following helpful exposition of the combined effect of the different provisions of the relevant statutes, taking into account section 105 Vocational Education Act 1930 in conjunction with sections 7 and 8 Vocational Education (Amendment) Act 1944:

> There is an obligation on the Minister upon such report of suspension by a VEC under section 7(2) Vocational Education (Amendment) Act 1944 being made to him or her to inquire into the alleged grounds of the suspension.
>
> There **is not** an obligation on the Minister to make that inquiry in any particular **way** and he may either make inquiries through his servants or agents in the ordinary way or he may exercise the powers conferred on him by section 105 of the Act of 1930 and direct a local inquiry, commonly called a sworn inquiry.

---

[1] See Crompton J. in *Re Newport Bridge* (1859) 2 E.& E. 377, 380.
[2] Unreported, High Court, 27 May 1982, Supreme Court, 18 March 1983.

If the Minister as the result of either form of inquiry is satisfied that no disciplinary action is necessary or that disciplinary action **less** than removal from office is necessary, he can accordingly direct.[3]

The need to hold an inquiry was highlighted in *Ridge v. Baldwin,*[4] where it was argued that an inquiry was essential:

Even where a case seems plain on the face of it, an inquiry cannot be dispensed with . . . if a barrister were reported to have been drunk in court, the Benchers would not act without an inquiry. Again, a man apparently drunk in the gutter may be a diabetic who has run out of insulin.[5]

See also *Franklin v. Minister of Town and County Planning.*[6]

"May appoint an officer of the Minister"   The meaning of the word "may" here is not permissive or discretionary, as was the case with the earlier use of the word in this section. In effect, the person appointed has to be an officer of the Minister.[6a] The Minister is not empowered to appoint anyone else other than an officer of his/her own. In *Julius v. Bishop of Oxford,*[7] Lord Blackburn stated that enabling words are construed as compulsory whenever the object of the power is to effectuate a legal right and Cockburn C. J. in *R.v. Bishop of Oxford*[8] is cited by Bennion[9] "So long ago as the year 1693, it was decided in the case of *R. v. Barlow*[10] that when a statute authorises the doing a thing for the sake of justice or the public good, the word 'may' means 'shall' and that rule has been acted upon to the present time."

13.2 Costs of Inquiry

Section 105(2) Vocational Educational Act 1930 provides:

Where the Minister causes a local inquiry to be held he **may**, if he so thinks fit, make an order directing the costs **incurred** in relation to such inquiry to be paid by the vocational education committee concerned, and any such order shall certify the amount of such costs and the amount so certified shall be a debt due by such committee to the Minister and

---

3   See also Suspension *ante.*
4   [1964)]A.C. 40
5   *Ibid.,* p.61
6   [1948] A.C. 87 at pp.102-103.
6a See, however, n.19 post.
7   (1880) 5 A.C. 214, 241.
8   (1879) 4 Q.B. D. 245, 258.
9   Bennion, p. 285.
10 (1693) 2 Salk, 609.

shall be recoverable by the Minister from such committee as a civil debt in a court of competent jurisdiction.[11]

"may" here is discretionary. *Halsbury's, Laws of England,*[12] cites *Re Wood's Application*[13] where it was held that that the discretion of the Secretary of State as to costs arising out of a Town Planning inquiry would not be controlled by *mandamus.*

"Incurred in relation to such inquiry" does not just relate to the Ministers own costs but also to the costs of the parties involved. In section 250(5) of the British LGA 1972 the Minister can make an order as to the parties by whom the costs are to be paid, and every such order may be made a rule of the High Court on the application of a party named in that order.

The phrase "incurred **in relation to**" is wide enough to cover the costs of legal advice and assistance as well as legal representation at the inquiry. There is no provision as regards the granting of legal representation. Hogan & Morgan,[14] referring to the social welfare appeals system, point out: "While constitutional justice does not require legal representation in all cases, the failure on the part of the appeals officer to permit representation in an appropriate case would probably amount to an unreasonable exercise of his discretion." In *Gallagher v. Revenue Commissioners,*[15] Blaney J. held that, because the plaintiff faced numerous serious charges which could result in his dismissal, it would be inconsistent with his right to fair procedures to deny him representation by counsel at an oral hearing.

Under the provisions of section 83 Local Government Act 1941, costs may be awarded against a local authority in respect of an inquiry held on the direction of the Minister for the Environment and, under section 6 of the Tribunals of Inquiry (Evidence) (Amendment) Act 1979, the Chairman of the tribunal may certify that all or part of the costs of a person appearing before a tribunal should be paid by another party.

The English Legal Advice and Assistance Act 1972 section 1 provides for legal advice and assistance in connection with statutory inquiries for persons who come within a means test. A free legal advice service is available through the TUI to their members.

Section 105(3) of the Vocational Education Act 1930 provides:

> (3) Any moneys due by a vocational education committee to the Minister under this section shall be paid by such committee out of its vocational education fund.

---

[11] Section 105(2).
[12] Vol. 28, para 1386.
[13] [1952] 3P&CR 238 DC.
[14] Hogan & Morgan, *Administrative Law* (London 1986) at p. 151.
[15] Unreported, High Court, 11 January 1991, Blaney J.

(4) For the purposes of this section the costs of any local inquiry shall be deemed to include such reasonable expenses of witness attending such inquiry as the Minister shall allow.

In Britain, by virtue of section 250(4) of the Local Government Act 1972, this sum is capped and must not exceed £30 a day for the services of an officer engaged in the inquiry.

Section 106(1) provides

An **officer** appointed to hold a local inquiry may by summons in the prescribed form signed by him require[16] any person to attend at the time and place (not being a place more than thirty miles from the residence of such person) named in such summons and there and then to give evidence or to produce any document in his power, possession, or procurement relating to any matter in question as such inquiry or to do both such things.[17]

13.3 Independence of Officer

Section 105 specifies that this is an **officer of the Minister**.[17a] Regrettably the independence of this officer has not been guaranteed by law. The independence of officers within departments of State deciding appeals etc., has been questioned in the past. In *McLoughlin v. Minister for Social Welfare,*[18] Ó Dálaigh J. stated that an appeals officer had abdicated his duty to act in an impartial and independent fashion. He had stated that he was bound to adhere to a direction, purported to have been given to him by the Minister for Finance.

13.4 Officer's Role

The nature of the officer's role in conducting the local inquiry under the Vocational Education Act is not specified in the Act. There is no provision that he is required to furnish a report **of** or **on** the inquiry. According to Henchy J. in *Geraghty v. Minister for Local Government:*[19]

A report **on** the oral hearing imports an accurate, but not necessarily exhaustive, account of what was presented at the oral hearing in the way

---

[16] The form of summons is Form V.31 S.L. No 58 1931.
[17] Section 106.
[17a] It is proposed to amend ss. 105, 106 and 107 of the Vocational Education Act 1930 to permit the Minister to appoint "a person" rather than "an officer" by s. 36 of the Education (No. 2) Bill, 1997. Introduced in the Dáil on Friday, 12 December 1997.
[18] [1958] I.R. 1.
[19] [1976] I.R. 153.

of evidence and submissions; the appointed person's findings of fact; together with such observations, inferences, submissions and recommendations as he thinks proper to put forward and which arise out of the evidence and submissions or out of any visit and inspection. . . . An accurate and reasonable account of what took place at the hearing is necessary — of the evidence, to support findings of fact and of the submissions. . . . It is inherent in the scheme for hearing the appeal that the facts shall be found by the appointed person.[20]

As already pointed out, this is not the case in relation to the inquiry under the Vocational Education Act, there is no report "of" or "on" the inquiry furnished to the Minister who must peruse the totality of the evidence produced at the inquiry without having seen or heard the witnesses.

Henchy J. in the *Geraghty* case[21] stated:

it should be inferred that the legislature intended, in order to preserve constitutionally guaranteed standards of fair and just procedure, that, where an oral hearing is provided for, conflicts of fact will not be resolved by a person who learns of the evidence only at second hand from a report and whose conclusions might conflict with those of the person who saw and heard the witnesses.[22]

13.5 Immunity of Witnesses

Section 106(4) Vocational Education Act 1930 states:

A witness before an officer holding a local inquiry shall be entitled to the same immunities and privileges as if he were a witness before the High Court.

This immunity from defamation is a mirror of the immunities in judicial proceedings and statements made at a local inquiry, therefore, have absolute privilege. In addition a witness also has the right to refuse to answer questions which might incriminate himself. In *Re Haughey*[23] Ó Dálaigh C. J. stated:

The immunity of witnesses in the High Court does not exist for the benefit of witnesses, but for that of the public and the advancement of the administration of justice and to prevent witnesses from being deterred, by the fear of having actions brought against them, from coming

---

[20] *Ibid.* at p. 174.
[21] Note 19 above.
[22] *Ibid.*, p. 174
[23] [1971] I.R. 217.

forward and testifying to the truth. The interest of the individual is subordinated by the law to the higher interest, *viz.* that of public justice, for the administration of which it is necessary that witnesses should be free to give their evidence without fear of consequences.

It is salutary to bear in mind that even in the High Court, if a witness were to take advantage of his position to utter something defamatory having no reference to the cause or matter of inquiry but introduced maliciously for his own purpose, no privilege or immunity would attach and he might find himself sued in an action for defamation....The fact that a witness may have been permitted or even encouraged to venture into the area will afford him no defence in such an action.

Furthermore, in the High Court it is the duty of the judge to warn **a witness that he is privileged to refuse to answer any question if the answer would tend to incriminate him.** That privilege is also enjoyed by witnesses before the Committee, but it does not appear from the documents before us that Mr. Haughey in this case was so warned.[24]

13.6 Evidence on Oath

Section 107 Vocational Education Act 1930:

> An officer appointed by the Minister to hold a local inquiry shall have power to take evidence on oath and for that purpose may administer oaths to persons attending before him as witnesses.

Nowadays, examination on a solemn affirmation might be acceptable where the taking of an oath is objected to. Section 212 of the Children Bill 1996 provided for taking the deposition of a child on oath or affirmation in certain circumstances. Section 22 of the Children Bill 1997 proposed the admissibility of a statement made by a child notwithstanding that it constituted hearsay evidence if the child is unable to give evidence by reasons of age, or the giving of oral evidence by the child would not be in the interest of the welfare of the child.

No person may be required by such summons to attend to give evidence or to produce documents unless the necessary expenses of his attendance are paid or tendered to him under (section 250(2) of the British Local Government Act 1972) and nothing in the section empowers the person holding the enquiry to require the production of the title or instruments of title of any land which is not the property of a local authority.

Every person who refuses or **deliberately** fails to attend in answer to such a summons, or who refuses to give evidence, or who deliberately alters, suppresses, destroys or conceals any book or document which he is required or liable to produce is liable on summary conviction to a fine not exceeding

---

[24] *Ibid.* at p. 264.

£100 or to imprisonment for a term not exceeding six months, or both. British Local Government Act, section 250(3).

A person unable to attend because of illness or accident would be excluded, likewise a person refusing to answer a question would have to be mute of malice in order to be culpable under the section.

13.7 The Rights of the Teacher

The rights of the teacher whose performance is being inquired into, are of crucial importance. In *Re Haughey,*[25] his counsel submitted that, in all the circumstances, the minimum protection which the State should afford his client was:

(a) that he should be furnished with a copy of the evidence which reflected on his good name. (In *Gallagher v. Revenue Commissioners*[26] *ante* the plaintiff was held entitled to be furnished, well in advance of the hearing with a copy transcript of an interview with investigators as well as a copy of the evidence to be tendered against him.)

(b) that he should be allowed to cross examine, by counsel, his accuser or accusers,

(c) that he should be allowed to give rebutting evidence, and

(d) that he should be permitted to address, again by counsel, the committee in his own defence.

For the Attorney General it was urged that a High Court witness is not allowed the protections mentioned at (b) and (d) *supra*. The answer was that Mr. Haughey was not just a witness but he had in effect, become a party because his conduct had become the subject matter of the inquiry.

Chief Justice Ó Dálaigh delivering the majority judgment in the Supreme Court stated:

> But the Constitution guarantees that the State "so far as practicable" (sa mhéid gur féidir é) will by its laws safeguard and vindicate the citizen's good name. Where, as here, it is considered necessary to grant immunity to witnesses appearing before a tribunal, then a person whose conduct is impugned as part of the subject matter of the inquiry must be afforded reasonable means of defending himself. What are these means? They have been already enumerated at (a) to (d) above.[27]

He then went on to comment that without the two rights, (b) and (d), ruled out by the Committee's procedures, no accused, within the context of the terms of

---

[25] *Ibid.* at p. 263.
[26] Note 15 above.
[27] Note 23 above at pp. 263-264.

the inquiry, could hope to make an adequate defence of his good name. "To deny such rights" he continued:

> is, in an ancestral adage, a classic case of *clocha ceangailte agus madrai scaoilte* (binding stones and unleashing dogs). Article 40.3 of the Constitution is a guarantee to the citizen of basic fairness of procedures. The Constitution guarantees such fairness, and it is the duty of the Court to underline that the words of Article 40.3 are not political shibboleths but provide a positive protection for the citizen and his good name.[28]

13.8 Right to Cross Examine

The Supreme Court, in *Re Haughey,*[29] has held that a person before the Dáil Committee on Public Accounts investigating his alleged improper conduct, has the same rights as those guaranteed by Article 38.1 of the Constitution to accused persons facing trial (*i.e.* the right to cross examine, the right to call rebutting evidence, and to make closing submissions.) The allegation of improper conduct places his good name in jeopardy and, under Article 40 of the Constitution, the State is obliged in such cases to ensure that the accused may vindicate his good name. The livelihood as well as the good name of a VEC officer may be at risk in a local inquiry under section 105 of the Vocational Education Act 1930.

Dr. Michael Forde points out[30] that where an Act does not set out the entire procedures to be followed it will be implied that constitutionally fair procedures are to be used.

Under subsection (3) of section 106 a person duly served with a summons who fails to attend in accordance with such summons, or refuses to take an oath legally required by the officer holding such inquiry, or to produce any document in his possession, power or control legally required by such officer to be produced by him, or to answer any question to which such officer may legally require an answer, is guilty of an offence and liable on summary conviction to a fine not exceeding twenty pounds.

13.9 Role of Person who Presides

Unlike the Housing Act 1966, the Vocational Education Act does require that the person appointed by the Minister to hold a local inquiry under section 106 (as pointed out earlier) must be "an officer of the Minister" under section 105(1), *i.e.* a civil servant. It appears, therefore, on the basis of the judgment of Walsh J. in *Murphy v. Corporation of Dublin*[31] that s/he would have the

---

[28] *Ibid.,* p. 264.
[29] Note 23 above.
[30] Michael Forde, *Constitutional Law of Ireland* (1987), p. 401.
[31] [1972] I.R. at p. 238.

privileges and protections (if any) which a civil servant in the business of the State assigned to him has. In the *Murphy* case, the Act did not require that the person appointed by the Minister should be a civil servant and thus he did not have these privileges, but the Minister was *persona designata, i.e.* the person designated to make the determination.[32]

The *Murphy* case, which arose out of a public inquiry after a compulsory purchase order by Dublin Corporation (under the 1966 Housing Act) over lands owned by Mr. Murphy in County Dublin, prompted the court to consider the role of the person appointed to conduct the inquiry. Mr Murphy asked the court to direct the Minister to make the inspector's report available to him, correctly suspecting that it was favourable to him. This then was the scenario which prompted Walsh J. to review the respective roles of the Minister and the person who conducted the inquiry as follows:

> In this context it is necessary to examine the precise function of the Inspector in this role. By statute the Minister is the one who has to decide the matter — not the inspector. In doing so, the Minister must act judicially and within the bounds of constitutional justice. No direct assistance is obtainable from the statute as to the precise functions of the Inspector or of his powers.
>
> It is clear, however, that in so far as the conduct of the inquiry is concerned he is acting as recorder for the Minister. He may regulate the procedure within the permissible limits of the inquiry over which he presides. In as much as he is there for the purpose of reporting to the Minister, the Inspector's function is to convey to the Minister, if not a verbatim account of the entire of the proceedings before him, at least a fair and accurate account of what transpired and one which gives accurately to the Minister the evidence and the submissions of each party because it is upon this material that the Minister must make his decision and on no other.[33]
>
> The Inspector has no advisory function nor has he any function to arrive at a preliminary judgement which may or may not be confirmed or varied by the Minister. If the inspector's report takes the form of a document, then it must contain an account of all the essentials of the proceedings over which he presided. In my view, it is no part of his function to arrive at any conclusion.
>
> If the Minister is influenced in his decision by the opinions of the Inspector or conclusions of the Inspector, the Minister's decision will

---

[32] *Ibid.*, p. 238.

[33] "The minister is bound to form his/her own independent judgment" — *per* Widgery J. in *Nelson v. Minister of Housing and Local Government* [1962] I W.L.R. 404. For decision making following public inquiries see *R v. Bolton M.B.C. ex parte Whitecroft plc* (*The Times,* October 12, 1983).

be open to review. It may be quashed and set aside if shown to be based on materials other than those disclosed at the public hearing.

In my view, in the exercise of the function which he was performing in this case, it was open to the Minister to refuse to produce the inspector's report on the ground that it is a document for which the executive privilege of non-production is available if granted by the Court, I refer to "executive privilege" for want of a better term. It follows that it was not open to the High Court to refuse to order production of the document in question on the grounds given by Mr Justice Kenny. I would allow the appeal.[34]

13.10 The Conduct of Inquiries

The Vocational Education Acts do not specifically provide that an officer whose performance is being inquired into must be afforded a hearing, but the conduct of inquiries in Ireland is governed by: (a) the common law, (b) the rules of natural justice, and (c) the 1937 Constitution which ensure that such an opportunity is available where appropriate. See Natural Justice *post*.

Although the right to be heard is enshrined as one of the principles of natural justice, it has also been regarded as a right at common law. Byles J. in *Cooper v. Wandsworth Board of Works*,[35] stated, "although there are no positive words in a statute requiring that the party shall be heard, yet the justice of the common law will supply the omission of the legislature".

Kenny J. in *Abbey Films v. Attorney General*[36] stated:

> one of the things which are conductive to the common good is that it should be seen that an enquiry [*sic*] by the State body is fair, impartial and unprejudiced. If it is not so, or appears not to be so, this is against the common good. . . . I consider it to have been unsatisfactory that radio and newspaper interviews were given during the course of the investigation.[37]

The Constitutional guarantee of fair procedures was expounded by Ó Dálaigh C.J. in *Re Haughey*,[38] as meaning that the citizen was guaranteed basically fair procedures by Article 40.3 of the Constitution

---

[34] Note 31 above pp. 238-239.
[35] (1863) C.B. N.S. 180 The right to be heard does not necessarily involve being heard *viva voce*. See *Rex v. Local Govt. Board* [1914] 1. K.B. 160.
[36] [1981] I.R. 158
[37] *Ibid* at p. 178. See also *Errington v. Minister of Health* [1935] I K.B. 249.
[38] Note 23 above. *Re Haughey* [1971] I.R. 217.

13.11 Swearing of Witnesses

There are no procedural requirements specified by statute and the person charged with conducting the inquiry, therefore, has a certain amount of discretion. For example, all of the witness at an inquiry may be sworn at the outset of an inquiry according to Griffin J. in *Kiely v. Minister for Social Welfare*,[39] where he described this as an acceptable practice, there being less formality than in court proceedings.

13.12 Evidence

> Provided that the rules of natural justice are observed, the strict rules as to evidence and procedure applicable in the courts need not be followed at public enquiries. Subject to any specific requirements applied by or under statutes, a person conducting such an inquiry is master of his own procedure and may admit hearsay evidence and act on any evidence which is logically probative.[40]

In *Kiely v. Minister for Social Welfare*[41] the Supreme Court held that requiring one party to a dispute to attend the hearing of proceedings and to adduce oral evidence in support of his claim and permitting the other party to contravene that evidence by furnishing a written statement made by a witness who did not attend the hearing, was an infringement of the requirements of natural justice.

In the High Court hearing of the same case Mr. Justice Kenny stated:

> I think that the law of the admission of evidence before tribunals, such as the appeals officer was happily stated by Diplock L.J. (as he then was) in *R. v. Deputy Industrial Injuries Commissioner, ex parte Moore*,[42] as follows: "Where as, in the present case, a personal bias or *mala fides*[43] on the part of the deputy Commissioner is not in question, the rules of natural justice which he must observe can, in my view, be reduced to two. First, he must base his decision on evidence, whether a hearing is requested or not. Secondly, if a hearing is requested, he must fairly listen to the contentions of all persons who are entitled to be represented at the hearing. In the context of the first rule, **'evidence' is not restricted to evidence which would be admissible in a court of law.** For historical reasons, based on the fear that juries who might be illiterate would be incapable of differentiating between the probative values of different methods of proof, the practice of the common law courts has been to admit only what the judges then regarded as the best evidence of any

---

[39] [1977] I.R. 267 at p. 286.
[40] *Halsbury's Laws of England*, Vol. 28, paragraph 1386.
[41] Note 39 above. Point No. 4 , p. 268.
[42] [1965] I Q.B. 456, 487.
[43] In relation to *mala fides* see *supra* at p. 182.

disputed fact", this practice he asserted excluded much material which, as a matter of common sense, would assist a fact-finding tribunal to reach a correct conclusion: *Myers v. Director of Public Prosecutions.*[44]

"These technical rules of evidence", he added:

> form no part of the rules of natural justice. The requirement that a person exercising quasi-judicial functions must base his decision on evidence means no more than it must be based upon material which tends logically to show the existence or non-existence of facts relevant to the issue to be determined, or to show the likelihood or unlikelihood of the occurrence of some future event, the occurrence of which would be relevant. It means . . . he may take into account any material which, as a matter of reason, has some probative value in the sense mentioned above. If it is capable of having any probative value, the weight to be attached to it is a matter for the person to whom Parliament has entrusted the responsibility of deciding the issue. The supervisory jurisdiction of the High Court does not entitle it to usurp this responsibility and substitute its own view for his.[45]

In relation to the second rule of *audi alteram partem* Kenny J. continued:

> Where, however, there is a hearing, whether requested or not, the second rule requires the deputy commissioner —
>
> (a) to consider such "evidence" relevant to the question to be decided as any person entitled to be represented wishes to put before him;
> (b) to inform every person represented, of any "evidence" which the deputy commissioner proposed to take into consideration, whether such "evidence" be proffered by another person represented at the hearing, or is discovered by the deputy commissioner as a result of his own investigations;
> (c) to allow each person represented to comment upon any such "evidence" and, where the evidence is given orally by witnesses, to put questions to those witnesses; and
> (d) to allow each person represented to address argument to him on the whole of the case.[46]

---

[44] [1964] 3 W.L.R. 145.
[45] Note 39 above, p. 26.
[46] *Ibid.*, p. 28.

13.13 The Minister

According to Henchy J. in *Geraghty v. Minister for Local Government*:[47]

> . . . the Minister may not allow himself to be informed, under the guise of expert advice or otherwise, as to factual matters not dealt with in the report which might be capable of augmenting, affirming or diminishing the degree of factual proof found by the appointed person in the report.[48]

This applies even more so in the case of a vocational teacher where there is no provision for a report by the person conducting the inquiry.

If the Minister were to do so there would then be only a partly local inquiry, furthermore since, in deciding what action to take, the Minister is acting in a quasi-judicial capacity and in Henchy J.'s opinion:

> . . . he must not act in disregard of natural justice, so if new facts or probative material in relation to the appeal are brought to his notice, he should not take them into reckoning for the purpose of the appeal until the parties have had an opportunity of dealing with them at an oral hearing, and until the appointed person has reported on them.[49]

13.14 Opinions or Conclusions

In *Kiely v. Minister for Social Welfare,*[50] Griffin J. expressed similar sentiments when he stated that it would be wrong for the party in charge of a quasi-judicial tribunal to receive evidence after the oral hearing had ended and the Supreme Court supported this contention by ruling that a letter written by an assessor to the appeals officer after the hearing could not be admitted without breaching the rules of natural justice. A similar ruling was brought about in *Murphy v. Dublin Corporation*[51] by the Minister wrongfully considering an inspector's report. Walsh J. held that a Minister's decision arrived at in such circumstances must be quashed.

---

[47] Note 19 above. *Geraghty v. Minister for Local Government.* [1976] I. R. 153.
[48] *Ibid* p. 175.
[49] *loc. cit.*
[50] Note 39 above. *Kiely v. Minister for Social Welfare* [1977] I.R. 286, 287 *op. cit.*
[51] Note 31 above. *Murphy v. Dublin Corporation* [1972] I.R. 215 *op. cit.*

CHAPTER 14

The Rules of Natural Justice

> By education most have been misled:
> So they believe, because they so were bred.
> The priest continues what the nurse began,
> And thus the child imposes on the man.

Dryden, Hind and the Panther, Pt. iii,1.389

Even though there is no specific provision in an Act of the Oireachtas to that effect, the principles of natural justice still apply to legislation because, as Lord Reid stated in *Ridge v. Baldwin*:[1]

> the older authorities clearly show how the courts engrafted the principles of natural justice onto a host of provisions authorising administrative interference with private rights. . . . Parliament presumes that the power it grants will be exercised fairly and regularly, and it is not bound to say so explicitly on every occasion.[2]

In relation to vocational education, this means that the powers and procedures in the Vocational Education Acts must only be used in accordance with these principles.

14.1 Meaning of Natural Justice

The term natural justice is difficult to explain but has some relationship with the application of equitable principles of what is fair and just and in accordance with principles of good conscience, but the relationship to moral principles propounded by De Smith,[3] *post,* must surely be questionable in view of the fact that natural justice was traditionally only applied selectively by the English courts to those who held an office.

De Smith, Woolf and Jowell[4] state:

> Although often retained as a general concept, the term natural justice

---

[1] *Ridge v. Baldwin* [1964] A.C. 40.
[2] *Ibid.* at p. 61.
[3] Note 4 below.
[4] De Smith, Woolf and Jowell, *Judicial Review of Administrative Action* (5th ed., London, 1995), pp. 376-378.

has since been largely replaced and extended by the more general duty to act "fairly". . . . The expression "natural justice" which is the source from which procedural fairness flows, has been described as one "sadly lacking in precision".[5] . . . Moreover, 'natural justice' is said to express the close relationship between the common law and moral principles, and in addition it has an impressive ancestry.[6]

In *McDonald v. Bord na gCon,*[7] Walsh J. commented that in the context of the Irish Constitution:

> natural justice might be more appropriately termed constitutional justice and must be understood to import more than the two well established principles that no man shall be judge in his own cause and *audi alteram partem.*[8]

Evershed M.R in *Abbott v. Sullivan*[9] stated:

> "The principles of natural justice are easy to proclaim, but their precise extent is far less easy to define. They came under the consideration of Mayham J. in *Maclean v. The Worker's Union*[10] and a useful note upon them is to be found in the final report of the Committee on Minister's powers known as the Donoughmore Committee of 1932 at pp. 75-80.[11]

14.2 Extent of the Rules

The rules of natural justice extend to evidential and procedural matters and rules, as well as an actual hearing or inquiry. In *Nolan v. Irish Land Commission*[12] it was argued by the defence that the rules did not extend thus far, that with the single exception of the principle which provides that a party is entitled to be informed of a charge against him, that they only related to the actual hearing. This construction was totally rejected by the Supreme Court, O'Higgins C.J. stating:

> If one party comes to the hearing with the scales of justice tilted against him because of procedural defect, then the requirements of justice are not fulfilled.

---

5 *Rex v. Local Government Board, ex parte Arlidge* [1914] 1. K.B. at 199.
6 De Smith, pp. 377-378.
7 [1965] I.R. 217
8 *Ibid.* per Walsh J. at p. 242.
9 [1952] 1 K.B. 189.
10 [1929] 1 Ch. 602.
11 Note 9 above at p. 195.
12 [1981] I.R. 23.

Griffin J. in agreement considered that without seeing the documents in advance the plaintiff could not cross-examine fully or adequately. Basic fairness and the essential interests of justice dictated that the plaintiff was entitled to discovery, limited to relevant documents, which may have come into existence between the date of the inspector's report and the date of the certificate.

14.3 Origin of the Rules

In *Garvey v. Ireland*,[13] the same judge pointed out that the application of the principles of natural justice to the different situations which competing interests in society create, has never been capable of precise definition:

> Natural justice, imprecise though the term may be, was something which came to be regarded as each man's protection against the arbitrary use of power. In his *Judicial Review of Administrative Action* (3rd. ed., p. 133) De Smith says of the term: "The term expresses the close relationship between the common law and moral principles, and it has an impressive ancestry."
>
> That no man is to be judged unheard was a precept known to the Greeks, inscribed in ancient times upon images in places where justice was administered, proclaimed in Seneca's Medea, enshrined in the scriptures, mentioned by St. Augustine, embodied in Germanic as well as African proverbs, ascribed in the Year Books to the law of nature, asserted by Coke to be a principle of divine justice, and traced by an eighteenth-century judge to the events in the Garden of Eden.
>
> Whatever its true origin may be and however imprecise its principles there can be no doubt that the concept of natural justice is part and parcel of the common law which we inherited from England. . . . Many office holders who were removable for cause could be so removed at the discretion of the employing authority, that authority exercising the right to act on what it alone regards as sufficient cause. In such cases, since the right to remove from office could not be questioned, it became important to ensure that what was done was done fairly.[14]

14.4 Application of Natural Justice

per Evershed M.R. in *Abbott v. Sullivan*:[15]

> When some person or body of persons exercising judicial or quasi judi-

---

[13] [1981] I.R. 75.
[14] *Ibid.,* p. 91.
[15] [1952] 1 K.B. 189, 195.

cial functions disregards any of the principles of natural justice which our courts recognise, the court will interfere to protect the party aggrieved. It is, however, equally clear that in giving effect to these principles no particular procedure has to be followed.

The Supreme Court has held, in *Hickey v. EHB*,[16] that an officer of a statutory or Local Authority Board or of the State, has no special rights to a hearing irrespective of the reason for his or her dismissal. Accordingly, where a temporary officer had not been dismissed for any fault committed by her in the discharge of her duties, nor on the basis of not performing her duties properly, the application of the relevant rules of natural justice to dismissal of a person for misconduct, did not apply. The appellant was made redundant because the EHB did not renew her temporary periodic engagement. There was no question or allegation that the decision to do so was arbitrary or capricious or induced by a wrong motive and there was no suggestion of any wrongdoing or misconduct on the part of the appellant.

Lord Hodson, in *Ridge v. Baldwin*,[17] pointed out that one of the difficulties felt in applying principles of natural justice was that there was a certain vagueness in the term, and as Tucker L.J. said in *Russell v. Duke of Norfolk*:[18]

> There are . . . "no words which are of universal application to every kind of inquiry and every kind of domestic tribunal. The requirements of natural justice must depend on the circumstances of the case, the nature of the inquiry, the rules under which the tribunal is acting, the subject matter under consideration and so forth". If it be said that this makes natural justice so vague as to be inapplicable: I would not agree. No one, I think, disputes that three features of natural justice stand out, — (1) the right to be heard by an unbiased tribunal; (2) the right to have notice of charges of misconduct; (3) the right to be heard in answer to those charges.[19]

In *McDonald v. Bord na gCon*,[20] the Supreme Court stated that, before the finding of any investigation held under the provisions of the Act could be relied upon as justification, the investigation must have been conducted in accordance with the dictates of natural justice, and must have been decided objectively.

---

[16] [1990] I.T.L.R., 22 October 1990. Giving a person an opportunity to be heard does not necessarily mean a *viva voce* hearing. *Rex v. Local Govt. Board, Ex parte Arlidge* [1914] 1. K.B. at 160.
[17] Note 1 above.
[18] [1948] 65 T.L.R. 263.
[19] Note 1 above at p. 132.
[20] [1965] I.R. 217.

Lord Morris, in *Ridge v. Baldwin*,[21] extolled the importance of natural justice stating:

> It is well established that the essential requirements of natural justice at least include that before someone is condemned he is to have an opportunity of defending himself, and in order that he may do so, that he is made aware of the charges or allegations or suggestions which he has to meet; see *Kanda v. Government of Malaysia*.[22] My Lords, here is **something which is basic to our system; the importance of upholding it far transcends the significance of any particular case.**[23]

14.5 Standard of Natural Justice

The standard of natural justice to be upheld by Irish tribunals or bodies has been established over the years in a number of cases, *e.g. R. v. Corporation of Dublin*,[24] *R. (Wexford Co. Co.) v. Local Government Board*,[25] *In the matter of the estate of Roscrea Meat Products Ltd.*,[26] and various other cases[27] including *Abbott v. Sullivan*.[28]

14.6 Oral Hearings

The removal of an office holder from office is the exercise of a quasi-judicial function as indeed, is the function of the Army Pensions Board. In *The State (Williams) v. Army Pensions Board*[29] the Supreme Court disagreed with Keane J. in the High Court who held that the functions of both the first and second named respondents were administrative rather than quasi-judicial, and that

---

[21] Note 1 above.

[22] [1962] A.C. 322, 337.

[23] *Ridge v. Baldwin* [1964] A.C. 41

[24] 2 L.R.Ir. 371.

[25] [1902] 2 I.R. 349.

[26] [1958] I.R. 47.

[27] Maguire C. J. in *Re Ó Laighléis* S.C. [1957] I. R. 113: See *R. v. Corporation of Dublin*, 2 L. R. Ir. 371; *R. v. (Wexford County Council) v. Local Government Board* [1902] 2. I.R. 349; *The State (Crowley) v. Irish Land Commission* [1951] I. R. 250; *Foley v. Irish Land Commission* [1952] I. R. 118; *General Medical Council v. Spackman* (1943) A.C. 627; *In re estate of Roscrea Meat Products Ltd.* [1958] I.R. 47.

[28] *Abbott v. Sullivan* [1952] 1 K.B. 189 at 195.

[29] Unreported, High Court, 13 January 1981. On appeal to the Supreme Court: *The State (Williams) v. Army Pensions Board*, 14 February 1983 [1983] I.R. 308, the High Court decision was reversed and Mrs. Williams was granted an order of *certiorari* quashing two reports of the Army Pensions Board to the effect that she and her children were not entitled to any allowance or gratuity. The fact that she was denied access to the Board's medical evidence amounted to a breach of natural justice. In *Rex v. Local Govt. Board* [1914] 1 K.B. 160, Hamilton L.J. in the Court of Appeal stated that where a report was involved there was a judicial proceeding.

while even purely administrative acts might be affected by the requirements of natural and constitutional justice, the submission that those requirements necessarily involved an oral hearing seemed to him to be misconceived.

This view as to the functions of the Board was not shared by the Supreme Court on appeal, where Henchy J. (Hederman J. concurring) said:

> "I incline to the contrary view. Their functions, which are conclusively adjudicative after consideration of the evidence tendered seem to me to have a judicial rather than an administrative flavour.

McCarthy J. (Hederman J. concurring) said:

> Reluctantly, I cannot agree with the learned judge that the function of the first and second-named respondents are more properly described as administrative. I accept that the function of the second named respondent is administrative, but, having regard to the observations of Henchy J. in *Kiely v. Minister for Social Welfare*,[30] I would hold the functions of the Army Pensions Board in an application of this kind are quasi-judicial in nature.[31]

14.7 Removal from Office held at Pleasure in England

In *Re Haughey*[32] one of the grounds of complaint was the admission of evidence on affidavit and the consequent denial of the right to cross-examine. In England, whether fair procedures are owed to an office holder or not depends upon the terms on which the office was created. In *Ridge v. Baldwin*,[33] Lord Reid examined cases of dismissal under three classes, dismissal of a servant, dismissal from an office held at pleasure, and dismissal from an office for cause.

In relation to the third class he concluded:

> I find an unbroken line of authority to the effect that an officer cannot lawfully be dismissed without first telling him what is alleged against him and hearing his defence or explanation. An early example is *Bagg's* case[34] . . . *Rex v. Gaskin* arose out of the dismissal of a parish clerk,. and Lord Kenyon referred to *audi alteram partem* as one of the first principles of justice. *Reg v. Smith*[35] was another case of dismissal of a parish clerk, and Lord Denman C.J. held that even personal knowledge

---

[30] [1977] I.R. 267 at 281.
[31] Note 29 above at p.189. *The State (Williams)* [1983] I.R. 308
[32] In *Re Haughey* [1971] I.R. at p. 261.
[33] Note 1 above.
[34] (1615) 11 Co. Rep. 93b.
[35] (1844) 5 Q.B. 614.

of the offence was no substitute for hearing the officer: his explanation might disprove criminal motive or intent and bring forward other facts in mitigation, and in any event delaying to hear him would prevent yielding too hastily to first impressions.[36]

Lord Reid also stressed the importance of *Ex parte Ramshay*[37] which dealt with the removal from office of a county court judge. The Lord Chancellor was empowered, if he thought fit, to remove from office on the ground of inability or misbehaviour but Lord Campbell the Chief Justice stated[38] that this was "only on the implied condition prescribed by the principles of eternal justice." Lord Reid also cited the judgment of Lord Hatherley L.C. in *Osgood v. Nelson*[39] to the effect that:

> the Court of Queen's Bench has always considered that it has been open to that court to correct any court, or tribunal, or body of men who may have a power of this description, a power of removing from office, if it should be found that such persons have disregarded any of the essentials of justice in the course of their inquiry, before making that removal, or if it should be found that in the place of reasonable cause those persons have acted obviously upon mere individual caprice.[40]

There are, of course, cases like *Malloch v. Aberdeen Corporation*,[41] where a statute imports the right to due process before removal but according to Lord Wilberforce in the same case:[42]

> A comparative list of situations in which persons have been held entitled or not entitled to a hearing, or to observation of rules of natural justice, according to the master and servant test, looks illogical and even bizarre.[43]

In Ireland, while certain offices may be held at pleasure, Article 40.3.1° and 2° of the Constitution imports a requirement of due process and imposes obligations on the State to vindicate the personal rights and the life, person, good name, and property rights of every citizen. (See Removal by VEC.)

---

[36] *Ridge v. Baldwin* at p.66.
[37] (1852) 18 Q.B. 173.
[38] *Ibid.*
[39] (1872) L.R. 5 H.L. 636, 649.
[40] Note 189, above at p.67.
[41] [1971] 2 All E. R. 1278.
[42] *Ibid.* at 1294.
[43] *Stevenson v. United Road Transport* [1976] 3 All E. R. 29 at p. 34.

14.8 Effect of Vocational Teachers being Officers

The Vocational Educational Act 1930 draws a distinction between officers and servants. The Unfair Dismissals Act 1977 applies to servants but not to officers of a VEC established by the Vocational Education Act 1930.[44]

Until 1982, vocational teachers could not claim the protection of the Trade Disputes Act 1906 because the definition of "workman" meant persons employed in trade or industry, and teachers, nurses and civil servants were not so employed. This affected, *inter alia,* the right to picket and, in the case of *Maguire v. Cullen,*[45] the plaintiff applied for an injunction to prevent former teachers in the NCAD picketing the private offices of the Chairman on the grounds, *inter alia,* that he was not the employer and that they were not workmen (*i.e.* persons engaged in trade or industry) On legal advice the teachers gave an undertaking that they would not continue the picket and this was accepted on behalf of the plaintiff.

The Trade Disputes (Amendment) Act 1982 substituted a new definition of "workman" which encompassed "any person who is or was employed whether or not in the employment of the employer with whom a trade dispute arises but does not include members of the Defence Forces or of the Gardaí"; thus Primary and Secondary teachers came within the protection of the 1906 Act.

A vocational teacher may be removed from office at will or pleasure solely, but the Vocational Educational Acts also specifically provide that he may be removed for cause. The Acts specify the grounds for removal from office[46] after a local inquiry is held, removal by the Minister without holding a local inquiry[47] and removal by a VEC under section 23, which it is submitted, must be in accordance with the principles of natural and constitutional justice. (See chapter on Removal by VEC.)

14.9 Procedure

The procedure to be followed where there is no enquiry is specified by section 8(3) of the Vocational Education (Amendment) Act 1944 as follows:

> Where the Minister is satisfied that the holder of an office has failed to perform satisfactorily the duties of such office and is of opinion that he is unfit to hold such office[48] the Minister **may** —

---

[44] Section 2(i)(j) of the Unfair Dismissals Act 1977.

[45] Unreported, High Court, but see *Irish Independent*, 10 December 1974.

[46] Section 8(1) of the Vocational Education (Amendment) Act 1944.

[47] Section 8(3) of the Vocational Education (Amendment) Act 1944.

[48] The Minister has to be satisfied of one thing and be of the opinion of the other -the section also refers to duties, *i.e.* plural.

(a) send by registered post to such holder at the principal office of the vocational education committee under which he holds office a notice stating the said opinion, and

(b) on the day on which he sends the notice, send by registered post a copy thereof to the said vocational education committee, and if the Minister, after the expiration of fourteen days from the day on which he sends the notice and the copy thereof and after consideration of the representations (if any) made to him by such holder or the Vocational Education committee, remains of the said opinion, he may by order remove such holder from such office.

14.10 Right of Access to Evidence

While the statute does not require that the notice must be sent, in practice it is, and, in the opinion of the author, advisedly so because of the requirements of natural and constitutional justice. Admittedly it can be argued that an individual who has been inspected on a number of occasions has knowledge of unsatisfactory performance of his duties, but this would not be sufficient. The officer should also be invited to make representations. In any such disciplinary matter, the accused must be formally told the charge against him and he must have an opportunity of answering the charge. He cannot have such an opportunity until he knows what the charge is. Deputy Judge Dillon, in the trade union case of *Stevenson v. United Road Transport Union,*[49] held:

> The failure to supply the plaintiff with a fair statement of all the charges which he would have to meet within a reasonable time before the meeting, and the failure to adjourn the meeting to enable the plaintiff to consider the charges, constituted a breach of the rules of natural justice.[50]

The importance of formal communication of charges was at the nexus of the Irish Supreme Court decision in *Glover v. B.L.N. Ltd.* when it held:[51]

> the inquiry held by the board of the holding company had not been conducted fairly as the plaintiff had not been given prior notice of the charges made against him or an opportunity to refute those charges.[52]

---

[49] [1976] 3 All E. R. Ch.D. 29.
[50] *loc. cit.*
[51] [1973] I.R. 388: In *Rex v. Local Government Board* [1914] 1 K.B. 160, a dismissal without disclosing the content of an inspector's report was held contrary to natural justice.
[52] *Glover v. B.L.N. Ltd.* [1973] I.R. 388, 389.

In *Williams v. Army Pensions Board,*[53] where the Board had refused the applicant access to medical evidence it was held that this one-sidedness amounted to a breach of natural justice.

In *O'Brien v. The Commissioner of An Garda Síochána,*[54] it was held by Kelly J. in the High Court that consideration of an undisclosed report from the applicant's superior breached his right to a fair hearing under the *audi alteram partem* rule.

Appendix A to C/L 43/85 section 2.2 does state "Where the Department issues a report in respect of the work of a teacher, such report will be made available to the teacher." Non-disclosure of the content of the inspector's report (not the production of the report itself) was the basis of the Court of Appeal judgment in *Rex. v. Local Government Board* (1914). (See note 38). In *Fountaine v. Chesterton,*[55] it was held that **a statement of reasons is not required by the rules of natural justice**.

14.11 Right to be Notified of Reasons by Agreement

In *O'Flynn v. Mid Western Health Board,*[56] clause 24 of the General Medical Services Scheme provided that a medical practitioner should be notified of the reasons for the belief that he had failed to comply with the terms of the agreement. He was only given an outline of the complaints alleged against him. Judicial review was granted and the decision to refer the complaint to the Minister, for him to appoint a committee of investigation and his order appointing such a committee, were both quashed. The plaintiff's solicitor had written asking to be furnished with the name or names of the person or persons making the allegations, the date or dates the transactions were supposed to have taken place and the nature of the goods allegedly involved. No reply was made to this request.

Barr J. held that the failure to disclose further particulars of the complaints or copies of documentary papers substantiating such complaints meant that the applicant was denied any opportunity of making proper representations as prescribed by clause 24 and the Health Board were not entitled to set in train the disciplinary procedure.

14.12 Principles Applied regardless of Status

In *Gunn v. Bord an Cholaiste Naisiúnta Ealaine is Deartha,*[57] it was held that, in the context of section 17 of The National College of Art and Design

---

[53] [1983] I.L.R.M. 334 *op. cit.*
[54] I.T.L.R. November 18 1996.
[55] *The Times*, 20 August 1968.
[56] [1989] I.R. 429.
[57] [1990] 2 I.R. 168.

Act 1971, the term "officer" must mean office-holder: consequently for the purposes of the Act, it appeared that the plaintiff, being a member of the academic staff of the College, was an officer or office-holder of the Board. In the absence of any particular procedure prescribed, the principles of natural or constitutional justice would govern the relationship between the plaintiff and the Board. These principles were not the monopoly of any particular class — *per* Mc Carthy J. In the same case Walsh J. explained:

> There is one matter I wish to refer to, to clear up what appears to be a misapprehension concerning the application of the rules of natural justice or of constitutional justice. The application of these rules does not depend upon whether the person concerned is an office-holder as distinct from being an employee of some other kind.

He then referred to *Ridge v. Baldwin* as follows:[58]

> "In that case, the person who had been dismissed was a Chief Constable and was the holder of a statutory office. He could only have been dismissed from it in accordance with particular statutory provisions. The persons who had the power to dismiss him were not his employers in the strict sense. Because of that fact, and that he was by statutory instrument designated as an "officer" as distinct from another type of employee, it was held that the particular statutory provisions referable to the dismissal of an officer had not been complied with. . . . In the present case, the agreed procedures are those set out in the agreement with the Federated Workers Union of Ireland, and they did not in any way depend upon whether the employee in question was an officer or not. In any case, where there is no particular procedure prescribed either by agreement between the parties or by statute and where the case falls to be determined by the application of the principles of constitutional justice, or the principles of natural justice, they are applicable without regard to the status of the person entitled to benefit from them.[59]

It must be pointed out that notification of grounds for disciplinary action is totally different from notification of reasons and that the latter is not required to be given by the rules of natural justice. (See chapter 10 *ante*.)

14.13 When Rules must be Observed

Determining the circumstances in which the rules of natural justice must be observed by persons entrusted with the conduct of inquiries but who do not

---

[58] *Ridge v. Baldwin* [1964] A.C. 40.
[59] Note 57 above at p. 181

have power to make a binding decision, has been described as one of the most troublesome problems in the whole of administrative law because of the apparent conflict of authorities. The formulation of general legal principles particularly from English decisions is complicated by the absence of a written constitution and the existence of offices held at pleasure (*durante bene placito.*) This is not so in Ireland because rights to constitutional due process come into effect in all cases, even in those where natural justice may not be applicable, *i.e.* regardless of whether the person involved is an office holder or an employee.[60]

14.14 The Scope of the *Audi Alteram Partem* Rule

De Smith[61] outlines the circumstances in which there is an implied obligation to observe the rule as follows:

(1) The presumption that courts and tribunals with functions and procedures similar to courts must observe the rule is rebuttable and such a body may be expressly empowered to act *ex parte* or to depart from the requirements of the rule.

(2) Bodies may be obliged to observe the rule —

    (a) if the language applicable to them indicates a duty to conduct an inquiry or hearing before coming to a decision; or

    (b) they are empowered or required to decide matters analogous to *lites inter partes*; or

    (c) they are empowered or required to determine disputable questions of law and fact or to exercise limited judicial discretion and the effect of their decisions will, unless successfully challenged have a substantially adverse impact on the interests of an individual.

---

[60] See Walsh J. in *Gunn v. NCAD*. Note 44 above.
[61] See De Smith, p. 233.

CHAPTER 15

Conditions of Appointment and Memo V.7

> With them the Seed of Wisdom did I sow,
> And with my own hand labour'd it to grow.
> And this was all the Harvest that I reap'd-
> I came like Water, and like Wind I go.
>
> The Rubaiyat of Omar Khayyam, xxviii

All appointments of permanent whole-time teachers in the vocational sector are made on the conditions specified in Memo V.7. It is a document published by the Department of Education from time to time and deals with appointment, qualifications and salary scales. It has no legal status in the sense of being a statutory instrument or an order, but it is an indication of the manner in which the Minister for Education will exercise his/her statutory powers under the vocational education Acts. In certain instances it is likely that the Minister would be estopped because of its contents.

As Mr. Justice Costello remarked in *O'Callaghan v. Co. Meath VEC:*[1]

> ... many hundreds perhaps thousands of rules and regulations, memoranda, circulars and decisions are issued by the Department and the Minister (dealing sometimes with the most important aspects of educational policy), not under any statutory power, but merely as administrative measures.[2]

In 1989, a confidential document presented by a senior official in the Department of Education, pointed out that the Department was conducting its day to day affairs within a "legalistic minefield" because of delay in updating its rules and regulations. No updating of the 1965 Rules and Regulations for National Schools were available with the document.

Few persons have ready access to Circular Letters and Memos and actions taken by such means are not subject to parliamentary control. In *McCann v Minister for Education,*[3] Costello P., referring to the non-statutory Rules for Payment of Incremental Salary to secondary teachers 1958, stated:

---

[1] *O'Callaghan v. Co. Meath VEC*, unreported, High Court, 20 November 1990.
[2] *ibid.*, p. 2
[3] [1997] 1 I.L.R.M. 1

"This method of administering funds voted by the Oireachtas has the advantage of flexibility and informality, but also has the disadvantage that the exact terms of a ministerial scheme may not be readily available and may, indeed, be difficult to ascertain.[4]

On the other hand they undoubtedly allow for a quicker, more negotiated response to sensitive issues. To some extent at least, this matter will be resolved by the introduction of a new Education Act. Mr. John Walshe, the Education Correspondent of the *Irish Times* has reported:

half our community schools operate without deeds of trust and without contracts for teachers. We also have legal difficulties over the vesting of sites for secondary schools, while the rules governing primary schools have not been updated since 1965.[5]

Rules   In *McCann v Minister for Education*,[6] it was held that the Minister could properly adopt a scheme that contained Rules[7] under which the payment of incremental salaries could be made. The Rules for Payment of Incremental Salary to Secondary Teachers 1958 were valid although they were purely administrative rules for the purpose of administering a scheme for which the Oireachtas had voted monies and were not made under the Intermediate Education (Ireland) Act 1914 or any other express statutory power. The test of reasonableness can be applied to administrative measures made by a minister for the purpose of administering public funds. The scheme adopted by the Minister for payment of incremental salaries to secondary teachers was a perfectly reasonable one (as were the amendments to it).
    Having dismissed the applicant's claims in a final comment, the President of the High Court referred to the fact that the law should be certain and be readily accessible and added:

The same applies to non-statutory administrative measures. In the case of primary and secondary education, hundreds of millions of pounds are administered annually by means of a large number of administrative measures whose existence is known only to a handful of officials and specialists, which are not readily available to the public and whose effect is uncertain and often ambiguous. If administrative ministerial rules and regulations were dated, if they were identified by reference to the sub-head in the book of estimates to which they relate, if amendments

---

4   *Ibid.,* pp. 8-9
5   See *Irish Times*, 27 November 1990.
6   Note 3 above
7   As the Rules for Secondary Schools see Farry, M., *Education and the Constitution* (Dublin, 1996), p. 109. Rules for National Schools pp. 28-30 and 104-105.

bore the same reference and were dated by reference to the ministerial order which made them, if a register was kept of the original measure and amendments to it, if the original measure and amendments were regularly consolidated and meanwhile made available in loose leaf form to members of the public, this would be one way of obviating the danger of injustice which is inherent in the present highly informal procedures. Such changes might also reduce the likelihood of the institution of proceedings like the present one.

Circular Letters, Conditions and Explanatory Notes   The Irish Courts have considered the implications of documents issued by ministers on a number of occasions. Such documents include "Circular Letters", "Conditions", and "Explanatory Notes".

15.1 Circular Letters

The legal consequences of a Circular Letter were examined in *Staunton v. St. Laurence's Hospital Board and the Attorney General*,[8] where Lardner J. held that:

> when the hospital acted in accordance with and in reliance upon the terms of a Circular Letter, a clause in it gave rise to a contractual obligation which bound the Minister to adjust, that is, in this case, to increase the hospitals financial allocation, to the extent that was necessary to cover the additional cost incurred by the hospital in respect of the common contract made with the plaintiff.[9]

Mr. Justice Costello, in *O'Callaghan v. Co. Meath VEC*,[10] pointed out that a Circular Letter was merely a notification that the Minister had authorised the implementation of an agreed set of procedures. It had no statutory force:

> If the VEC acted in breach of Circular 7/79 it would not follow that it acted *ultra vires,* as might well be the case if the procedures had been included in a statutory instrument.[11]

Whether or not the Circular Letter gave rise to contractual rights between the parties to the agreement was a matter which did not arise in this case.

---

[8] *Staunton v. St. Laurence's Hospital Board & Attorney General*, unreported, High Court, 21 February 1986.

[9] *ibid.* at pp. 8-9.

[10] Note 1 above.

[11] *ibid.* at p. 6.

15.2 Conditions

In *Lachford and Sons Ltd. v. Minister for Industry & Commerce,*[12] the Supreme Court considered the legal effect of conditions prescribed by the Minister under which a subsidy would be paid. Murnaghan J. concluded:

> After having made and published the conditions on which payment of subsidy would be made, the Minister can alter these conditions from time to time or withdraw them; but, until altered or withdrawn, the conditions apply, and persons who have complied with the published conditions are entitled to claim that they have qualified for payment of the subsidy.[13]

In *The State (McMahon) v. Minister for Education,*[14] the prosecutor sought to apply the reasoning in *Lachford* by analogy to the system of appointment and selection of staff set out in paragraph 7 in the second schedule to the Draft Deed of Trust which governed the administration of Pobalscoil Rosmini. He submitted that a candidate who had gone through the selection procedure set out in paragraph 7 and been selected as the successful candidate, would be entitled to the appointment.

The Minister withheld approval because she took the view that the post did not exist. She was held to be wrong in doing so and the correct issue was Mr. McMahon's suitability to fill the existing vacant post for which the Board had recommended him. The Court made an order of *certiorari* quashing the Minister's decision and an order of *mandamus* directing the Minister to consider in accordance with law, the question of whether she should approve the appointment of Mr. McMahon to the post.

15.3 Explanatory Notes

A similar but more recent case involving entitlement to the payment of a subsidy is that *of Kylemore Bakery Ltd. v. Minister for Trade, Commerce and Tourism,*[15] where Mr. Justice Costello concluded that a contractual relationship had arisen between the parties:

> by sending the "Explanatory Notes" to Kylemore, by inspecting their products and then informing them that certain of their products were eligible for subsidy the Minister was I think, making an offer to make subsidy payments to Kylemore. The terms of this offer were to be found

---

[12] *Lachford & Sons Ltd. v. Minister for Industry & Commerce* [1950] I. R. 33.
[13] [1950] I.R. 33 at p. 42.
[14] *The State (McMahon) v. Minister for Education*, unreported, High Court, 21 December 1985.
[15] *Kylemore Bakery Ltd. v. Minister for Trade, Commerce and Tourism* [1986] I.L.R.M. 529.

in the "Explanatory Notes" and in the official application form which he supplied to Kylemore.[16]

This offer could have been withdrawn at any time by the Minister and could have been varied by him, either by amending the rate of subsidy payable, or by amending the terms and conditions of the scheme or the application form. Mr. Justice Costello then held that once Kylemore complied with the terms and conditions contained in the "Explanatory Notes" and the application form, the Minister had no discretion to refuse payment, he had made an offer from which he could not subsequently resile once it had been accepted. Kylemore had reduced the prices of a number of their products in the expectation that they would be paid the subsidy.

In both the *Staunton* and *Kylemore* cases, the judges had no hesitation in finding for the plaintiffs on the grounds of representations leading to contracts. In the *Lachford* case, declarations were given, the court being satisfied that "There was no contract in the sense in which contract is used as creating mutual rights and duties." The plaintiff did not sue the Minister for damages for breach of contract, and in the opinion of Murnaghan J., had they done so, they could not have succeeded.

In all cases, regardless of the status of the documents, the courts held in favour of the plaintiffs, albeit on different grounds, having no doubt as to the legal consequences. A commentator might find a comparison of the basis for these decisions difficult to reconcile and suspect that they are based more on pragmatism than principle.

15.4 Conciliation and Arbitration Schemes

It is also significant that the High Court regards Conciliation and Arbitration schemes as contracts between the Minister and the associations which sign them and has held that the parties are entitled to rely on the fact that the terms of such a scheme must be observed.[17] Section 3 of the Industrial Relations Act 1946 excludes civil servants and local government staff from access to the Labour Court. The Industrial Relations (Amendment) Act 1955 extended access to many local authority staff but not to vocational teachers, presumably on the basis that they have access to Conciliation and Arbitration.[18] If a vocational teacher is not a member of a trade union, or is a member of a union which is not a party to the Conciliation and Arbitration scheme, he is also denied access to Conciliation and Arbitration.

---

[16] *loc. cit.*

[17] *McMahon and Lynch v. Minister for Finance,* unreported, High Court, 13 May 1965, Kenny J. See also Farry and Asmal, *The Law of Collective Agreements in Ireland* (Dublin, forthcoming 1998).

[18] The present teacher C&A scheme is under review and it is proposed to extend the range of issues and representation to all education unions and management.

Appendices

AGREEMENT BETWEEN THE TUI AND THE IVEA

Suspension Procedures for Vocational Teachers

1. It is recognised that disciplinary matters can and should be resolved locally, informally and without acrimony. However, where this is not possible, it is recognised that a clear procedure should exist through which serious disciplinary matters can be progressed.

2. Where it is reported to a C.E.O. that a teacher has failed to satisfactorily perform his/her duties, the terms of C/L 43/85 should apply or Clause 6.2 of Memo V.7 as appropriate.

3. Where the C.E.O. is of the view that a teacher may have misconducted himself/herself in relation to their duties or may otherwise be unfit to hold their office the following procedure shall apply:

Part I The teacher to be orally advised by the C.E.O. of such alleged failure and be given an opportunity to remedy the matter. The teacher, should he/she so wish, may be accompanied by his/her Trade Union representative(s) or other friend(s).

Part II Where no improvement is deemed to have been made after a reasonable period of time, normally 3 months, the warning to be given in writing stating the specific areas of dissatisfaction and indicating that if after a reasonable period of time, normally 3 months, no improvement is made then the matter to be reported to the Committee.

Part III If, following the written warning and the elapse of a reasonable period of time, normally 3 months, no improvement is deemed to have been made, the C.E.O. may report the matter to the Committee. If the Committee so decide, a final written warning may be issued (again detailing specific areas of dissatisfaction and detailing the manner in which it is alleged the teacher has failed to remedy the matter or matters as set out in the earlier correspondence) and a reasonable period of time, normally 3 months, allowed for improvement.

Part IV If, following the final warning and the elapse of a reasonable period of time, normally 3 months, the Committee considers that the problem, as detailed to the teacher in the oral warning (and as formally set out in the first and second written warnings to the teacher) remains unresolved, the teacher shall be invited to meet a small Sub-Committee of the V.E.C., and shall be advised of its composition, or, if the teacher so wishes, the full Committee. At least 10 working day's notice of the meeting will be provided to the teacher, the notice to be accompanied by a statement setting out full details of the allegations against the teacher in accordance with the earlier written and oral warnings, and in addition, detailing how the teacher has failed to remedy the allegations against him/her. The notice should state clearly the purpose and the seriousness of the meeting and further state that depending on the outcome of the meeting, the Committee may decide to take disciplinary action which may include exercising its right to suspend the teacher under section 7 of the Vocational Education (Amendment) Act 1944.

The teacher, should he/she so wish, may be accompanied by his/her Trade Union representative(s) or other friend(s) at the meeting.

The teacher together with his/her Trade Union representative(s) or other friend(s) to be given an adequate opportunity to respond to the allegations both orally and in writing.

The proceedings of the meeting will be recorded in full. This record of the proceedings to be given to the Committee at its next meeting for consideration and to the teacher. Any observations which the teacher may wish to make in writing to the record will accompany the record when it is made available to the Committee.

Following consideration of the record, the Committee may:

(i) exonerate the teacher;

(ii) allow a further period of time for improvement(not exceeding one calendar year);

(iii) take appropriate disciplinary action.

Where the Committee allows a further period for improvement as set out in (ii) above and the teacher fails to effect the required improvement on the subject of the complaint, then Part IV of the procedure to be reactivated.

In the event of the C.E.O. or the Committee, as appropriate, becoming satisfied that the teacher has remedied the subject of complaint as set out in a written warning, then the procedure will be terminated and the teacher written to, advising to that effect within 10 working days.

In the event of the C.E.O. or the Committee, as appropriate, not proceeding from one stage of their procedure to the next stage within 6 calendar months, then the procedure to that point to be deemed null and void.

It is the intention to seek the Minister's agreement in respect of the following procedure:

1. Where a teacher is suspended from office, the Minister shall be advised of

the suspension within one week of the suspension date. All relevant documentation shall be forwarded to the Minister at the time of notification and a copy of the documentation forwarded to the teacher.

2. The Minister shall, on receipt of the notification of the suspension, either terminate the suspension within one month or alternatively:

(i)   Cause a local sworn inquiry to be held not later than one month from the date of notification of the suspension by the Committee. The subject of the inquiry to be the matters as set out in the oral and written warnings.

(ii) The inquiry shall in all cases be a sworn inquiry conducted by an Official of the Department.

(iii) It shall be open to the Committee or its representatives and the teacher or his/her representative to introduce witnesses and to question any witnesses who are party to the inquiry.

(iv) The officer conducting the inquiry shall report to the Minister on the results of the inquiry within two weeks from the completion date of the inquiry.

(v)   The Minister shall, within a further two weeks, issue to the Committee and to the teacher the results of the inquiry and his/her decision on the suspension.

APPENDIX 2
C/L No. 43/85

INSPECTION OF SCHOOLS, COLLEGES and COURSES CONDUCTED UNDER VECs and DEPARTMENTAL PROCEDURES in connection with ADVERSE Reports on TEACHERS employed by VECs

Appendix A Inspection of Schools, Colleges and Courses conducted under VECs

1.0 This document deals with the inspection of schools, colleges and courses under vocational education committees.

2.0 When inspecting the school/college/institution, the inspector will be concerned with the inspection of:

(i)   the organisation of the school/college/institution;

(ii) the learning environment;

(iii) the interaction of the school/ college/ institution with the community;

    (iv) the quality of the teaching and learning;

    (v) any other elements which are accepted as being of educational import or are likely to have an effect on (i) to (iv).

The inspector may offer advice and direction on these matters and report to the Department as appropriate.

2.1 When making his/her observations of the teaching/learning situation, the inspector takes three main elements into consideration:

(i) *Planning*   The inspector will observe the way in which the subject relates to the curriculum, its relationship with other subjects, the teaching arrangements, etc. He/she will look at the way in which the syllabus is being interpreted in the light of identified objectives, the overall target of the course and the perceived needs of the students. He/she will have regard to such factors as immediate preparation, use of resources and learning aids, continuity etc.

    The inspector may seek evidence of preparation and planning and records of work covered to date and use such evidence as a basis for an initial discussion with the teacher. To ensure that questions do not unknowingly cover matters not already dealt with in the course of instruction, the inspector will take cognisance of the records of course work already covered.

(ii) *Presentation*   The inspector will note, with due allowance for his/her presence, the relation between the teacher and the learners. He/she will observe the techniques of teaching employed by the teacher, the nature of communication with the class, the use of learning and other aids, the measure of class control and pupil involvement and classroom performance in general. The inspector may require, in relation to this aspect, that the teacher continue with the particular lesson the teacher had planned for that period.

(iii) *Student attainment*   The inspector may question the students, covering the course work done and projects in hand or contemplated, examine their written work and practical work, and otherwise determine their attainment and their progress in relation to the objectives set out for them.

2.2 The inspector will report on the quality of the teaching/learning but a visit by an inspector or a report on such visit does not always imply an assessment of the teacher's work. Where the Department issues a report in respect of the work of a teacher, such report will be made available to the teacher.

3.0 *Inspector/ Teacher relationships*
The inter-relationships in the classroom between the teacher and inspector are rooted in mutual interest, responsibility, respect, courtesy and profes-

sional integrity.

3.1 A teacher may make a request, through the principal and the VEC for an inspection of his/her work.

4.0 Generally the purpose of the inspector's visit will be fulfilled when the inspector makes his /her observations, offers advice to the teacher and reports to the Department.

If, however, the inspector finds that learning is not proceeding satisfactorily and that this is attributable to a deficiency on the part of the teacher, the inspector will make known to the teacher any shortcomings he/she has observed and before concluding the inspection will make suggestions on means of overcoming them.

The inspector will, on a subsequent visit, observe how the teacher is coping with these difficulties and give further advice and suggestions. Where, in the opinion of the inspector, the work of the teacher continues to be unsatisfactory, the inspector may recommend the issue of an Adverse Report. Adverse Reports are dealt with in a separate document.(Appendix b).

5.0 *Probationary Service*
The conditions of Memo V.7 in relation to probationary service apply to all teachers appointed for the first time to a permanent whole-time post. As far as possible, inspectors will inspect teachers on probation during the teacher's probationary period and will provide advice, support and help to those teachers.

                                                        Deireadh Fomhair, 1985.

Appendix to Circular Letter No. 43/85

Departmental Procedure in connection with Departmental Reports on
Teachers employed by Vocational Education Committee.

Note: The procedure described below relates to probated teachers only. The present provisions in relation to teachers serving their probationary period will continue to apply.

1. *First Report*
Where the Department, on the basis of an inspector's report, decides that an adverse report on the teacher should be issued, an adverse report will be issued to the Committee as soon as possible after the inspector's visit, normally within two months.

The Committee will be requested to keep the report confidential and it should only be discussed in Committee.

The Chief Executive Officer will be requested a copy of the report, within seven days of receipt, to the teacher concerned and a copy also to the principal. The teacher should forward to the Committee, within 21 days, excluding holiday periods, any observations which he/she wishes to make on the report. The teacher's observations and those, if any, of the Committee, should be submitted to the Department at an early date, and will be taken into account in connection with the next inspection. Similar procedures will be followed in relation to all adverse reports.

2. Second Report

A second inspection will be conducted by two inspectors, one of whom, as a rule, will be a specialist in the subject area in which the teacher is timetabled, after a reasonable period has elapsed after the issue of the first adverse report, normally from two to six months.

At least three days' notice of the week in which inspection will be held will be given to the teacher. However, if it happens that the teacher is absent on the day of the visit for inspection, notice need not be given of the next visit. At least two separate classes will be inspected in the teacher's main subject(s) in the timetable.

Should the teacher's work be found satisfactory, a letter (with copies for the teacher and the principal) will be issued to the Committee drawing attention to the previous report and stating that the Department is now satisfied that the work of this teacher is of a satisfactory standard. Should the teacher's work be found unsatisfactory at the second inspection, a second adverse report will be issued, normally within two months. If more than twelve months, excluding periods of teacher absence, elapse before this inspection is held, an adverse report issuing will be considered only as a first adverse report.

3. Third Report

After a reasonable interval following the issue of the second adverse report (normally from two to six months) has elapsed, a third inspection will be conducted by a Senior Inspector and another inspector, one of whom is a specialist in the subject area for which the teacher is timetabled. The same conditions of notice will apply as for the second inspection. At least two classes will be inspected in the teacher's main subject(s) in the timetable.

Should the teacher's work be found satisfactory at this stage, a letter to this effect (with copies for the teacher and the Principal) will be issued to the Committee.

If more than twelve months, excluding periods of teacher absence, elapse before this inspection is held, any adverse report arising as a result of it must be considered only as a second adverse report.

Should the teacher's work be found to be still unsatisfactory, a third adverse report will be issued, normally within two months.

It will be open to the teacher at this stage to avail of the appeal procedure described below.

4. Appeal Procedure

Where an appeal by the teacher invoking the following procedure is received by the Department within 21 days, excluding holiday periods, of the issue of the third adverse report, the appeal will be referred to the Chairperson of an Appeal Board to be constituted as follows. The Appeal Board will consist of an agreed Chairperson, a representative of the Department, a representative of the Vocational Education Committee by whom the teacher is employed and not more than two representatives of the teacher's union.

It shall be the function of the Chairperson of the Appeal Board, having considered the appeal made by the teacher, the adverse reports issued by the Department, and any other evidence or views which the members of the Board may put forward, to make a recommendation in his/her own name to the Minister. The Chairperson may:

(a) advise that he/she sees no adequate reason why the adverse reports issued by the Department should not be taken as a basis for action; or

(b) may recommend that a further inspection be held, and may recommend that it be carried out by an Assistant Chief Inspector together with another inspector, one of them being a specialist in the main subject area in which the teacher is timetabled. Where a further inspection takes place, a copy of the report issued by the Department as a result will be made available to the Appeal Board and will be taken into consideration by the Chairperson in making his/her final report to the Minister; and/or

(c) make any other recommendation he/she deems appropriate.

Before finalising his/her report the Chairperson will invite the observations of the members of the Board on his/her draft report.

The proceedings of the Appeal Board shall be confidential.

5. Action by the Minister

The report of the Chairperson will be considered by the Minister before deciding on whether to take action in accordance with the relevant provisions of the Vocational Education Acts. Where no appeal is received within the time specified in paragraph 4 above, the question of such action by the Minister will arise at that stage.

Meitheamh, 1985.

APPENDIX 3
Interview Panels

Education Panel

1. University personnel Lecturers.

2. Educationalists from Teacher Training Institutions.

3. Educationalists from DIT and Regional Technical Collegs.

4. High Diploma in Education monitors.

5. Retired Department of Education Inspectors.

6. Serving VEC Principals (except within their own scheme).

7. CEO's and Education Officers (except within their own scheme).

Personnel Panel

1. Civil Service Commission nominees.

2. Local Appointments Commission nominees.

3. State or semi-State companies in the area.

4. Large companies or enterprises in the area.

5. Personnel Officers from educational institutions.

6. Persons retired from senior positions in the Department of Education, the Civil Service or, state bodies.

7. CEO's and Education Officers serving or retired (except within their own scheme).

A minimum of one person from the Specialists Panels must be from outside the VEC sector.

The panels will be reviewed on an annual basis starting from December 1997.

Index